Our Walk of Faith

Our Walk of Faith
The Journey to Bill's Healing

Barbara Hollace

Published by
Hollace House Publishing
Spokane Valley, Washington

For more information or to contact the author:

Email: barbara@barbarahollace.com

Website: www.barbarahollace.com

Book and cover design: Ann Mathews

ISBN: 978-1-7345159-9-2

Printed in the United States of America

Dedication

This book is dedicated to my amazing husband, Bill.

Thank you for the honor and privilege of walking by your side on this incredible miraculous journey to God's healing.

Thank you for sharing the lessons God has been teaching you.

I am blessed to be your wife and so proud of the man of God you have become through the refining fire.

Your faith and trust in God continue to light the way to the future God had planned for us.

The best is yet to come, Mr. Bill.

Forever, you are my love.

Acknowledgments

Every book has a team of people that brings it into being. As an author, editor, and publisher myself, I can appreciate this labor of love.

First, all praise and honor and glory go to God because without Him, there would be no book and definitely no "happy ending." Every day the Lord faithfully gave me these lessons in my quiet time with Him to share with you. Thank you, Lord!

To Ann Mathews, you have been a silent partner in many of my editing book projects. God chose you to help me bring this book to life from the cover design to the formatting. You are a treasure. I am forever grateful.

To the prayer warriors who have covered Bill and me these two years, your prayers have changed our lives. There are several women that are my frontline prayer warriors that I call upon when the battle is intense. Thank you for fighting in the spiritual realm with me.

To our senior pastors, Dave and Alice Darroch, Spokane Dream Center, Bill and I are forever grateful for your prayers and standing with us through this incredible journey. You were always the first place I reached out for prayer.

To Joe and Kelly Lachnit and Bob and Janice Cepeda, you stood with us through our most challenging hours when Bill's life hung in the balance. Thank you for praying and staying when we needed you most.

To my "blood" family, church family, friends, and Facebook family, you have been our strong foundation with your prayers and encouraging words on this journey to Bill's healing. We are forever grateful.

To Evelyne Ello Hart, many months ago you spoke of having this book translated into French because you knew people who needed to be touched by our journey. From your mouth to God's ear, I am open to have our journey touch lives around the world. Have Your way, Lord.

Introduction

Suddenly life changed… in the twinkling of an eye, life went from "normal" to a fight for my husband's life. We had just returned from celebrating Christmas with my family in Western Washington. A couple of days later, Bill had symptoms of a cold and wasn't feeling well.

Our apartment was undergoing some renovations including replacing all the windows in the month of January. Bill, not feeling well, was in our apartment in the cold, with a cold for several hours. That night, Bill slept on the couch since he didn't want to keep me awake with his coughing.

About 4 am the next morning when I got up, I took one look at Bill and knew he was in trouble. His breathing was labored, he was gasping for breath. I told him I was calling 911 now! He wanted to wait. We couldn't wait. His life depended on immediate action.

After calling for help, I laid my hands on Bill and prayed asking God to spare Bill's life and to fill him with the breath of life. When the paramedics came, it was clear that Bill needed to go to the hospital.

Even in his weakened state, Bill was determined to walk down the stairs from our apartment to the ambulance. It was an indication of the fighting spirit he would need in the days, weeks, and months ahead.

The diagnosis: pneumonia and his heart was in afib (irregular heartbeat). They found a bed for him in ICU at the height of the flu epidemic that year. I stayed there in the hospital with him.

That night about midnight, the doctor came into his room and announced that it appeared Bill was having a heart attack. Bill was feeling no pain. It was a surprise to both of us.

A few days later, Bill came down with influenza A and the following morning had a brain bleed followed by brain surgery at a second hospital. All this happened in the first five days.

This was only the beginning of our incredible journey that still continues to the completion to Bill's healing. His initial hospital stay spanned 168 days, five hospitals and a skilled care facility in two different states. (There will be other books written about those adventures.)

God directed me to share our story on Facebook because He wanted to "do a work there." Daily, I posted of our challenges and prayer requests. In addition to that, every morning God was sharing new insights with me. They became a daily devotion that I posted (Hubby Health Update) that God used to encourage others in their own lives and challenges.

Many people commented that my devotional posts became part of their morning devotion time with the Lord. God's gift to me became my gift to them. That's how it works in God's economy, nothing is wasted.

As we continued on Bill's healing journey, I was encouraged by others to collect these posts and put them into book form. It was a dream, but as Bill's full-time caregiver and working with my own editing clients, I didn't have the time.

Late in 2019, God impressed upon my heart that now was the time to create the first book. January 10, 2020 was the two-year anniversary of the beginning of this journey. God said, "Now is the time."

What you hold in your hands is a compilation of my daily posts from January 10, 2018 through December 2018. It is designed to be used as a daily devotional which includes highlights from our journey to Bill's healing.

Many of these entries were written in hospital rooms on my Kindle or at home on my computer. Every morning, I asked God what He wanted me to share. God gave me the Bible verse; the Holy Spirit supplied the words. You will see recurring themes, but I believe it is God emphasizing His message to each of us. I am honored to be His messenger of hope.

God continues to download daily lessons so expect the next volume to be ready by year's end covering the 2019 posts.

My prayer is that God would speak to you and encourage you in the face of your challenges. I pray that our journey will inspire you to trust the Lord even when you can't see the outcome. And most of all, that you would believe in the God of miracles, and open your hands and heart to receive the gifts He has for you.

Our lives have been forever changed – transformed by His love. God used a butterfly to illustrate this transformation. In fact, one day while Bill was in the hospital, God brought a unique butterfly to the window. God showed me this was Bill and that one day Bill's transformation – body, mind, and spirit would be complete. You will find butterflies throughout the book as a reminder of God's transforming power in our lives.

Enjoy your time in the presence of the Lord. He is worthy of our praise. Hallelujah! #Godisfaithful

Blessings,

Barb Hollace

January 2018
Holding on to Hope

Day #1 January 10

Anchor Verse: Psalm 18:6
But in my distress I cried out to the Lord; yes, I prayed to my God for help. He heard me from his sanctuary; my cry to him reached his ears. (NLT)

The day it all started…1.10.18… the day our lives were forever changed.

In my distress, I cried out to the Lord. Yes, I did! I prayed to my God for help, and He heard me from His sanctuary, from the throne room of heaven. My cry reached God's ears and God's heart – it moved Him to action, it moved me to action.

When faced with a crisis situation, people usually respond one of two ways. They either embrace it (run toward it) or they shut down (run away from it) mentally, physically, emotionally, or sometimes all three ways.

Over the last few days as my husband had what we thought was just a cold, we watched and waited. Maybe we waited too long to take action, but early this morning, about 4 am when I heard my husband's labored breathing, I knew it was time for action. There was no time to wait.

Calling 911 for help was the first step, but as soon as the phone disconnected, I cried out to the Lord. I laid my hands on my husband and asked God to spare his life, to fill him with the breath of life. I chose faith instead of fear. Do you cry out to the Lord in your time of trouble?

As we wait here at the hospital for the next steps on this healing journey, God is listening. It's the height of the flu epidemic and the ER doc said, "We have no beds." We might have to send you to Seattle, Washington or Missoula, Montana, hours away from our home. My heart cried out to the Lord for a miracle. God knows the way that we take. We will trust Him in the storm. When God is all you have, God is all you need.

In the storms of your life, believe God is faithful. Thank you for standing with us. I'm believing for a healing miracle. #pray4bill #Godisfaithful

Day #2 January 11

Anchor Verse: Isaiah 54:17
No weapon formed against you shall prosper. (NKJV)

This morning my faith and my feet are firmly planted on my favorite spiritual warfare verse from Isaiah 54:17, "No weapon formed against you will prosper!"

I'm not in my "normal" place spending time with the Lord. In fact, there's not much that is normal about our lives right now. I am with my husband in ICU at the hospital near our home. It still feels a bit surreal. Will I "wake up" and find out that all of this is a bad dream? Unfortunately not, it's the real thing. And I'm not talking about Coke's marketing motto either.

Bill has pneumonia and a heart that's out of rhythm. It's not just a little bit "bad", it's really bad. In fact, last night it got a little worse. Around midnight, the doctor came into Bill's room and asked if he was having any chest pains, because they believed Bill was having a heart attack.

What?? How could that be? We thought he was healthy, or at least as healthy as the average guy walking the street. We were wrong. We are grateful that God is so gracious and that He spared Bill's life.

There will be times in your life when God calls upon you to shout a battle cry against illness or an enemy in whatever form it may take. With the armor of God in place, it is imperative that we "stand on the wall" and fight from a place of victory.

Scripture verses, the "sword of the Spirit", are some of the most effective weapons we have to fight the enemy and defeat him. Thank you, Lord, for the Bible and Your powerful promises.

Thank you, Lord, that You are Bill's healer, Your grace is sufficient. Holy Spirit, move through the hospital hallways and heal all our diseases. You are faithful and You can do it. #pray4bill #Godisfaithful

Day #3 January 12

Anchor Verse: Psalm 13:5
But I have trusted and relied on and been confident in Your lovingkindness and
faithfulness; My heart shall rejoice and delight in Your salvation. (AMP)

Who do you trust and rely on in your time of trouble?

Psalm 13 says, I can trust and rely on God and also be confident in His lovingkindness and faithfulness. Hallelujah! God is always faithful.

More than that, my heart will rejoice and delight because of Christ's gift of salvation. The gift of salvation is not only for this life but for all of eternity.

When you are walking through a health challenge, a health scare, what a blessing to know that your faith is secure on Christ, the Solid Rock, He is unchangeable!

So much has changed so quickly in our lives. 2017 had its own challenges, but stepping into 2018, returning from Christmas with my family, only to step into what feels like a nightmare was totally unexpected.

Another night in ICU as we wade through this journey to conquer restored health for Bill's heart and lungs and body. We had a good night. We only had the normal interruptions instead of any troubles. My husband Bill was asking me this morning how they were going to get his strength built up again – a very good sign.

His heart rate is down, for which we are grateful. (High 70s/low 80s.) I'm still praying for his heart to convert out of afib. That would be a nice gift today. All his other vitals look great. We are rejoicing in the Lord this morning and His faithfulness. Will see what the doc says when she does rounds this morning. We continue to trust and rely on the Lord.

Thank you for all your prayers. They are bearing much fruit. The Lord is good! #pray4bill #Godisfaithful

Day #4 January 13

Anchor Verse: Psalm 56:3
When I am afraid, I will put my trust and faith in You. (AMP)

Have you ever been afraid? I have. As a child, the darkness between the house and the garage looked very dark. When I mustered up enough courage, I would run to the garage quickly, deposit the garbage, and run back. Whew! I was safe once again.

We all have had experiences with "monsters" under the bed… maybe you still do. Most of those "scary things" are ones that our imagination conspires to use against us. In "real life", there are "real" things that cause us to worry or become anxious – physically, mentally, emotionally, and even spiritually.

Walking through scary places is part of life. This week as I have faced my husband's serious health issues, I have chosen to trust in God. And God's peace that passes all understanding has surrounded me, has surrounded us, and all those who have been in ICU with us.

Lord, we praise and thank you for the gift of Your love. We thank you for the gift of faith that releases us from fear. Thank you, Lord, that when we choose faith, You are faithful to meet every need. Thank you for the gift of community. We are one in the spirit; we are one in the Lord.

Be with those who are facing challenges today, even the things that make us afraid. In the name of Jesus, we rebuke every doubt that the enemy would send our way. We pick up the shield of faith that repels every dart of the enemy.

We are very grateful this morning! The twinkle in Bill's eyes gives testimony to the power of your prayers. His sense of humor is evident. His lungs are sounding better than 24 hours ago. Prayers still needed for complete recovery from the pneumonia, a strengthened heart, and the procedure next week to determine the cause of the heart weakness.

Thank you for standing with us. Bill won't be dancing a jig soon, but he's so much better than Wednesday. #pray4bill #Godisfaithful

Day #5 January 14

Anchor Verse: Jonah 2:2
  In my great trouble I cried to the Lord and he answered me. (NIV)

"In my great trouble"… yes, being in the belly of a whale definitely counts as great trouble. Jonah had been given a task to do by the Lord and he chose to run the other way. Not the best idea.

You might ask, how did he get in the belly of a whale? Well, when you are on a ship and the storm of all storms has suddenly come up, and the sailors on board don't know what to do, they ask you for any suggestions. Jonah said, the storm was his fault, so just toss me overboard. That didn't seem like such a great plan either.

As the storm persisted, it was either do what Jonah said or they would all die. So overboard Jonah went!

However, God in His mercy didn't let Jonah die in the stormy waters. God sent a whale "to the rescue"… so to speak. In this second chapter of Jonah, we read that Jonah cried out to the Lord and God answered him in his time of trouble.

You may not be in the belly of a whale, but I know that today God will hear and answer your cries for help.

1.14.18 It's been a rough day for Bill. He has a high fever, but it's coming down. Bill tested positive for influenza A, didn't have this when he walked in the door, they tested him for it. Lord, we need your help!

Bill is in his own great time of trouble. Hear and answer our cries for mercy, O Lord. Thanks for standing in the gap with us and praying. #pray4bill #Godisfaithful

Day #6 January 15

Anchor Verse: Romans 8:31
So, what does all this mean? If God has determined to stand with us, tell me, who then could ever stand against us? (TPT)

What does all this mean? That is the question I asked early this morning (1.15.18) as I watched my husband have a brain bleed (stroke) in front of my very eyes. But God was there and so were a team of nurses. One of them quickly assessed what was happening and took action.

Watching his left arm and then his left leg fall lifeless to the bed, my heart shattered. What does this all mean?

As they quickly rushed him to have a CT scan to confirm what happened, I was led to another room to call someone to come and be with me. I wasn't sure who to call. I called our pastors. And then as the prognosis was confirmed, Bill had a stroke, I lost it. I sobbed as a nurse held me in her arms. Bill was still conscious. I needed to pull it together and comfort him.

Two church friends arrived to give me a ride to the next hospital. There was no ICU bed available for him, we needed to pray. I still remember the prayer of faith offered by my friend, Fawn, "Bill needs a bed in ICU. God, we'll give You 10 minutes." Wow! Talk about bold prayers!

About 15 minutes later, just as we finished praying we were notified that a bed was available. Surgery was scheduled for 4 pm to remove the blood clot. Bill is alert. He can follow directions. There is hope. God is here.

If God is for us, who can be against us? No one! We walk forward in faith as God holds us in His arms of love.

Today, God's promises are true for you. What does all this mean? That God loves you and you won't face any trial alone. Thank you for standing with us. #pray4bill #Godisfaithful

Day #7 January 16

Anchor Verse: Psalm 23:4
Yea, though I walk through the valley of the shadow of death, I will fear no evil;
For You are with me; Your rod and Your staff, they comfort me. (NKJV)

It's a new day... and God is faithful. That is the truth I am standing on this day and every day. This morning, life looks differently than it did yesterday.

Bill's brain bleed yesterday morning followed by LifeFlight transfer to a second hospital for brain surgery was not how we had planned to live our day. What seemed to be the path of healing had just taken on a new dimension. Truly we walked through the valley of the shadow of death, and the Lord was with us.

My husband and I have a new path to walk... together. Today a new chapter in our life begins post-surgery. It is uncharted territory - a new place, but with the same purpose - that God would be honored and glorified in our lives.

We need continued prayers after Bill's surgery yesterday and through the recovery and rehab process. God has us wrapped in His arms of love. Personally, I am expecting a God-sized miracle – complete restoration. Believing that for you in your life and the ones you love as well.

Lord, thank you for the gift of life for it is precious. Thank you, Lord, that You are faithful. Thank you, Lord, that Your healing miracles were not just for those who lived so many years ago but they are available for us today As my dear husband wakes up to an altered path, remind him that he does not walk alone. Lord, complete his healing.

I pray for those who are waiting for their own miracle – we know that Your timing is always perfect. Lord, do what we cannot do ourselves. We trust you, Lord. In Jesus' name we pray, amen.

Thank you for your continued prayers. God hears and answers. #pray4bill #Godisfaithful

Day #8 January 17

Anchor Verse: 2 Kings 6:15-17

When the servant of the man of God got up and went out early the next morning, an army with horses and chariots had surrounded the city. "Oh no, my lord! What shall we do?" the servant asked. "Don't be afraid," the prophet answered. "Those who are with us are more than those who are with them." And Elisha prayed, "Open his eyes, Lord, so that he may see." Then the Lord opened the servant's eyes, and he looked and saw the hills full of horses and chariots of fire all around Elisha. (NIV)

How we wake up in the morning often sets the tone for the day. We all have heard the expression about getting up on the wrong side of the bed.

Elisha's servant had such a morning. Stepping outside to get some fresh water, the servant was surprised by what he saw. During the night, an army with horses and chariots had surrounded the city. The servant was overwhelmed.

Running back to Elisha, his servant is worried and anxious as he relays the news. Elisha's response, "Don't be afraid." That sounds like a common response when trying to calm someone down. Elisha goes on to say, "Those who are with us are more than those who are with them."

That made no sense to the servant. He didn't see an army ready to defend them. How would they make it out of this situation alive? Elisha asked the Lord to open his servant's eyes so he could "see" into the spiritual realm those who were fighting for them. God heard Elisha's prayer. The servant saw the hills full of horses and chariots of fire all around them.

They were not alone! The Lord, the God of angel armies, was fighting for them. They were not outnumbered; the numbers were in their favor!

Today as we fight the battle for Bill's healing, God has an army of angels fighting for us. God is fighting for us, just as He is fighting your battles.

Lord, open our eyes today to the armies of the Lord that surround us and are fighting for us. With God, the victory has already been won! Hallelujah! #pray4bill #Godisfaithful

Day #9 January 18

Anchor Verse: Psalm 91:14-16

Because he loves me," says the Lord, "I will rescue him; I will protect him, for he acknowledges my name. He will call on me, and I will answer him; I will be with him in trouble, I will deliver him and honor him. With long life I will satisfy him and show him my salvation. (NIV)

Psalm 91 is filled with verse after verse of powerful promises, powerful weapons to use when the enemy of our soul comes calling, day or night. There are powerful things that are spoken here about our love for God, acknowledging God, and calling out to God.

What does God supply in return? He will rescue us, protect us, answer us, be with us in trouble, deliver us, honor us, and satisfy us with long life, and show us His salvation. God delivers so much more than what we offer Him. And the best part, Jesus paid the price for all of it. We just need to accept His gift of love.

What must we do? 1. We must love God. Invite God into every circumstance of your life, not just the good times, or the bad times, but all the time. 2. We must acknowledge God. Taking a stand for what is good and holy and right in the sight of the Lord is imperative. In Matthew 10:32, it says, "Whoever acknowledges me before others, I will also acknowledge before my Father in heaven." (NIV) We must not let our light be hidden, but to let it shine. 3. We must call out to God. We often take pride in being independent but that independent spirit can be our downfall. Asking for help from God or others is so important, don't skip that lesson! You don't want to go around that mountain again.

Even though we have come so far, God is telling me not to settle for the miracles that have already happened, but press in and receive the greater joy and healing that are yet to come. All glory and honor belong to God.

Thank you for your prayers and continued outpouring of love. With the armor of God and the mantle of praise, we fight the good fight today and take back ALL the territory the enemy tried to claim. #Godisfaithful

Day #10 January 19

Anchor Verse: Psalm 118:1
Give thanks to the LORD, for he is good; his love endures forever. (NIV)

Praise is the best way to start our day. Lift your hands in praise this morning to the King of kings and the Lord of lords. He alone is worthy of our praise. Hallelujah!

It seems so much longer than 10 days since this all began. The depth and breadth of the challenges in our life when a minute seems like hours, an hour seems like a day, a day like a whole week. But through all of this, God's presence and the love and prayers of His people have made all the difference.

As we stand on the truth that God loves us with an everlasting love and that will NEVER change, we are moved into the cleft of the rock, under the shadow of the Almighty and we can rest in the storm.

At some point, the rain will stop, the wind will cease, the clouds will part, and the sunshine of the Lord's favor will rest upon us once again.

I slept all through the night... what a gift! I am ready for what lies ahead of us today. Praying that through the night Bill was blessed with that same restorative sleep and clarity of mind with healing in his brain and body, so he might walk into a new day of healing.

We need your continued prayers ... the battle is still raging. Most wars are not won on the first charge up the hill. Healing is a process. Sometimes our brain tells us it wants to move ahead before our bodies are ready. Patience comes hard for many of us.

Thank you for your prayers for Bill in the in-between place. We are carried in His arms of love. "She is my #1 girl" – Bill's words were music to my ears.

My friend, may the darkness recede in your life today. God is still on His throne. Truly, it is well with our souls. Praise God from whom all blessings flow! Thank you for your continued prayers! #pray4bill

Day #11 January 20

Anchor Verse: Genesis 50:20
You intended to harm me, but God intended it for good to accomplish what is now being done, the saving of many lives. (NIV)

As I read Genesis 50:20, where we find Joseph talking to his brothers, "You intended to harm me, but God intended it for good to accomplish what is now being done, the saving of many lives.", I thought about our present situation and Bill's health issues.

"God intended it for good" - that is the promise I am holding on to this morning, for me and for you. Why? God's perspective is so much different than ours. We see a small sliver and He sees the whole picture.

We see the beginning, He sees the end.

We see the problem. He knows the solution.

We see the sickness, He sees the healing.

As believers, we trust God on the darkest night when there is no sunshine, just the light of the Word of God to pave the way. Just the joy burning in our hearts as we recount the testimonies of His faithfulness, both in our own lives and the lives of others.

That is why living in community, coming together with the family of God is so important. That is why God called me to include you on our journey because we need each other.

When we are weary, others will lift our arms. When we are discouraged, others can sow seeds of joy into our heart and lives. When we are lost, God will send someone to show you the way back to the path of life, the path of healing.

Today I go with expectation, believing that when I walk into Bill's hospital in ICU that I will see the manifestation of his healing. All it took was one word from Jesus and the blind received their sight, the lame could walk, even the dead returned to life. The Bible says He is the same yesterday, today, and forever. I believe that He is still the God of miracles. God is Bill's healer. #pray4bill #Godisfaithful

Day #12 January 21

Anchor Verse: Isaiah 55:9
As the heavens are higher than the earth, so are my ways higher than your ways and my thoughts than your thoughts. (NIV)

God's perspective is what changes our trials into testimonies. It's what brings praise out of the pain. It's how we stand firm in Him when our knees are shaking because in the natural, it looks pretty scary.

But God... His ways are higher than our ways and His thoughts than our thoughts. We should be grateful for that truth because our perspective isn't always the best, neither are our "brilliant" ideas.

With Him in the equation, we walk in victory. We are not bowed, we are not broken.

The peace of God will guard your heart and mind this morning and all through the day. Trust Him. Entrust your loved ones to Him. He is faithful. He can do it.

When I left Bill last night, he was still sedated but sleeping more peacefully. As I hold his hand and touch his head, and pray over him out loud, I can feel the power of the Lord working in him.

Just below the surface, like rushing water under a thick layer of ice, I can feel the river of life surging through my dear husband. God is doing a deep healing work inside of him.

Today I am trusting God when my eyes can't see. I pray that is your stance as well – trusting in spite of the fog before you.

This morning I am praising God from a place of victory. Thank you, Lord, that Your thoughts and Your will are paving Bill's path to healing and victory. #pray4bill #Godisfaithful

Day #13 January 22

Anchor Verse: Matthew 14:30-32
But when he realized how high the waves were, he became frightened and started to sink. "Save me, Lord!" he cried out. Jesus immediately stretched out his hand and lifted him up and said, "What little faith you have! Why would you let doubt win?" And the very moment they both stepped into the boat, the raging wind ceased. (TPT)

Peter had walked some distance on the water before he took his eyes off Jesus. Then looking at his circumstances, he was afraid and began to sink.

It was when Peter was "beginning" to sink... just beginning, not when the water was up to his neck that Peter cried out to Jesus for help.

"Immediately" Jesus reached out his hand and took hold of Peter. Together they went back to the boat and once they got "into" the boat the raging wind stopped. Maybe Jesus wanted Peter to know that it was possible to walk with his Savior through the storm.

The storm doesn't always stop as soon as we cry out to Jesus. Sometimes we will walk with Him a distance, to our destination, before the wind is calm once again.

Jesus is walking with Bill and me through that stormy sea. The wind is still roaring but there is peace knowing He is the Master of the storm, and in His time, the wind will cease.

Did you know that God reached out His hand to invite you into our journey? God wants to do something in your life too.

As You call us out of the boat to walk on the water with You, Lord, we ask You to walk with us, we can't do it alone. But we know that with You, Lord, ALL things are possible – ALL things. Hallelujah! #pray4bill #Godisfaithful

Day #14 January 23

Anchor Verse: Hebrews 4:16
So let us come boldly to the very throne of God and stay there to receive his mercy and to find grace to help us in our times of need. (TLB)

God is faithful and the enemy is a liar, just in case you missed the memo.

You may have memorized this verse, Hebrews 4:16, in your youth and the words just flow by rote memory. Let's stop and see what it really says.

How? "Come boldly" ~There is no place for doubt! Come expecting, God will not let you down. Come as bold as a lion, now is not the time to be as meek (or weak) as a lamb.

Where? "The throne of God" ~As we come before the throne of God, we are in the presence of the King of kings and the Lord of lords. It is a place that we are invited and where we have free access as His children.

Why? That we may "receive His mercy" ~ Without God's mercy, we would surely perish. His mercies are new every morning, hallelujah!

What? "To find grace" ~We receive His amazing grace that will help us in our time of need. It's grace to last a lifetime. Grace in our hour of need, grace to not only receive, but grace to offer others.

Today, I challenge you to come "boldly" into the throne room of grace. On this journey to Bill's healing, I have learned that is the only way to fight our battles when life and death are at stake.

If you are like me, you might need to camp in the places this verse talks about today and every day. God has a plan to meet every challenge that I face this day, and all the days of my life.

Thank you, Lord, for the refining fire that we might shine more brightly for you when we emerge. Thank you for your continued prayers! #pray4bill #Godisfaithful

Day #15: January 24

Anchor Verse: John 16:33
These things have I spoken unto you, that in Me you might have peace. In this world you will have tribulation; but be of good cheer, I have overcome the world. (NKJV)

In this world you will have tribulation, but be of good cheer, I have overcome the world! Hallelujah! What a promise! What a prediction and warning that life will not always be easy.

However, the beginning of this verse says, Jesus did it so that in Him we might have peace. Amen!

Four a.m. on Wednesday, January 10, 2018, our lives changed as I called for an ambulance to take my husband to the hospital because his breathing was so labored. Over the course of the last two weeks, wave after wave of health issues have struck like relentless tsunami waves: pneumonia, heart issues, the flu, a stroke (brain bleed), brain surgery, and then after the surgery, seizures, heart rate issues, and ICU delirium. Sounds like a grocery list you wouldn't even wish on your worst enemy.

In the midst of all of this, God has been shining like the pillar of fire that led the Israelites by night through the wilderness. We have seen miracles. We have heard the blessings that have come to you as you have stood with us and believed for God's ultimate restoration of my dear husband.

"I have overcome the world." That is the encouragement He whispers to me and to you. Are your ears open to hear those words? Is your heart ready to receive His gift that is wrapped in unusual wrapping paper?

Lord, thank you for empowering Bill and me on this journey as Your light shines through us. We expect nothing less than Your best for us. In Jesus' powerful name we pray, amen. #pray4bill #Godisfaithful

Day #16 January 25

Anchor Verse: Ecclesiastes 3:11
He has made everything beautiful in its time. He has also set eternity in the human heart; yet no one can fathom what God has done from beginning to end. (NIV)

God makes everything beautiful in His time. Read it again. God makes all things beautiful in His time.

There is power and peace – that's God's promise. When it seems like things are taking forever, we need to remind ourselves that God's timing is perfect. Truly, He is making ALL things beautiful. Not just some of them or a few of them, but all of them.

The days seem to run together when your loved one is in crisis - no matter if that is a physical illness, emotional turmoil, the loss of a job or stretching their faith. It's amazing how life becomes so simple. The things you thought were so important are quickly stripped away – set aside – at least for a time. And it's a good thing. To be shaken out of our "routine" as the Lord brings us to a new place.

This morning I am home getting ready to start a new day. I miss him here with me, but I know that Bill is where he needs to be in ICU and being held in God's arms of love. I also know it's only for a season and then we will be reunited with a new appreciation for each other and the gift of life.

God makes ALL things beautiful in His time. Trust the Lord's timing in your life. He is never early. He is never late. He is always right on time.

We are feeling the love! Thank you for your continued prayers. You are a blessing! #pray4bill #weareloved #thankyouLord #Godisfaithful

Day #17 January 26

Anchor Verse: Exodus 14:14
The Lord will fight for you; you need only to be still. (NIV)

Sometimes God calls us to move out like a mighty army and be actively involved in fighting the battles of life, and other times, our most powerful position of strength is to be still and rest in the shadow of the Almighty. It is there under His wings of love that we have new strength, we have new hope, and we have victory.

Along this journey, Bill and I have been in both of those places. At times, he has been so sick that all Bill could do was rest in God's arms of love and hold on, believing that the Lord would carry him. In fact, most of these 17 days that has been the truth.

For me, there have been many moments when by God's strength He called me to stand on the wall and fight for my husband's health, in fact, for his very life. With your prayers, we fought valiantly and God heard us and answered. There have also been moments where I was wrapped in God's arms as He held me when I cried because the intensity of the battle and the relentless attacks of the enemy took my breath away.

Today, we stand together. Today, we know that God is faithful. Today, we know that God is fighting for Bill's life and health and wholeness and the amazing future God has for him. We will quiet our hearts before the Lord this morning. Hallelujah!

Your prayers have turned the tide. Praying for clear lungs when I get to the hospital this morning. He is Lord! And nothing is too hard for God! Nothing! #pray4bill #Godisfaithful

Day #18 January 27

Anchor Verse: Romans 15:13
May the God of hope fill you with all joy and peace as you trust in him, so that you may overflow with hope by the power of the Holy Spirit. (NIV)

Good morning! After an incredibly restful night, I am at peace because I know that God has been at work in Bill during the night. Last night as I left the hospital, Bill was sleeping comfortably. His lungs sounded so much better. He, too, was at peace. Thank you, Lord.

As I look at this verse from Romans, it says that as we are filled with joy and peace as we TRUST God, we will overflow with HOPE by the power of the Holy Spirit.

I have been able to stand in that place these last 18 days. Because of God's grace, I have been able to encourage the medical team when they got discouraged when wave after wave of adversity continued to hit us. Jesus has been our solid rock through all of it. And He isn't finished yet!

Extreme makeovers often look like they are destroying the original structure but instead they are making room for the "new thing" that God is doing. Praising the Lord this morning for the plans God has for us, to give us a future and hope!

My prayer is that you, too, will be filled with God's hope and peace. It comes through trusting Him. It's your choice.

Let our praises reach heaven's gates this morning. Hallelujah! #pray4bill #Godisfaithful

Day #19 January 28

Anchor Verse: Isaiah 43:2
When you go through deep waters, I will be with you. When you go through rivers of difficulty, you will not drown. When you walk through the fire of oppression, you will not be burned up; the flames will not consume you. (NLT)

For a very long time, this Bible verse has been an anchor for me. This trip with my dear husband is not the first time I've been through deep waters or the rivers or through the fire.

It's not your first rodeo either. Each time we face a new challenge, especially related to someone we love, God asks us to trust Him when we cannot see the outcome.

Today is a new day, the first day of the week, the day we celebrate Jesus' resurrection, the day He overcame death and the grave. That's what Isaiah 43:2 is talking about, I believe, Jesus walking with us through all those tough places and coming out the other side unharmed. And oh so much wiser, and more intimately in love with our Savior and Lord.

I can't wait to see my husband this morning. To be with the one I love. I told Bill the other day while he was sleeping that I missed hearing his voice. Maybe today will be the day, God gives me that gift.

Attentively listen to the voice of the one you love today. Appreciate the gift of their voice. I haven't heard Bill's voice in several weeks. It's one of the things I miss the most, hearing him say, "I love you."

Thank you for your continued prayers and faithfulness. I'm believing for the miracles still to come. #pray4bill #Godisfaithful

Day #20 January 29

Anchor Verse: Philippians 4:13
I can do ALL things through Christ who strengthens me. (NKJV)

We made it through the night. (Thank you, Lord.) No phone call from the hospital, but I didn't expect one. I am quite rested this morning and ready to walk into the day with the full armor of God in place and the prayers of God's people all around us.

Yesterday I was reminded of how powerful God is. He does hold our lives in His hands and God knows the number of our days. Today we will not focus on yesterday's close call. We will focus on the rebuilding, the restoration, and how we can be part of Bill's recovery. We pleaded for his life last night and God heard our heart cries. Today we will stand and pray for the new path God has ahead of him.

His heart, his lungs, continued healing for his brain, his blood pressure, restoration of all his body functions to "normal" is vital. My prayer is also for Bill's spirit that God has been wooing into a deeper place with Him.

I can't wait for Bill to share with us his conversations with God over these last 20 days and also the angels that minister to him. Miracles – every day.

Bill and I are private people and like to live our lives under the radar. When we began this journey, God asked me to go "public" with it because He wanted His glory to be seen! It has been seen and He is not done yet. Greater things are yet to come! Hallelujah!

I can do ALL things through Christ who strengthens me. That is God's promise to you as well. Thanks for praying. #pray4bill #Godisfaithful

Day #21 January 30

Anchor Verse: Matthew 19:26
But Jesus looked at them and said, "With man this is impossible, but with God all things are possible." (NIV)

It's hard to imagine how fast your life can change. Many of you have stood at a similar crossroad, not just once but many times. When we choose to put our hand in God's hand, we win.

Many of you have spoken words of encouragement and prophetic words into our lives. You have lifted up our arms when we grew weary, just as Moses needed support during the battle to assure the Israelites' victory.

It takes 21 days to create a new habit or break an old one. Just so you know, my new habit will not be hanging out in the ICU unit, even though that's what I have done for the last 21 days.

I believe God has been remaking Bill at a deep level. Bill has an inquisitive mind and asks lots of questions. God likely has had His hands full with Bill's questions but I believe the answers are transforming Bill's life.

In Daniel 10:12-14, Daniel had a vision from the Lord. Verse 12 says, "Fear not, Daniel, for from the first day that you set your heart to understand and humbled yourself before your God, your words have been heard, and I have come because of your words. The Prince of the kingdom of Persia withstood me 21 days but Michael, one of the chief princes came to help me."

Since day #1 we have been in a battle for Bill's life, but God is encouraging us through this passage. There has been great opposition from Satan and his cohorts. But every attack from the enemy has been neutralized because of our prayers and using God's Word as our most powerful weapon.

Yesterday I saw stirrings in Bill, indications of life and hope I have not seen in many days. Thank you for your prayers. They have moved heaven. God has heard and He will complete the miracle He started. #pray4bill #Godisfaithful

Day #22 January 31

Anchor Verse: Matthew 21:21a
"...if you have faith and do not doubt..." (NIV)

As I was spending time with the Lord this morning after a great night's sleep, I saw this verse and I was reminded that faith is a marathon and not a sprint.

Bill and I are on this roller coaster ride with his health issues where every day requires a new step of faith. The other day I described it to one of the doctors like a shooting range where you never know what is going to pop up in front of you.

This one thing I do know is my faith in God and holding on to His hand has given me the strength to make big decisions and to face unimaginable situations with peace in my heart. God loves us so much and truly He provides all we need.

It has been the outpouring of love, your prayers and encouraging words that have brought tears of joy. The road to recovery may take a while or God could say it's time today.

Whatever it looks like, I am committed to have faith and not doubt. Thank you for standing with us. There are many of you that span the globe! Our God is an Awesome God.

I am believing that God can touch and heal you as well.

Bill note: Last night when I left the hospital, we were seeing more movement and alertness in Bill. The nurse and I were encouraged. Looking forward to what lies ahead of us today. #pray4bill

February 2018
Love Never Fails

Day #23 February 1

🜲 *Anchor Verse: Psalm 59:16*
But I will sing of your strength, in the morning I will sing of your love; for you are my fortress, my refuge in times of trouble. (NIV)

When we started on this journey on the morning of January 10, I never imagined that we would be entering the month of February with Bill still in ICU in a different hospital. But God knew, and I rest in the knowledge that God knows the race He has set before us.

Nothing surprises God.

If there's a problem, God knows the solution.

That gives me peace.

That gives me hope.

That puts a song in my heart.

I've never been much of a runner, although at one point in my life I had aspirations of walking the course of the Boston Marathon. Maybe this is my marathon.

On Day #23, I am learning about pacing myself for the race. I can't run at a sprinting pace or I won't be able to finish the race. That's why this verse meant so much to me this morning. He is my strength. He is my song. He is my fortress and my refuge in times of trouble. He is my all and all.

As I left last night, Bill was tracking better with his eyes, we are praying this continues today and the breakthrough comes.

PRAYER REQUEST: The neurologist is adjusting the dosage of one of his anti-seizure medications today. Pray that God would direct this move, that it is just enough to improve Bill's overall condition but not too much that the seizures return. Nothing is impossible with God. Standing and believing there is victory in Jesus' name! Thank you for standing with us! Be blessed!

#pray4bill #victoryistheLords #Godisfaithful

Day #24 February 2

Anchor Verse: Jeremiah 29:11
"For I know the plans I have for you," declares the Lord, "plans to prosper you and not to harm you, plans to give you hope and a future." (NIV)

This verse has been "my verse" for many years. This morning the Lord brought it to my mind, because sometimes we need to focus on God's plans for us, not what our physical eyes may be seeing in the present. Do you know what I mean?

God asks us to walk by faith and not by sight. I'm glad. God equips us to walk through the difficult places in our lives with HIS help. We can't do it on our own and have it end well.

Yesterday I had to smile about God's sense of humor.

2017 ended in a flurry of activity in its last months so I didn't have time to complete my normal preparation for 2018. Not all of our scheduled events made it to our big monthly calendar.

Yesterday when I turned the page to February, it was blank.

God reminded me that He would be scheduling our path in the days ahead. I just need to trust Him, for His plans are for good and not evil, to prosper us and not harm us, to give us hope and a future. I trust you, Lord.

Praying for another day of the manifestation of God's healing in Bill's life.

Thanks for praying us through this storm. God is faithful and so are you!#pray4bill

Day #25 February 3

Anchor Verse: Exodus 33:14
My Presence will go with you, and I will give you rest. (NIV)

What a great promise from the Lord. Not only will God go with us and fight our battles and provide all that we need BUT He will also give us rest. How amazing is that!

Fighting our way through our daily battles, we can be exhausted by day's end - mentally, physically, emotionally, and yes, even spiritually. However, if we do it with God's help, and not in our own strength, He will give us rest.

I have experienced both His presence and His rest in these last 25 days that Bill has been in ICU. Yep, Bill is still in ICU, right where he needs to be and God continues to be there too.

As I pray and speak the name of "Jesus" in Bill's room, the power of His presence crescendos just like the fullness of sound in a symphony.

I can almost reach out and touch it in the air. You can, too. That's the kind of intimate relationship God wants with His children.

Today is a new day. I have seen God lead us through deep waters, I have no doubt it is His hand leading us on this journey. Yesterday was a good day. I can't wait to see what God did while He was on the night shift.

Thanks for standing with us and praying us through and speaking encouraging words and scripture into our lives.

Praise God from whom all blessings flow! #pray4bill #Godisfaithful

Day #26 February 4

Anchor Verse: Isaiah 54:17
No weapon forged against you will prevail, and you will refute every tongue that accuses you. This is the heritage of the servants of the Lord, and this is their vindication from me," declares the Lord. (NIV)

Good morning. I slept very well last night because of all your prayers. Hopefully Bill slept well too. The Isaiah verse that I listed above, I really thought I was supposed to share it yesterday, but then God gave me the verse about His presence and being at rest instead.

It was exactly what I needed yesterday – to be reminded of His presence no matter what it looked like in the flesh as I found rest in God alone.

From the beginning of this journey, God impressed upon me the beginning of this verse that "no weapon forged against you will prevail"... but it was just the other day, He told me to claim ALL of the verse.

I love the line, "This is the heritage of the servants of the Lord and this is their vindication from me."

Wow... what a promise! It's our heritage – the attacks of the enemy won't prevail. How cool is that!?!?!?!?

That's what I am seeing lived out before my eyes in Bill's life. God will not be stopped. His plans for us will come to pass.

Today is the Super Bowl. Bill's favorite team is playing, the Patriots. Oh how I pray that today would be the day of that healing miracle God promised, overcoming all these illnesses that have come against Bill.

God's timing is perfect. Lord, I trust You with my husband's life. You make all things beautiful in Your time. I trust you, Lord.

Thanks for your continued prayers. #pray4bill #Godisfaithful

Day #27 February 5

Anchor Verse: Psalm 62:2
Truly He is my rock and my salvation, He is my fortress I will never be shaken.
(NIV)

What a powerful declaration by King David! This is where I take my stand as well. I am proclaiming the truth that God is able to support me, not just in times of crisis but everyday living.

You may not be going through a family health crisis right now. You may be flourishing in the fields of grace and abundance where life is good, that's great. God is your rock and salvation and fortress there as well.

This one thing I know, if I put God first in my heart, my mind, my life, then He will take care of everything else. It all falls into place. I am resting in that fortress this morning. So is Bill.

Come and join us and the peace that passes all understanding will guard your heart and mind in Christ Jesus.

Looking forward to the next steps forward God has for us today. They will be good.

Thanks for praying for Bill's lungs and brain and heart and overall physical status. God makes all things beautiful in His time.

The EEG monitoring will conclude this morning to see if anything is off kilter there as his brain is healing. Today I am praying that Bill has the mind of Christ. (Three weeks ago today was his surgery.)

Thank you for standing with us. God hears and answers your prayers. #pray4bill #Godisfaithful

Day #28 February 6

Anchor Verse: Proverbs 3:5-6
Trust in the Lord with all your heart and lean not on your own understanding in all your ways submit to him, and he will make your paths straight. (NIV)

As Bill and I walk this journey together, I am learning the power of the Word of God in a whole new way. Often, daily, I stand over Bill and I speak Bible verses to him, whether he is awake or asleep, sedated or more with it. I speak them not only so he can hear them but I can hear God's promises as well. Having Scripture memorized is so powerful and essential in times of trouble. The cool thing is that God brings to mind the verses that you need when you need them.

These verses from Proverbs mean something deeper to me today than they did 28 days ago. It starts with trusting God. Trusting God with all your heart and entrusting to Him the person you love with all your heart. God doesn't ask for anything in half measures. God wants all of us, but He is also willing to give ALL of Himself and His blessings to us in return.

I have definitely exceeded all of my understanding with the medical issues we have faced in these last 4 weeks. However I have a greater appreciation and understanding for those God has gifted with the ability to be His hands and feet in hospitals. And most of all, how God has so intricately designed our bodies and created us to live for His honor and glory.

What areas of your life is God asking you to trust Him beyond your understanding? Submit, surrender to God, and He WILL make your path straight. I can't wait to walk on the new path that God has for me and Mr. Bill.

Have a blessed day! Love you all. Thanks for standing with us. #Godisfaithful #pray4bill

Day #29 February 7

Anchor Verse: Matthew 18:19-20
Again, truly I tell you that if two of you on earth agree about anything they ask for, it will be done for them by my Father in heaven. For where two or three gather in my name, there am I with them. (NIV)

Today as I wake up I am reminded of the power of prayer. Isn't it amazing how God has invited us to be part of His work here on earth? God can do anything... yes, anything! Yet, He invites us to touch lives in many ways. You all have been part of our journey together through one health crisis after another.

There is power in agreement when we pray together. It's important to pray in our own prayer closet, but the impact is multiplied when we pray together.

Do you have a prayer partner or a group that prays with you? I have found that having a prayer team in your life is essential for survival in this world. There are some people I can call upon day or night to pray for me and my prayer requests. When we are engaged in spiritual warfare, we need to have others covering us in prayer. It's a practice we all need to follow.

On the days when it seemed that sickness was winning the battle, together we stood in the gap for Bill, and declared, "No weapon formed against him would prosper." The enemy is defeated. We believe it and we fight from that place of victory.

Today (2.8.18) is a Day of Prayer and Fasting for Bill. It is a day of breakthrough. Today I expect to see the manifestation of Bill's healing on many fronts. I invite you to join with us in intentional prayer. There will be specific posts throughout the day and I will post the 12 prayer points God placed on my heart.

My shield of faith is up. My sword is drawn. The army of God, prayer warriors of faith, will have the victory this day! Hallelujah! Amen! Thank you! #pray4bill #Godisfaithful

Day #30 February 8

Anchor Verse: Psalm 100:5
For the Lord is good and his love endures forever; his faithfulness continues through all generations. (NIV)

God's faithfulness is how we have survived these last 30 days. I don't know how people make it through a crisis in their lives without the Lord.

As a believer, I can run to God's Word, the Bible, and read His promises. I can recite those I have memorized and speak them over Bill to encourage him too. I can pray because I know that my heavenly Father will hear and answer me. And I am surrounded by all of you who are praying as well and offering amazing support.

I was teasing the nurse and respiratory therapist yesterday that this wasn't exactly what I had planned for a month's "vacation." Not that we were planning a vacation, but 30 days out of your life away from home should be spent at a great vacation location, don't you agree?

I told them that I probably wouldn't invite them along on our next vacation when we go to the ocean, one of Bill's favorite places, even though we have met many great people during Bill's 30 days in ICU.

In the midst of this journey, I remember that the Lord is good and His love endures forever. He is a good, good Father.

The Bible says that His faithfulness continues through all generations. That is God's promise for all those in generations past and generations yet to come. I am so grateful not only for God's faithfulness, but the many prayers that were prayed on my behalf from my grandparents, and great-grandparents, and those who would never know my name. It's our turn to sow good seeds in prayer for the next generation starting today.

Thanks for standing with us! Yesterday was an amazing day. Let's see what God had planned for today. #Godisfaithful #pray4bill

Day #31 February 9

Anchor Verse: Romans 8:35, 37
Can anything ever separate us from Christ's love? Does it mean he no longer loves us if we have trouble or calamity, or are persecuted, or hungry, or destitute, or in danger, or threatened with death? No, in all these things we are more than conquerors through him who loved us. (NLT)

Christ's love is closer than our own breath. As a Christ follower, it is woven into every cell in our body. When trouble comes, it must meet our Defender, Jesus, before it encounters us. Isn't that good news?

As Bill and I have walked through these last 31 days, I will tell you that I have never doubted Christ's love for us or even His plans for us.

His arms have been wrapped around us as we have taken one of the scariest roller coaster rides of our lives. God is faithful.

Paul, the author of Romans, goes on to say, we are MORE THAN conquerors. Not only do we win the battle but there is a great reward for the journey as well.

Today is a new day. Today would be a good day to win the battle, to have the tide turn. Pray for the neurologist especially as he looks at Bill's anti-seizure medications. This may be the crux of the problem.

Lord, give him wisdom. I pray that You gave him a dream in the night with the right medication and the right dosage. May today be our day of victory, in Jesus' name, amen.

Thank you for standing with us. May the Lord's blessings flow over you abundantly today and every day. #pray4bill #Godisfaithful

Day #32 February 10

Anchor Verse: 1 Corinthians 13:7
It (Love) always protects, always trusts, always hopes, always perseveres. (NIV)

When we started this journey 32 days ago, I had no idea we would still be in ICU on February 10, but God did. God knew how long it would take to complete the miracle that He wanted to do. Also the miracle God wanted to do in your life and those we have encountered through our hospital experience.

If you missed my last update last night, Bill took himself off the ventilator. He pulled one piece out and the doctor finished the job. Bill is on a high-flow oxygen nasal cannula and was doing well last night when they called from the hospital about 7 pm.

When I was asking the Lord what verse to share with you this morning, He directed me to 1 Corinthians 13, the Love chapter, but more than that to verse 7, as a reminder of how we can show our love to our loved ones.

Am I willing to ALWAYS protect, trust, hope, and persevere in my love for Bill? Yes! I am willing to trust God with Bill. Last night I had to make that choice as I laid down to sleep. I could choose to worry that Bill may have prematurely removed himself from the ventilator or I could trust God that He was walking out the steps of the miracle He promised. I chose to trust God. As I went to sleep, I imagined that with every breath I took, Bill was taking one just like it. We were in cadence with each other during the night, no hiccups.

Valentine's Day is next week, but I invite you to walk out this verse today with the love of your life, whether you are married or single. It may be that God is asking you to have that 1 Corinthians 13 love relationship with Him.

We will see what this day brings forth. We have declared that nothing is impossible with God. We have prayed for the miracles. May we believe and see with our eyes the manifestation of them. Lord, complete what You have started in Jesus' name.

Thanks for praying with us! #pray4bill #Godisfaithful

Day #33 February 11

Anchor Verse: 1 Peter 5:7
Cast all your anxiety (cares) on Him because He cares for you. (NIV)

Anxiety is a weapon the enemy uses against us to chisel away at the truth of God. Anxiety robs us of peace and often keeps us from experiencing the fullness of His joy.

When Bill first went into the hospital with pneumonia, it had stolen his breath. His breathing was filled with anxiety as if the next breath might not come. There have been times in recent days when that shallow, short breathing happened again, even on the ventilator where there is an endless supply of oxygen.

We speak to Bill and try to reassure him to relax and just breathe. When we are in situations where we are filled with anxiety and distress, logic sometimes flies out the window.

Bill's lungs, the mucus secretions, and the oxygen level in his blood are our battlefield right now. This is where the enemy is camped and we can uproot him and destroy him through prayer. Let's do it!

The Lord's shoulders are big enough to carry our worries, our cares, and our anxiety. He has the answers. His presence is filled with peace. His arms of love restore our strength and our hope.

I invite you today to cast all your anxiety, worries, and cares on the Lord, because He cares for you. Victory is assured in Jesus' name.

Thank you for standing with us. Today the banner of victory is raised high as we go out to fight for Bill in Jesus' name! Love you all! #pray4bill

Day #34 February 12

Anchor Verse: Psalm 3:3
But you, LORD, are a shield around me, my glory, the One who lifts my head high. (NIV)

Holding your head high... it says something about your attitude. It conveys a message that you are confident and you are looking at the road that lies ahead of you.

When we are burdened or ashamed or scared, we look down at the ground, at our feet. Our line of sight doesn't extend beyond the crack in the sidewalk in front of us.

As believers in God, where does our confidence come from? Not ourselves. Our God who is a shield around us, our glory, and the lifter of our head is our source of strength and confidence.

During these last 34 days, I know this has been true for me. God has been my strength. God has given me the faith to look beyond my immediate circumstances, the trials, and life-threatening places Bill has walked through, to see God's face smiling upon us.

Today I declare that God is the lifter of my head. I pray that is your testimony as well.

You don't have to carry life's burdens alone... you can't, none of us are strong enough for that. But with God... all things are possible!

Thank you for standing with us. Praying for a day filled with answers and miracles. We are blessed by your faithfulness. #Godisfaithful #pray4bill

Day #35 February 13

Anchor Verse: Psalm 29:11
The Lord gives strength to his people; the Lord blesses his people with peace.
(NIV)

Strength and peace - what an amazing combination. With these two weapons, any battle can be fought and won. This strength we speak of is God's strength, not our own. In fact, the sooner we come to the end of our strength, the better off we are.

On this journey with Bill's health challenges, I probably came to the end of my own "personal" strength about midnight the first night, January 10th, when the doctor came into Bill's room and said, "Are you having pain in your chest? We think you're having a heart attack." My stomach dropped. This on top of pneumonia, but we were only starting the roller coaster ride.

There has been abundant strength in the Lord. Strength to face medical decisions, my husband in a hospital bed for 35 days when he loves to go, go, go, and most of all, the strength to stand against the wiles and strategies of the enemy in prayer and declare victory in Jesus' name.

In the middle of the day at the hospital or the dark hours of the night, the Lord has been with me. He has never left me or forsaken me. God will never forsake you either.

Thank you for your continued prayers for Bill. God's greatest miracle hasn't been revealed yet. The doctors are amazed that any person could have come through all Bill has in the last 35 days and still be alive... only God. We are believing for his COMPLETE healing. Love you, all!

P.S. Please pray for Syneal, Bill's roommate, if God didn't do a healing miracle overnight, today will likely be his last day on earth. Pray for his family especially Darlene as they walk through this difficult time.

Thank you for your faithfulness. #pray4bill #Godisfaithful

Day #36 February 14

Anchor Verse: 1 Corinthians 13:13
And now these three remain: faith, hope and love. But the greatest of these is love.
(NIV)

Today is Valentine's Day. This year I have a different perspective than ever before. Today I look beyond the chocolate, gifts, and candlelight dinners, to the heart of the matter, the commitment of love.

Thirty-six days ago, Bill and I walked into the refining fire that would purify our love for each other. Even though he hasn't always been able to communicate along this journey with words, I feel the power of our love coursing through our hands as he grasps mine. Our hearts are connected by a language that is far beyond the confines of the English alphabet.

As we enter this Lent season, I am reminded of Jesus' love for us. It was unconventional as well. It wasn't what society expected. As believers, our desire to follow the Lord and love as Jesus loved will be viewed the same way. People won't always understand, but don't let that stop you.

One of the medical staff commented yesterday on my loyalty and faithfulness, day after day being there with Bill. I can't imagine it any other way.

Now that I know the circumstances that have torn his body down, I can be part of the rebuilding process as God creates a new and improved "temple" in Bill.

What about you? Faith, hope, and love - the triad of Christian living. Truly God's abiding love for us and our love for Him will stand for all eternity. Are you willing to love as Jesus loved?

Happy Valentine's Day! I'll be spending the day with my valentine. You are loved! #pray4bill #expectingmiracles #Godislove

Day #37 February 15

Anchor Verse: Hebrews 11:1
Now faith is the substance (assurance) of things hoped for, the evidence of things not seen. (NKJV)

Faith in God is what separates believers from unbelievers. Faith is what keeps us going another day when the world seems to be in chaos and totally out of control. Faith gives us peace in the midst of the storm.

This verse in Hebrews talks about assurance and evidence, two things that are opposites. Evidence is scientific, something you can hold in your hands and "prove" – doctors and scientists live in this world. But assurance is confidence that isn't always supported by evidence, it's a gift from God.

From the beginning of Bill's health challenge journey, God has assured me of His promises regarding Bill's life that something beautiful would come out of all his pain and suffering. That lives would be touched and forever changed beginning with our lives. We are seeing that daily.

Across the nation and the world, more people than I can count are praying for Bill, and me, and all those who are working with us. God's work is being fulfilled in us.

Yet, the evidence of his completed healing has not yet been seen. But I have the assurance that God will make all things beautiful in His time.

Today is an important day. God is going to have the victory. We walk by faith and not by sight. Lord, be glorified in us!

Thanks for your prayers, your hope, and your faith, it is changing the course of our lives. Love you all! #Godisfaithful #pray4bill

Day #38 February 16

Anchor Verse: 1 Corinthians 2:9
No eye has seen, no ear has heard, and no mind has imagined what God has prepared for those who love him. (NLT)

God is amazing! We cannot even begin to understand the depth and breadth and height of who He is and what He can do – what He has already done and what is yet to come!.

Daily as I sit in the ICU unit with Bill, I am amazed at not only the wealth of resources available to help heal people but also the skills that God has given individuals to operate those machines and administer treatments and medications.

This morning as I was praying for Bill and thinking about him (I do that a lot), I was just wondering what it will be like for Bill to wake up today into a "new world." We are not sure how much he will remember of these last 38 days, and more importantly, how to get reoriented into his "new" life.

Then God brought this verse to mind to reassure me that God's plans for Bill are so incredible that I cannot even fathom them. They are so good that we can't even imagine what they will be like. God will help him take the next step and the one after that.

Today we will take another temporary measure to facilitate his healing. The feeding tube that has been down his nose will be removed and a feeding tube placed into his stomach to provide nutrition as his body gets stronger and heals. Please lift us up in your prayers.

Our hearts are filled with gratitude for the blessings we have experienced on this journey.

Thanks for standing with us. May God be honored and glorified in us today! #pray4bill #Godisfaithful

Day #39 February 17

Anchor Verse: 2 Corinthians 5:17
Therefore, if anyone is in Christ, the new creation has come: The old has gone, the new is here! (NIV)

Good morning. Today is a new day, a fresh start, a day of hope. As this verse came to mind this morning, I was thinking about Bill and the path he has taken these last 39 days. It is not a path that we would have chosen, but it is a path that God ordained for our good and for His glory.

It is a powerful testimony when the God of the universe who created you walks with you through the refining fire so that you can become all that He created you to be. Sometimes we need to get the gunk stripped away so God can use us to accomplish His will in His way.

Are we willing? Are we willing to let the old pass away and allow the new to come? We probably all have things that we have held on to for years — possessions, ideas, opinions, beliefs, and even self-imposed limitations.

Then one day God said, "It's time, it's time for 'surgery.' I love you, my child, too much to let you settle for a life of mediocrity. It's time to go through the refining fire with Me. I will never leave you or forsake you. I will hold your hand through all of it — from the beginning to the end."

I believe that is what is happening right now in Bill's life and all of ours as well, as we are part of this army of prayer warriors and the cloud of witnesses who are viewing his transformation.

When Bill is fully restored - mind, body, and spirit, it will be interesting to see God's finished work. As I have talked with nurses about this waking up process, after being sedated to some extent for many, many days including the 2-week intubation process, people often don't remember any of it. I think that would be a blessing. However, I do believe Bill will emerge a new creation in Christ. The best is yet to come!

Thanks for standing with us. Your prayers are moving the hand of God. #pray4bill #Godisfaithful

Day #40 February 18

Anchor Verse: John 11:4
When he heard this, Jesus said, "This sickness will not end in death. No, it is
for God's glory so that God's Son may be glorified through it." (NIV)

Today is the 40th day we have been on this journey, since the day we entered Valley hospital in those early morning hours with Bill's breathing so difficult.

It was there we stepped into God's place of healing and hope, a place of quiet rest and trust, even when our eyes couldn't see in the middle of the blinding storm.

In the Bible, the number "40" is associated with some pretty spectacular events, but this morning, the Lord reminded me that "40" is just a number, many amazing miracles happened on other days as well.

God wanted me to see the bigger picture, that's why He brought me to this verse in John about Lazarus. Bill's circumstances are different, but I believe God's message is the same... ALL of this is for the glory of God in order that the Son of God (Jesus) would be glorified through it.

Bill and I have been touched by the Lord in an amazing way. I know that you have been as well. Our intimacy level with God, and each other, has been magnified as we have walked through the calm and the storm holding Jesus' hand.

Whether Bill is able to verbalize what happened or not, I believe his life will never be the same.

May the Lord be glorified in your life today. My prayer is that you won't have to follow this route through ICU for 40 days (and counting). But wherever God leads you, know that is it for your good and God's glory.

Thanks for standing with us. #pray4bill #Godisfaithful

Day #41 February 19

Anchor Verse: Habakkuk 3:19
The Lord GOD is my strength [my source of courage, my invincible army]; He has made my feet [steady and sure] like hinds' feet And makes me walk [forward with spiritual confidence] on my high places [of challenge and responsibility]. (AMP)

There is victory in Jesus this morning. As I read this verse, I was encouraged, I was emboldened, my strength soared just like an eagle!

Many of you may be familiar with the classic book, "Hind's Feet on High Places" by Hannah Hurnard, the story of Much-Afraid who goes on a spiritual journey as she overcomes many dangers and finally climbs the High Places with the Lord's help.

The Lord impressed upon my heart this morning that Bill and I are on a similar journey as He leads us to the High Places where He is calling us to go with Him. We are not alone on this journey, neither are you.

God has already equipped us to walk this path, with His help. He knows how long it's going to take to get to the top of the mountain and overcome these circumstances, we don't have a clue. We trust His perfect timing. As I was reading about Jesus healing the sick this morning, I realized that none of those who were healed knew that morning when they woke up that it was the day that Jesus would heal them.

He doesn't send a text message or an email or a telegram or call you and say, "By the way, today is the day I will set you free from your pain or illness." And that is a good thing. Every day we live in expectation. We live in dependence on Him.

More than that, we live in victory! Because we know that God is our strength and that He will make our feet secure and will lead us upon our high places singing psalms and songs of victory in Jesus' name. Hallelujah!

Remember to pray for Bill's procedure at 1:30 pm PST. Thank you for standing with us.#pray4bill #Godisfaithful

Day #42 February 20

Anchor Verse: Philippians 3:12-14

Not that I have already obtained all this, or have already arrived at my goal, but I press on to take hold of that for which Christ Jesus took hold of me. Brothers and sisters, I do not consider myself yet to have taken hold of it. But one thing I do: Forgetting what is behind and straining toward what is ahead, I press on toward the goal to win the prize for which God has called me heavenward in Christ Jesus. (NIV)

Forgetting what is behind and straining toward what is ahead. I am reminded of a couple of things. As we watch the Winter Olympics, we see men and women who put behind them their falls and fears, and are totally focused on that particular competition, there is no room for looking back. It's time to win the prize!

Second, when we choose to dwell in the past, it's really difficult to gain traction for the future. Jesus reminds us that the old is gone and the new has come. If He is willing to forget about our past then we should too.

Today is 42 days since we entered ICU. It would be easy to get caught up in the enemy's web of doubt and discouragement. Paul reminds us that we need to forget what is behind and strain toward what is ahead.

Since I have been very transparent, I am going to share another area God is healing me. My first husband had cancer when we got married and for the three years of our marriage, it overshadowed us on a daily basis.

Today, February 20, is the 25th anniversary of the day my first husband died. Our current journey has been covering the same calendar days that I walked 25 years ago... BUT this story has a different outcome. Bill's path is the path to life and healing, for my first husband, it marked the end of his journey. God is healing me from past wounds, so that I might forget what was behind and press on toward the goal for which God had called me heavenward in Christ Jesus.

Praise the Lord for what He is doing in Bill's life. Thanks for praying! May the Lord's blessings flow over you. #pray4bill #Godisfaithful

Day #43 February 21

Anchor Verse: 1 Peter 5:10
After you have suffered for a little while, the God of all grace [who imparts His blessing and favor], who called you to His own eternal glory in Christ, will Himself complete, confirm, strengthen, and establish you [making you what you ought to be]. (AMP)

I love reading the Bible. It's my blueprint for living, but more than that, it tells the stories of those who have gone before us and were overcomers - more than conquerors!

This morning God laid the word "grace" on my heart and I went searching for the verse to share with you today. God led me to 1 Peter 5. It's a powerful verse.

Peter, the author of this book in the Bible, tells us that we will suffer, but only a little while. And then the God of all grace, and I would include mercy here as well, who called us into His glory with Jesus, will Himself, God himself will do this for YOU, and me. He will restore, empower, strengthen, and establish you. Doesn't that cover all we need?

If you have been doubting that God can rescue you out of the mess of your life or your trials or your pain or your loss, I pray that this word encourages you. Hold on to it and don't let go.

We don't know how long "a little while" is. I didn't expect Bill would still be in ICU 43 days later, but he is. God's work isn't completed yet. I choose to trust my heavenly Father to do what is best for Bill, for me, and for us as a couple, that He might be glorified and that we would be restored, empowered, strengthened, and established.

Thank you for standing with us! May the Lord bless you and keep you today. He will carry you through. Much love! #pray4bill #Godisfaithful

Day #44 February 22

Anchor Verse: 1 Thessalonians 5:16-18
Rejoice always, pray continually, give thanks in all circumstances; for this God's
will for you in Christ Jesus. (NIV)

Rejoicing, praying, and giving thanks ~ what a great trilogy! What a great way to live our lives. From the moment we started walking through Bill's health challenges, I knew that we would be facing some extraordinary circumstances. But trust me, I never imagined they would rise to the magnitude we have experienced. I am grateful I didn't know on day #1 that Bill would still be in ICU 44 days later. But God did.

As I began my quiet time with God this morning, "pray without ceasing" came into my heart and mind, and how God has developed that discipline in so many of you, and enhanced that way of life for me. I couldn't tell you when the turning point was for me when I surrendered my will to the Lord and asked Him to use me to stand in the gap for others in prayer. What a privilege it's been to see the hand of God move in powerful ways.

I thought that "praying without ceasing" was where God wanted us to focus this morning, but He expanded my vision to include rejoicing ALWAYS, and praying without ceasing AND giving thanks in ALL circumstances for this is God's will for us.

Did you notice that God wants it ALL? Not just rejoice and pray and give thanks when you feel like it or it lines up with your plans... but ALWAYS!

I believe that God is using Bill's health journey to teach those lessons to us. And He is rewarding us with the treasures that come when prayer is answered.

Rejoice, pray, and give thanks in every circumstance today. Share what happened with a friend. It will rock your world!

Thank you for standing with us! #pray4bill #Godisfaithful

Day #45 February 23

Anchor Verse: Numbers 6:26
[May] the Lord turn his face toward you and give you peace. (NIV)

Peace is not found in our circumstances, but in our heavenly Father. He is unshakable, unmovable, unstoppable! That's my God! That's why we can go through deep waters, through the river, and through the fire, and walk out unharmed, strengthened in our faith and flesh.

The last few days as I have watched Bill begin to emerge from his cocoon, it has been a challenging experience. Just like birth, there's a process to waking up. There's a process to coming alive again after you have been through so much in your mind, body, and spirit. I have seen God's faithfulness, hour by hour, minute by minute.

I see Bill exploring the world and even feeling the whiskers on his chin, a man who is always clean shaven. I see him stretching his arms and legs, as if God has been telling Bill the exercises he should be doing to build up the muscle tone he lost.

I see hope. I see a man who needs time to reclaim what the enemy tried to steal from him. That's why God showed me this verse in Numbers. I see God turning His face toward Bill and offering peace when it must be very chaotic in his mind and body.

Coming off the effects of sedation for a man who other than his blood pressure medication rarely takes anything, detoxing will take a while. This morning I envisioned Joshua and his troops marching around Jericho. For six days all they did was walk, one step at time claiming the territory that God promised them.

When God said it was time, they shouted the victory and the city was theirs. Our journey is like that too. For now, it's one step, one breath, one heartbeat at a time. God's face and favor are surely upon us.

Thanks for standing with us. Praying for Bill's peace of mind today and clarity of thought. God is faithful. #pray4bill #Godisfaithful

Day #46 February 24

Anchor Verse: Psalm 32:8
I will instruct you and teach you in the way you should go; I will counsel you with my loving eye on you. (NIV)

God is better than any GPS system. Our journey with Bill's health challenges in the last 46 days didn't come with a map when we entered ICU on January 10, 2018. There wasn't a magic decoder ring from the cereal box. All we had was God to lead us through a maze we never could have imagined... I'm glad we didn't know.

We are nearing another crossroad in our path. God led me to Psalm 32 this morning to reassure me that He knows the way. And more than that...God is going to instruct me and teach me the way to go and He will counsel me with love. How cool is that! The God who created the universe wants to teach me how to navigate the decisions ahead of us. He's not going to make those decisions for me, because God wants me to learn how to "fly" so that I can fully be used by Him. It's like graduating from training wheels to riding the bike without them.

There's a certain amount of performance anxiety at play this weekend. The days right after Bill's surgery to remove the blood clot (January 16 and 17) Bill was talking to us and swallowing and beginning to eat again. There was some weakness on his left side from the stroke but the neurologist's belief was that with time and therapy that could be restored. Then we entered this tunnel when a lot of other stuff happened, and now we are coming out of that tunnel.

As Bill is "waking up", my belief is that God has been restoring him internally through the fog we have seen outwardly. In these last couple of days as the sedation has been removed, I have seen more mobility and strength on his left side. There's a lot of overall body weakness, but I see a strong spirit. Bill, it's time to shine! What God has started, He will complete!

Thanks for standing with us. #pray4bill #Godisfaithful

Day #47 February 25

Anchor Verse: Galatians 6:9
Let us not become weary in doing good, for at the proper time we will reap a
harvest if we do not give up. (NIV)

I have heard it said that the race is not always to the swift but to those who
keep on going. There are seasons in our lives when the race is a sprint and
the challenge quickly passes. There are other seasons when we are in a
marathon, and then another marathon, and another.

This morning I was thinking not only of our journey with Bill's health
challenges but for those who have medical conditions that they battle daily
and have done so for years. Whether that is MS or diabetes or those
battling heart disease, high blood pressure, depression or anxiety, just to
name a few, the battle is relentless but God is faithful.

When a loved one is taken down in a battle like Bill is facing, it doesn't
mean the rest of your life stops. The world still spins, the bills still need to
be paid, and evil doesn't take a holiday. But God in His mercy and grace
gives more grace when the burdens are greater. He encourages us Himself
in the depths of our soul. We are blessed He sent amazing faithful people
like you to pray, stand, and speak words of encouragement into our lives.

In due season, we will reap the harvest, and see the manifestation of Bill's
complete healing. In the meantime, daily we are filled with gratitude for the
baby steps. We rejoice even on the days when the victory seems elusive
because God does His best work in the dark.

My closing thought for you today is DON'T GIVE UP! If you are listening
to the Lord's voice and walking the road of truth and righteousness, then
He will bless your obedience. If you have wandered off into the weeds,
then ask for God's help and forgiveness and get back on the path that leads
to life. You are loved. Hold on to God's hand. He will carry you through.

Thanks for standing with us. #pray4bill #Godisfaithful

Day #48 February 26

Anchor Verse: Revelation 3:8

I know your deeds. See, I have placed before you an open door that no one can shut. I know that you have little strength, yet you have kept my word and have not denied my name. (NIV)

God's word is alive and powerful! It gives us hope and instruction and encouragement just when we need it. Last night as I was getting ready to leave the hospital, I was reflecting on what was going to happen today. There will be an evaluation for Bill's placement in a rehab facility which will include his present health condition and what he is capable of doing at this point and his future prospects.

For those of you who have followed us on this journey, you know that it has been very eventful from a medical standpoint. The first five days included pneumonia, a heart attack, the flu, and a brain bleed (stroke). And we were just getting started... so much more has followed that as well. Any one of those could have taken him out, but God had a plan for His glory to be seen in Bill and his life. How else would we all have been brought together and learned about the power of prayer and God's amazing ways?

As I was led to this verse in Revelation 3:8, tears filled my eyes. God knows exactly where Bill and I are. He has been here with us every step of the way. Our heavenly Father knows that we have little strength on our own. God has seen how we have trusted Him and that the name of the Lord has been lifted high through this journey. And now He has set before us an open door that no man can shut.

God knows where Bill needs to be. God will smooth out the logistics for all of it –placement in the best facility, paperwork, insurance coverage, finances, the when and where and why and how of it. All we need to do is trust Him and walk in obedience just as we have done in the 47 days prior to this.

We shout hallelujah this morning. Our God reigns! He will accomplish His purposes in Bill. Thank you, Lord! #pray4bill #Godisfaithful

Day #49 February 27

Anchor Verse: Psalm 95:2
Let us come before His presence with a song of thanksgiving; Let us shout joyfully to Him with songs. (AMP)

Yesterday was quite an amazing day in Bill's health journey. With every passing hour, it seemed there was something new to celebrate. The smile didn't want to leave my face and tears of joy were barely below the surface while shouts of hallelujah were heard in the depths of my soul. Someone hollering hallelujah in ICU might have caused quite a scene – for the good!

Then last night as I went to bed I found myself on my knees, on my face before the Lord, thanking Him and worshiping Him for what He had done. Not only to come into His presence with thanksgiving but also as a defense against the enemy. Because God was not the only one who saw what happened yesterday.

I want to focus on the praise part this morning. It's important to stop and praise the Lord when He answers our prayers, but it's also important to praise Him while we are still in the storm.

I am rejoicing over all that happened yesterday and still aware that there are more steps that lie ahead, Mr. Bill isn't home sleeping next to me in bed... yet. So I press on in the battle. I am encouraged by yesterday's victory. I'm heading into this day with expectation about what God can do, He showed us that yesterday. Donning the armor of God, I am aware there are still skirmishes that lie ahead, a fight to be fought!

If you haven't done so already, I would encourage you to thank the Lord for yesterday's miracles and sing a song of praise to His holy name. May the angels in heaven hear our songs of joy and words of gratitude. They are a sweet aroma to the Lord.

Thank you for standing with us. There is victory in Jesus' name. #pray4bill #Godisfaithful

Day #50 February 28

Anchor Verse: Matthew 16:24
Then Jesus said to his disciples, "If any of you wants to be my follower, you must give up your own way, take up your cross, and follow me. (NLT)

Life is not always easy. In fact, many of you know that sometimes it's really difficult to just put one foot in front of the other. The good news is that Jesus is with us every step of the way. He doesn't skip a beat. God doesn't send you to His voicemail or go on vacation. Day or night, your heavenly Father is available to hear the cries of your heart.

This morning as Bill and I stand on the threshold of yet another leg of our journey, the Lord's words to me this morning were, "Follow Me." I found encouragement there because it means I don't have to figure out the way ahead, I just need to follow the Lord. For 50 days, He has been leading the way through tight curves, times when it seemed like we had hit the wall, and even in the joy-filled places Jesus continued to say, "This is not our destination. Keep on going. Follow Me."

Yesterday as Bill was making some incredible steps forward, I had to remind him that we needed to follow the medical staff and their instructions. As much as he was raring to go, Bill could only attempt to stand with help from two other people. It was a great reminder to me as well. When we go through the deep valleys, we need to follow our guide, not try and make our own way.

The verse in Matthew spoken by Jesus is very appropriate for where we are right now. Jesus tells us if you want to follow me, you must give up your own way (ouch!) and take up your cross (there will be sacrifices and challenges), and follow Me. But the good news… it is the path to victory.

Bill and I have given up our own way, and He may be calling you to do the same. Jesus knows the better way, the BEST way, trust Him and follow where He leads.

This morning the NIACH Admissions committee will meet to determine if Bill is going there. Pray not only for God's favor, but God's best for Bill. He knows the way. We will follow where He leads. Thanks for standing with us. #pray4bill#Godisfaithful

Our Walk of Faith

March 2018
Transformed in the Storm

Day #51 March 1

Anchor Verse: Joshua 1:9
Have I not commanded you? Be strong and courageous. Do not be afraid; do not be discouraged, for the Lord your God will be with you wherever you go. (NIV)

During the night, God woke me up to remind me of Joshua as they were about to enter the Promised Land. God reminded me that where the Israelites were headed was uncharted land for them. They knew what was behind them, they were familiar with it, even though there had been lots of trials, but what they faced was unknown. Frankly, I bet they were afraid.

God reminded Joshua to be strong, courageous, and not be afraid or discouraged, but that God was with Him EVERYWHERE he went.

Today Bill is moving to the rehab facility in Post Falls, Idaho. It is our Promised Land, because it is there that God will complete what He started. It is there where Bill will walk again in all God has for him. It is there that we will know God in a more intimate way.

Letting go of the old to grasp the new is a big leap. Bill just wants to come home. I understand that, but God needs to complete the miracle first. The ICU unit has become a familiar place to me. I know the staff here from doctors to nurses to therapists, blood drawers, and housekeepers. Even the people in the cafeteria want to give me an employee discount because we have been here so long. So today, I take a leap of faith as well. Just like Joshua, God is telling me to be strong and courageous. His angels are already waiting for us at NIACH (North Idaho Advanced Care Hospital) this morning.

Where is God calling you to be strong and courageous? God will be with you wherever you go. He promised.

Thanks for standing with us and praying us through. It's your day of victory as well. #pray4bill #Godisfaithful

Day #52 March 2

Anchor Verse: Job 23:10-11
But he knows the way that I take; when he has tested me, I will come forth as
gold. My feet have closely followed his steps; I have kept to his way without
turning aside. (NIV)

So grateful that God's mercies are new every morning! After a good night's sleep, I am ready to take on the challenges of this new day.

I learned a couple of really important things yesterday. 1. Familiar places bring us comfort, even if that place is one of chaos. Life in ICU at Deaconess had become our home away from home. There was both joy and loss when we left there yesterday. The familiar was stripped away. A good but unfamiliar place is where we are now. 2. Spiritual warfare is everywhere. It's important to keep your shield of faith up no matter where you go. The enemy is a sneaky bugger.

Others have compared our journey to that of Job. This morning God brought me to this verse. It wasn't what I thought I was going to share, but it's the right verse. God does know the way that we take. He is with us. The location of the test may have changed, but the outcome is still the same. We have victory in Jesus.

Thank you for holding up my arms when I have been weary in the flesh. Your prayers have reached the throne room of heaven.

Today more evaluations will continue. Bill will have an opportunity to use some of that strong spirit to help him walk in his healing. We are motivated! We are blessed! We are empowered by the Spirit of God! We will not be defeated because the Lord is on our side.

Come and join us as we walk in His steps of victory today!
#pray4bill #Godisfaithful

Day #53 March 3

Anchor Verse: Mark 8:29a
"But what about you?" he (Jesus) asked. "Who do you say I am?" (NIV)

My relationship with Jesus has taken on a new dimension as I have walked through this health journey with Bill. My faith has been stretched and strengthened. Like your house in a storm, you discover how sound it really is when the winds, rain, and snow come or the heat of the day beats down upon you.

That's how your relationship with Jesus is tested as well. Are you a fair weather follower or are you willing to trust Him in the storm even when your eyes can't see?

My relationship with my husband has also taken on a new dimension. There have been many days, most days, when he couldn't communicate, frankly, wasn't responding much at all. If my love for Bill was dependent on hearing him say, "I love you" every day or kissing me before I went to sleep, or receiving gifts, our relationship would have fallen apart days ago.

Instead, I have learned about abiding in God's love, not only as I love Bill through this storm, but as I love my heavenly Father and Jesus Christ with all of my heart and soul and mind.

I believe that it is in the storms of life that Jesus asks us, "Who do you say I am?" Is He your Savior, your Lord, your friend that is closer than a brother?

Only you can answer that question. He wants all of you. I am willing to give Him all of me. Are you?

Today is a new day. In an effort to have Bill more awake, they were trying something different with his overnight meds. Will keep you posted on how Bill did through the night. After all, as my friends tell me, God is on the night shift.

Thanks for standing with us. Your prayers are still needed as we run another leg of this marathon race. #pray4bill #Godisfaithful

Day #54 March 4

Anchor Verse: Daniel 9:19
O Lord, hear! O Lord, forgive! O Lord, listen and take action! Do not delay, for Your own sake, O my God, because Your city and Your people are called by Your name. (AMP)

When was the last time you reminded God of the promises He made in His Word, the Bible? Do you pray the truth of God back to Him?

What God promises, He will fulfill. The Bible is filled with example after example of that and our lives are as well. Sometimes it seems that the fulfillment of His promises are long in coming, and other times, they seem to happen overnight.

As we are walking this faith journey, I am constantly reminded that His promises are true. Yesterday as I was reflecting on the week that had just passed and some of the difficult places, God reminded me of Moses and the promise God made to the children of Israel as they left Egypt. He was taking them to the Promised Land. For days and weeks and months and years, all that Moses had to hold on to was the promise, because the manifestation of it did not happen for years. Many days of desert travel, and trials and tribulations, and grumbling people for companions, yet every day Moses and all those in his entourage took the next step, one step at a time toward the Promised Land.

When Daniel cries out to the Lord in this verse, he recognizes that it is God's reputation on the line. He asks the Lord, not to delay the fulfillment of His promise. That is my prayer today as well. Lord, we desire to see the beautiful butterfly of Your healing power in Bill's life. Don't delay it one minute longer than it needs to be. Complete Your transformation, in Jesus' name. Amen.

Hold on to the promise today. Don't give up! Never give up! The fulfillment of His promise is near.

Thanks for Your continued faithfulness through prayer. God hears and answers. #pray4bill #Godisfaithful

Day #55 March 5

Anchor Verse: Psalm 73:26
My flesh and heart may fail but God is the strength of my heart and my portion forever. (NIV)

I didn't wake up in my own bed this morning. I am sleeping on the window seat in Bill's ICU room in Kootenai Medical Center in Idaho.

For those of you who saw my posts last night and into the morning hours, you will see that life took an unexpected turn.

It looks like there was some bleeding in his lungs from the blood thinner. Bill is sedated and resting comfortably.

The doctor is hoping this is just a small bump in the road and Bill can get back to rehab in a couple of days. God knows the way that we should take.

When your phone rings during the night, it's usually not a good thing. After I received the news something had happened and they were working on a solution, I ran to the Lord and poured out my heart and tears to Him. Then I enlisted help in the physical and spiritual realm and for you all to pray.

My flesh failed in that moment when I heard Bill's oxygen levels had fallen and they didn't know why and were figuring out what to do.

But God truly renewed my strength. I held on to His hand as He promised not to let me go. I can watch Bill as he sleeps and the entourage of machines and medicines that surround him.

I am grateful that God is the Great Physician. There is healing in His hands. The Lord will carry us through.

Thanks for standing with us. We are grateful #Godisfaithful #pray4bill

Day #56 March 6

Anchor Verse: Psalm 34:3
Glorify the Lord with me, let us exalt His name together! (NIV)

I am reminded this morning that God can work through those who praise Him. We bring our prayers and petitions before Him but it is in praise that our heart beats with our heavenly Father's heart. Do you want to turn your defeated countenance around? Praise the Lord! Do you want to defeat the enemy in your life? Sing praises to the Lord. Fill your heart and soul with songs of deliverance!

The book of Psalms is filled with many of King David's songs of praise and we know that man faced all kinds of trouble. Magnify the Lord with me! Let us exalt His name together. Not only is there power when you tap into the Lord on your own, but in the company of others, our voices and songs of praise are magnified as the hosts of heaven join with us.

In church on Sunday morning, a body of believers singing to the Lord shifts the atmosphere and God can do His work there and change your mourning into dancing and magnify your joy.

This morning I stop to remember the miracles God has done in Bill's life, the times He saved his life from destruction. The times God woke him up from a place of cloudiness and sedation and said, "Bill, it's time to rejoin life again." And the times when God renewed Bill's strength like the eagle's and said, "Bill, it's time to sit up. It's time to stand again that My glory might be seen in you." (God used an angel named Emma.)

There was no phone call during the night because God's angels have been watching over Bill. I lift my hands toward heaven and thank the Lord for the great things He has done and the greater things that are yet to come.

I often sing over Bill, mostly while he is sleeping. "I sing praises to Your name, O Lord." The room is filled with His peace and glory, and so am I.

May the courts of heaven be filled with our praises this morning. We come with expectation. We love you, Lord. In Jesus's name, we ask all these things, amen. #Godisfaithful #pray4bill

Day #57 March 7

Anchor Verse: James 1:4
Let perseverance finish its work so that you may be mature and complete, not lacking anything. (NIV)

Perseverance...it means you are in it for the long haul, it's not like going through the drive-through at your favorite coffee stand.

It's definitely not a sprint, it's a marathon race. How many of us are actually prepared for that? Have you or I been training to be in a marathon, not just in the physical realm, but also the spiritual realm?

Preparation is key to this journey. The best preparation is the time we spend in the Lord's presence, in the Bible, in prayer and fasting, and in the company of other believers. It is there that our spiritual muscles are built up. It is because of this discipline that in the day of trouble we will stand and not fall. It is there that we will find the fullness of God's joy instead of being pulled under and drowned in sorrow and hopelessness.

As I was led to this verse this morning, I felt like I was home. This is where I am living right now. I want God to do this in me. I want perseverance to finish its work in me. The days that are hard. The days when I am choked up with emotion. The days I stand in victory singing His praise. The days when Bill's healing is so evident.

Why am I willing to walk this path? So I may become mature and complete, not lacking anything. Wow! That's powerful. I was talking to a friend yesterday about this whole situation. God has given me eyes to see that this is preparation for the days to come when there will be other difficult situations, not just in my life but in yours. He is equipping me, He is equipping us to know how to stand and fight from a place of victory.

Hallelujah! We praise you, Lord! Lord, I am willing for You to do Your work in me that You would be honored and glorified.

Thank you for all your prayers. God is on the move in Bill's life. #pray4bill #Godisfaithful

Day #58 March 8

Anchor Verse: Joshua 24:15
Choose for yourselves this day whom you will serve... but as for me and my house, we will serve the Lord. (NKJV)

Clarity about life often comes through times of crisis. Quickly so many layers are peeled away like the layers of an onion. And yes, there are times that peeling away involves tears, just like cutting an onion.

Our moments of revelation are often thrust upon not because we have chosen to take a sabbatical or embark on a journey to "find God." Instead we find God in glimpses of His glory when a miracle happens and we are filled with joy. Or in the alternative, the bottom falls out and He is the only one who is still holding our hand.

The other thing I have learned is about serving God every day. It's about choosing obedience as He shows me the way I should go. Rebellion has been the downfall of many, whereas as obedience leads to life.

This morning, Joshua 24:15 rang loud in my ears. I have chosen where I will stand, I am on the Lord's side and so is Bill. God is using our journey as a clarion call to all of you, "Choose you THIS day whom you will serve." Will you and your household serve the Lord?

Wherever you are standing today, my prayer is that you will choose Him. When the wind, waves, and storms of adversity hit your life as it has done in ours, I pray that your feet are planted on solid ground, Jesus Christ. He will not be moved. He will not be shaken. And neither will you, if you are standing with Him.

Today you may be called upon to choose between God's way and the way of the world, may you choose wisely. Now that Bill has improved so much cognitively, he is able to participate in these next steps of healing. I am praying for the mind of Christ and that the Lord would continue to renew Bill's mind and strengthen his body in the next steps He has for Bill.

The Lord is good and His love endures forever. Thanks for standing with us. Your prayers have moved the hand of God!#Godisfaithful #pray4bill

Day #59 March 9

⚓ *Anchor Verse: Galatians 5:22-23*
But when the Holy Spirit controls our lives he will produce this kind of fruit in us: love, joy, peace, patience, kindness, goodness, faithfulness, gentleness and self-control. (TLB)

We all bear fruit. What kind of fruit is seen in your life? The other day as I was sitting with Bill and we were going through one of our transition places. I was asking the Lord how to pray for him. As Bill is recovering from injuries and assaults to so many parts of his body, like almost every part of his body, much has been stripped away but what needs to be added back in?

The Lord led me here to Galatians 5. These are the next ingredients that God is adding to Bill's recovery: love, joy, peace, patience, kindness, goodness, faithfulness, gentleness, and self-control. The enemy tries to sow the opposite kind of seed into our lives. He sows weeds into God's beautiful garden. We can choose to pull out those weeds or they will grow and choke out the good fruit.

One of the areas I have been focused on for Bill is peace. Because of the brain bleed and surgery, his brain is still healing. There is much of this journey he doesn't remember. Waking up in the middle of what must seem like a nightmare to Bill causes anxiety. Daily, I pray for God's blanket of peace over him and the complete healing of his mind.

What about you? Are the fruit of the spirit evidenced in your life? As we have walked this path, we have been touched by you and so many others we have encountered, including medical personnel, who are filled with love, joy, peace, patience, kindness, goodness, faithfulness, gentleness, and self-control. As a patient and family member, it has been a blessing straight from the heart of God.

Let your light shine today. Thank you for standing with us. Your prayers make a difference. Much love! Barb and Bill #pray4bill #Godisfaithful

Day #60 March 10

Anchor Verse: Philippians 1:6
Being confident of this, that he who began a good work in you will carry it on to completion until the day of Christ Jesus. (NIV)

Completion - we are often in a rush to get to the finish line when there are so many lessons to learn on the journey. We often have our eyes on the prize and we miss the flowers, the beautiful smiles, the amazing people that line our path. Too often we miss the blessings. It must grieve the Lord's heart when that happens. Just like a good earthly father, God, our heavenly Father, wants us to experience ALL the joy, hope, and love that He has for us. Don't you want that for your own family?

Today marks 60 days we have been on this journey. From the moment Bill was taken by ambulance to the ER as he fought for breath with the pneumonia in his lungs to where we are now, NIACH, an advanced care hospital, to continue his healing, daily we have seen the blessings.

Daily, the Lord has brought amazing people across our path. Daily, we have seen the line drawn between life and death. Daily, we have made the choice to pursue hope. Daily, we strive for completion… but we're not there yet.

It's still coming. I believe that, too. One thing I have learned is that God is faithful. His promises are true. He will never leave me or forsake me. What God starts He completes.

What are you waiting for God to complete in your life? What action do you need to take? What choice do you need to make? Today I am holding on to hope. I am standing with you as we pray for Bill that God would complete the healing that He started, in Jesus' name. Amen.

Thanks for standing with us! God is good... all the time! Thank you for your faithfulness. #pray4bill #Godisfaithful

Day #61 March 11

🦚 *Anchor Verse: Deuteronomy 13:3b-4*
The Lord your God is testing you to find out whether you love him with all your heart and with all your soul. It is the Lord your God you must follow, and him you must revere. Keep his commands and obey him; serve him and hold fast to him. (NIV)

"The greater the test, the greater the testimony." Often we attribute our trials and tests to the enemy, the devil. However, in the Bible we find many situations where God himself is testing people, and even nations, to determine their level of commitment to follow God and God alone.

This verse in Deuteronomy really accentuated that for me this morning. "The Lord your God is testing you..." Why? "To find out whether you love Him with ALL your heart and soul."

How do we do that?

We must follow God, revere Him, keep His commands and obey Him, serve Him, and hold fast to Him.

That list might seem overwhelming to you. Daily, I am learning that all we have to do is let Him take us by the hand and He will guide our steps. God promised and He will do it.

Daily, hourly, minute by minute, He provides all I need. There is grace, mercy, and peace in abundance. I want to be found faithful as I walk through this time of testing.

As I lean on Him, His grace is sufficient and His power is made perfect in my weakness.

We are all going through something - either personally, with a family member or friend, or maybe it's in your business or workplace. The Lord will see you through this test. He is your #1 fan. Be blessed!

Thank you for your continued prayers. They have moved the hand of God.#pray4bill #Godisfaithful

Day #62 March 12

Anchor Verse: Isaiah 43:1
But now, O Jacob, listen to the LORD who created you. O Israel, the one who formed you says, "Do not be afraid, for I have ransomed you. I have called you by name; you are mine." (NIV)

This is one of my favorite verses. There is something about God calling me by name and that I belong to Him that not only fills me with joy but makes me feel secure. Like a child that needs to be comforted who finds refuge in their parent's arms that's what God does for us.

The Creator of the universe knows your name! You aren't some random thought. God's love is greater than any love you have ever experienced.

When I consider this journey we have traveled and where Bill is right now, in the place between death's door and complete healing, it gives me comfort to know that God knows Bill and He has called him by name. Bill belongs to God.

I don't have to worry, fret, or freak out! I just need to trust God with the man I love, the one I plan to love the rest of my life. Isaiah tells us not to fear for the Lord has formed us and redeemed us. When Bill's body systems aren't quite in balance, it might seem like a juggling act for the doctors to get it right, but God already knows how it's supposed to look and the Great Physician will guide them to what's best for Bill.

My hope and prayer is that this verse brings you comfort. There is security in being called by name by your heavenly Father, the one who created everything in the universe. You matter. What happens to you makes a difference to God. The choices you make are important. Trust Him. Even when you don't understand the circumstances you are walking through, God knows. Rest in His arms of love. Have a blessed day!

Thank you for your continued prayers. I had a great night's sleep. I hope Bill did too. I'm ready and refreshed to walk with Him today. #pray4bill#Godisfaithful

Day #63 March 13

Anchor Verse: Romans 8:28
And we know that in all things God works for the good of those who love him,
who have been called according to his purpose. (NIV)

All things... "all" is a big word, even though it is only three letters. It is often a word that God uses in the Bible. He's like that. God wants all of us - our heart, our mind, our soul, and our strength. He won't settle for just a little bit of us, God wants it all. Because He loves us that much, God wants us to love Him no matter our circumstances.

God also wants you to receive ALL that He has for you – all the blessings, all the wisdom, all the grace, all the love, and so much more.

Now that it's been over two months since we have been on this journey, I am beginning to understand the tenacity and endurance of those who run marathons. It's not just about our strength, it's about our mindset.

That's what I see in this verse today, I must believe that all things – even the things I don't understand, the potholes on the path, the people who are cheering us on, the everyday victories, and the enemy's ambushes – all of these will work together for my good, for Bill's good.

Bill and I are committed to finishing this race well. We love the Lord and nothing will change that. Nothing will change His love for us. Nothing will change His love for you.

Walk in confidence today holding on to the Lord's hand. He will never leave you or forsake you. May the Lord be glorified in you today. Hallelujah!

Thank you for standing with us. The race is not always to the swift but to those who keep on running! #pray4bill #Godisfaithful

Day #64 March 14

Anchor Verse: Song of Solomon 2:4
He has brought me to his banqueting place, And his banner over me is love
[waving overhead to protect and comfort me]. (AMP)

This morning I woke up to this Sunday School song, "He brought me to his banqueting table, His banner over me is love." As a believer, this is Jesus' gift to us. He honors us, protects us, and provides for us.

Two things struck me about this verse in relation to Bill this morning. First, the banqueting table...he is still on a liquid diet via a feeding tube... but that will change. My prayer is that in the restoration process the Lord will soon have Bill eating food by mouth again. It brings tears to my eyes to think of the smile on Bill's face when he sits at the table savoring every bite he takes. His favorite breakfast is biscuits and gravy. That's what I imagine him eating. (I know... sounds really heart-healthy, right?)

Second, God's banner over him is love. It is God's love and protection that has been over Bill all the days of this journey and even before that. God loves Bill so much that He was willing to let Bill (and me) go through this refining fire so that His honor, His glory would be seen in us, and in you, our faithful prayer warriors.

In one of the commentaries I was reading, it described His love like a military banner of protection. God delights in us and protects us! When I am with Bill, I feel the presence of God's love. Our love is getting stronger as we take one step closer to God's healing for Bill.

This promise is for you as well. Whether you are walking through a celebration or a challenge, He is with you and will never leave you or forsake you... never!

Three prayer points: 1. Bill's mind: Complete restoration. Each cell and neuron needs to be healed and rejuvenated. 2. His lungs: Chest x-ray shows improvement. Still on antibiotics. 3. His heart: Praying for healing of his aortic valve, good blood pressure, heart rate, and his heart back in sinus rhythm. Nothing is too hard for God.

May the Lord's love protect you and comfort you and fill you up with joy! Thank you for standing with us. #pray4bill #Godisfaithful

Day #65 March 15

Anchor Verse: Psalm 96:1
Sing to the Lord a new song! (NIV)

We often get stuck in a rut doing the same thing over and over and over again, not only at work or socially or even in our daily routine, but sometimes in our relationship with God.

But God calls to sing a new song! A song we have never sung before as we walk in a new place, new territory with Him at our side.

Two months ago, January 15, my dear husband, Bill, had a brain bleed early that morning after coming down with the flu the day before. It was one of the most horrific and helpless moments of my life. Yet the Lord was with me as I had to make big decisions about Bill's life and our future. He was teaching me a new song.

Today we are in a different place. God is restoring Bill! In the last few days, we have seen tremendous progress. Is Bill completely healed? No, not yet. But we have seen good progress. There is still some deficit but his growing alertness is encouraging to all of us.

To capture this verse in a picture, I see the contrast between a stagnant, stinky pond and a freshwater mountain stream. The pond has no new life flowing into it, but the mountain stream is filled with hope and joy and refreshes all who come near it – the sound of the stream brings new life!

God wants you to sing a new song today. He wants to transform your life from a stinky stagnant pond to a stream filled with life and hope and joy.

You get to decide. Come and join me as we sing a new song unto the Lord! He will turn your mourning into dancing. Your cup runneth over with joy!

Thanks for standing with us and celebrating the goodness of the Lord! #pray4bill #Godisfaithful

Day #66 March 16

Anchor Verse: Matthew 6:10
We ask that your kingdom will come now. May your will be done here on earth, just as it is in heaven. (TLB)

How much do you trust God? I mean really trust Him. It is easy to say that we are Christians and we believe in God. Do you trust Him with the details of your life, with your loved ones?

You may have learned the Lord's Prayer as a child. It can be found in Matthew 6 where Jesus' disciples asked Him to teach them how to pray. This is the model prayer that Jesus gave them and us to follow.

This passage in verse 10 where we pray for "His will to be done" is a powerful verse. To me, it signifies that I am willing to take a leap of faith right into my heavenly Father's arms.

For those of you who have been following us through these 66 days of Bill's health challenges, you know that we have looked death in the face on many occasions. It is in that place where truly our faith is tested. Am I willing to say to God, "Your will be done" no matter the outcome? I believe each one of you has faced or is facing right now a situation where you are being asked the same question.

Maybe it's your own health, or employment, a relationship, your finances, an issue with a loved one, you fill in the blank. You know what I'm talking about. Just like Abraham, am I willing to put my hopes and dreams and loved one on the altar, and give them to God? That is a question only you can answer. May the Lord give you the strength to take that leap of faith.

And the good news, we have a heavenly Father who loves us so much that when we pray for His will to be done, it's often way better than anything we could ever imagine!

Thanks for standing with us. There is power in the name of the Lord. #pray4bill #Godisfaithful

Day #67 March 17

Anchor Verse: Joel 3:10b
Let the weak say, "I am strong!" (NKJV)

There is power in the Word of God. There is even more power when we speak it out loud so we can hear it. What do you speak and declare over your own life, your own body?

This verse in Joel reminds us that our words are powerful. What we say to ourselves can change our outlook, even change our actions, and physical changes can take place as well.

We have all read stories about people who have overcome amazing odds, when it looked like they had no chance at all of recovering, yet they did. Bill and I are living our own story of victory right now. God is writing that story right in front of our eyes.

In one of Bill Johnson's messages, he commented, why reinforce what the devil says about you? We need to believe God's truth from God's Word. Too many times we have believed the lie rather than the truth

Every day I speak words of life over Bill. I speak scripture over him. I lay hands on him and anoint him with oil, as I pray from the top of his head to the soles of his feet. I have seen the hand of God at work. When circumstances looked pretty bad in the flesh, that is when I turned my eyes to heaven and declared, "Bill is strong in the strength of God."

Declare God's promises over your life today. Speak His truth. Don't believe the lies that are spoken about you or the seeds of doubt that the enemy flings your direction. Choose God. Choose life. Choose truth.

Ephesians 6:10 reminds us, "Finally, be strong in the Lord and in his mighty power." That is my encouragement for you today. Be strong, not in your own flesh, but be strong in the Lord, and watch what He can do.

We have a clean slate, a fresh start, with new mercies. Can't wait to see what God will do today in Bill's life. Thanks for standing with us and holding up our arms. #pray4bill #Godisfaithful

Day #68 March 18

Anchor Verse: Deuteronomy 33:25, 27
Your strength will equal your days. The eternal God is your refuge, and underneath are the everlasting arms. (NIV)

I love God's promises in the Bible. The Bible is a treasure trove of blessings and instruction. God's Word is alive and full of power.

This morning in my daily reading, these verses really resonated with me. Bill and I have been on a long journey as we have faced his health challenges. God in His faithfulness has supplied all our needs. Often the greatest need is strength for the journey, whether that is physical strength, or mentally, emotionally, or spiritually. Whichever one it is or all of the above, my strength, your strength, Bill's strength will equal our days and the day's demands. Isn't that wonderful? I don't need to worry about the "what ifs" of life, I just need to trust God. He is my refuge and strength, an ever-present help in time of trouble.

God is holding me in His everlasting arms, just like a parent holds their child, safe and secure. His arms are strong when I am weak. When I am walking the tightrope of life's challenges high above the floor of the arena, God is my safety net. He will never leave me or forsake me, never!

Every morning, I run to God and so many times during the day and night. When we faced moments where the veil between life and death was so thin, it was almost transparent, I ran to my heavenly Father first to plead for my husband's life before I ran to anyone else. I know that my life and Bill's life and your life are in His hands. He is a good, good Father. He is the Giver of life.

Whether we are weak or strong, He is faithful. Be mindful today of those around you. They may need your prayers, your listening ear, or your words of encouragement. Thank you, Lord, for the gift of Your strength today. I am forever grateful.

Thank you for standing with us. I'm praying for a day of victory for Bill in Jesus' name. #pray4bill #Godisfaithful

Day #69 March 19

Anchor Verse: Psalm 23:2
He makes me lie down in green pastures, he leads me beside quiet waters. (NIV)

Psalm 23 is one of the favorite psalms of all time. It is packed with powerful imagery as well as God's promises. Just as a shepherd must "make" his sheep lie down in those green pastures to rest and find nourishment, there are times in our lives when God does the same for us.

We are totally dependent on Him, the Good Shepherd, not only to meet our needs but to stand watch over us and protect us from our enemies – from all harm and danger. Sheep are pretty vulnerable creatures. We can be too. The enemy comes to steal, kill, and destroy, but God comes to give us abundant life.

The Lord is in charge of Bill's complete restoration and recovery. The Good Shepherd is in Bill's room every day. He is watching over Bill's care and I know He speaks to Bill in the stillness of the night reminding him to not be afraid, for the Lord is with him.

And the second part of the verse, "He leads me beside quiet waters" reminds me that in the midst of the chaos of our lives, He leads us to a quiet place where our thirst is satisfied, not only our physical needs, but our thirst to know Him more.

It may sound crazy, but even in ICU I have felt His peace and rested beside those quiet waters, when there was lots of noises, alarms, loud voices, even people crying out for help. Someone commented about the peace they felt in Bill's room. That is the presence of the Good Shepherd.

Are you in a timeout right now? Is He making you to lie down in those green pastures to rest and recover, or to slow down and appreciate the life you have been given?

Thank you for your prayers for Bill. May Bill be filled with God's peace as the Lord continues to heal his body, mind, and spirit. He is the Lord our Healer. #pray4bill #Godisfaithful

Day #70 March 20

Anchor Verse: Ecclesiastes 3:1
There is a season (a time appointed) for everything and a time for every delight and event or purpose under heaven. (AMP)

I am excited that today is the first day of spring! Spring is my favorite season as the whole earth comes alive and so do we! I am even more excited this year as we see Bill beginning to take more steps forward in his healing.

For everything there is a season – I'm so grateful that God created the earth with seasons. It reminds me that there are seasons in our lives we cherish and other seasons that are difficult, yet God is always faithful.

How do we graciously and gratefully make it through the seasons in our lives? Only by the grace of God. We must hold on to His hand and listen to His voice speak to us and only move when God says it is time.

During these last 70 days, I have learned so much about life, time, priorities, and the many things that fill the hours of our days. So much was stripped away the day we walked into the Emergency Room but so much was given to us as well.

Being with the one I love is so much more important than running here and there, even when the activities are good ones. Often our lives resemble our dear friend Chicken Little.

It's time to stop and breathe, my friends. God is the one in charge of the universe, not us. Today Bill is having a trach mask trial to see how he does with a new baby step forward. I am praying for success. It will be a step into a new season, a new place, a new frontier in his healing.

I am so grateful that there is a time for every purpose under heaven. May you walk in all that God has for you and may all the rest be pruned away as you blossom in this spring season. You are loved!

Thank you for your steadfast support! #pray4bill #Godisfaithful

Day #71 March 21

Anchor Verse: Proverbs 16:9
A man's mind plans his way [as he journeys through life], But the LORD directs his steps and establishes them. (AMP)

We make our lists, we make our plans, some people may even have elaborate systems to track what to do, when to do it, and when they have met their goals. Being organized is a wonderful thing; it helps us accomplish amazing things in life.

What I have learned on Bill's health journey is that my plans are often not God's plans. God is in charge of my life and He directs my steps.

This morning as I was thinking about the road ahead of us and Bill's current medical and support team and their plans for Bill, I found amazing comfort in this verse. The Lord directs my steps, not only that, He makes them sure, secure. It's like those hind's feet on high places; we won't slip and fall in the process of reaching our goal.

We have believed in miracles throughout Bill's entire journey. You have heard us testify of them. God has more of them planned. They may happen today, I don't know, but God does.

I'm not suggesting that you throw out your day planner, but I am proposing that you listen for His still small voice as He directs you through your day. There will be times when using a wrestling term, you are "body slammed" to the mat and it takes a while for the healing to happen. We know that wasn't part of your plan! During the healing process look up to God, seek His face, learn the lessons, and receive the miracles. Your life will never be the same. That's a good thing.

Trusting when my eyes can't see the miracles God has for Bill and me. Looking forward to another day in the Bill Hollace NASCAR Health Race with excitement at every turn.

Thanks for standing with us in prayer. We couldn't do this without you. #pray4bill #Godisfaithful

Day #72 March 22

Anchor Verse: Philippians 4:4
Rejoice in the Lord always. I will say it again: Rejoice! (NIV)

Giving thanks is a powerful tool in the hands of God. It is not just about how we feel but looking beyond our circumstances to the one who holds our hand. We can choose to look beyond the momentary struggles to the greater glory that God has planned for us. Trusting our heavenly Father who loves us far more than we can ever imagine!

When the way is clear and our life is looking good and we're healthy and so is our family, our bills are paid and there's emergency money, and our relationship with God is very close, we do feel like rejoicing. Our hearts may be singing praises to God from the moment we wake up in the morning until we go to bed at night.

What about when the opposite is true? We are unemployed. Our family relationships are broken and tension is running high, and there are unpaid bills, and there is no reserve – either financially or emotionally, and God seems so far away, are you willing to rejoice then?

This Bible verse says we are to rejoice always – even when our eyes can't see how God's promises will come true for us. That is the kind of faith that God is looking for – remember, faith as small as a mustard seed.

Today I rejoice, as I have in days past, not because I have all the answers, or there are no hiccups in my life, but because I know that God is faithful. Last night I was talking with my dad, and I said, I have two choices, either I trust God with the big and small things in my life, and in Bill's life, or I don't trust God. I choose to trust Him. No matter what it looks like today or tomorrow.

You may still be waiting for the manifestation of His promises, His healing, His restoration in your life, it's still on the way. It could be a miracle that is still in the making, just like we are waiting for Bill's complete healing.

Thank you for standing with us through the storms of life. Great will be your reward. #pray4bill #Godisfaithful

Day #73 March 23

Anchor Verse: James 1:12
Blessed is the one who perseveres under trial because, having stood the test, that person will receive the crown of life that the Lord has promised to those who love him. (NIV)

Trials, temptations, and tests – we all have them. We all walk through them, and sometimes Jesus carried us through them when our strength is gone and we can't even stand.

In the last 73 days, I have watched my husband go through some deep valleys. I have seen God lead him beside still waters. God is restoring Bill's soul. For a lot of this journey, Bill was so sick that he was sedated. The result is that Bill doesn't remember those chunks of time. And that's okay, because some things are best forgotten.

Together we are learning what perseverance means. I thought I knew what persevering meant, but God is taking the depth of my understanding to a new level. Just like when I attended law school and my brain was stretched, this lesson is stretching my brain and heart and soul. It's a good thing. Nothing is wasted in God's Kingdom, nothing.

I actually had chosen a different verse in James for today's verse but God put this one in front of me this morning. It's a promise that I am claiming this day. I pray that you will take it to heart as well. "Blessed" is the one who perseveres under trial, because "having stood the test" (that's what Bill and I are doing right now) we will receive the crown of life that the Lord has promised to those who love Him.

There is a purpose. There is a reward for persevering. Hold on to His hand today. Hold on to His promises. God will never let you go. Our heavenly Father loves you and me and Bill with an everlasting love.

Praying for another great day of next steps for Bill and healing throughout his body, mind, and spirit. God is able! Thanks for standing with us. #pray4bill #Godisfaithful

Day #74 March 24

Anchor Verse: Psalm 62:5
For God alone my soul waits in silence ana quietly submits to Him, For my hope is from Him. (AMP)

Silence - silence in the Presence of God is a powerful place. Many people run from silence. Often our days are filled with noise – music, television, videos, games, people, conversations, work, traffic, just life.

Have you every stopped to recognize that silence is filled with its own symphony?

I am an early morning person. It is in the silence that I come into the Lord's presence and I am filled to full and overflowing. It is in the silence that I find strength to meet the demands of the day. It is in the silence that God touches me and I am wrapped in His arms of love.

In this psalm, King David reminds us that our hope comes from God. Our hope comes from God, not our circumstances, not our bank account, not even our feelings – that is why we are hopeful. All life and hope and victory come from God.

My strength is renewed this morning because I am standing on that truth and it is the living water that quenches the thirst of my soul.

Today as I go to see Bill, there has been a mindset shift. I will not be on the defensive, which is what the enemy has been trying to do the last couple of days. Instead, I will boldly reclaim that hospital room for the Lord, all worry and fear and frustration and anxiety must flee in Jesus' name. There is victory in Jesus and I declare Bill's room as holy ground.

Thank you for standing with us. May His victory be yours. There is power in silence as you wait in His presence. May you seek it and find it today and every day.#pray4bill #Godisfaithful

Day #75 March 25

Anchor Verse: Psalm 138:1, 8
Lord, with all my heart I thank you. I will sing your praises before the armies of angels…The Lord will work out his plans for my life—for your loving-kindness, Lord, continues forever. Don't abandon me—for you made me. (TLB)

75 is a special number. If a couple has been married for 75 years, they celebrate their diamond anniversary. Today marks 75 days since Bill and I started this journey from his illness to his health and healing. A diamond is created by great pressure and polished to enhance its beauty. I believe that is a good description of what we have walked through these 75 days.

Most of all this morning, my heart is filled with gratitude and thanksgiving that the Lord has never abandoned or forsaken us, not for even a second. His words are true. His love never ends. He is faithful. He is a good, good Father.

On this journey, many times in the flesh things were a little dicey. Just like an airplane that goes into a dive and recovers before crashing, God rescued us before we crashed.

In this last week, it seems that Bill's healing in so many ways has hit warp speed. However, Bill's healing is not completed... yet... God's timing is always perfect and complete healing will be accomplished in His time.

This morning I am curious about God's gift for this Jubilee day. It will be good. As Psalm 138 proclaims this morning, with ALL my heart, I praise you, Lord, in the presence of the angels, I sing your praises.

Heaven's throne room is filled with my offering of praise this morning. I lift my hands and heart and voice before the Lord and praise His holy name.

Lord, I know that I was right to trust You and believe for the healing miracles that have happened and are still to come. We trust You, God, to complete what You started in Jesus' name. You are worthy of our praise. I love you, Lord. Thank you for standing with us. Thank you for your faithfulness and encouragement. #pray4bill #Godisfaithful

Day #76 March 26

Anchor Verse: Esther 4:14
...Yet who knows whether you have come to the kingdom for such a time as this? (NKJV)

For such a time as this... do you wonder if you are where you are supposed to be? Do you wonder if you have taken the wrong path and are in the wilderness because you took a wrong turn? Or are you able to get the 25,000 foot level perspective, God's perspective, that where you are is part of God's plan?

Last night I was talking to a friend about our current situation, and she made a comment about how God had equipped me to carry this message to others through His gift to me of writing and words. It led me to Queen Esther who was an orphan girl that God chose to be queen so that she could be in a position to save her people, the Jews.

When we started this roller coaster ride with Bill's health, I specifically asked the Lord about sharing our journey on Facebook. As you know, once you open the door here, you can't close it. "Lord, do you want me to take this to Facebook?" My first impulse was to keep it more private. God's response, "I want to do a work there (on Facebook)." How could I turn Him down? If God wanted to do a work on Facebook and touch lives through our journey, then there was only one choice – obey!

In exchange for my obedience, God has given me not only the words to share and the scripture passages, but He has given me His own perspective about this journey. God has given me joy, peace, and strength, and also stretched my faith to depths beyond my understanding.

What has He done for you? Only you can tell that story. I have heard testimony after testimony which includes miracles in your own life, a greater love for God, and an enhanced prayer life. How cool is that!

God has equipped you for a place, a plan, a purpose, even a very specific occasion. When you are walking in obedience, not walking in sin, He can use you in the lives of others as we bring Him honor and glory.

Thank you for your countless prayers. They are a sweet aroma to the Lord. #pray4bill #Godisfaithful

Day #77 March 27

Anchor Verse: Romans 12:2
And do not be conformed to this world, but be transformed by the renewing of your mind, that you may prove what is that good and acceptable and perfect will of God. (NKJV)

As I was spending time in the Lord's presence this morning, the renewal of my mind and transformation was the place He brought me, not only in my own life but in Bill's life.

As I watch God do Miraculous things (yes, with a capital "M") in Bill's natural body, my heart's cry was for the completion of Bill's transformation including the renewal of his mind as God puts everything back together in the right order.

Our mind is very powerful; it's like the quarterback on the team who directs traffic. It's the lighthouse. It's the command center of a military campaign. It's poetry and power in motion. I stand in awe of the way God created our brains... just as God created them He can restore them.

Paul reminds us in this passage that there is a purpose for this renewal and transformation, it's so we can know and prove what God's will is. God wants us to walk in all He has for us, but to do that, we need to be aligned with Him. We can't just walk around willy-nilly and expect it's all going to turn out for the best.

Just as I have watched the medical teams who have worked with Bill methodically move forward addressing every part of his body that needs to be repaired, I know that God does the same thing in our lives. Our heavenly Father is a God of order; all creation speaks of God's amazing plan. God wants order in your life as well.

Pray not only for Bill's brain to be healed, but in his recovery, he would not be conformed to the world but transformed by the renewing of his mind. I pray your heart's desire is to be more like Jesus.

Thank you for standing with us in our hour of need. Be blessed as you have blessed us. #pray4bill #Godisfaithful

Day #78 March 28

Anchor Verse: Judges 6:12
When the angel of the Lord appeared to Gideon, he said, "The Lord is with you, mighty warrior." (NIV)

You are a mighty warrior! I can hear your reply, "Not me!" Yes, you. Daily the Lord equips you to be a light for Him, to fight the battles that you are called to fight. That might be as a parent, spouse, pastor, teacher, business owner or employee, there are so many roles that we have in this life. However, our most important calling is to walk in obedience to God, to go where He tells you to go.

If you read the rest of Judges 6, you will see that even though God called Gideon a mighty warrior, Gideon didn't think he was. Gideon had lots of reasons why he couldn't do what God asked him to do. Lord, You've abandoned us. Lord, how can I save Israel? My clan is the weakest and I am the least in my family.

God wasn't moved by Gideon's doubt or excuses. God saw what Gideon couldn't see - God had already equipped Gideon for the task that was ahead of him.

God still works that way. Jeremiah 29:11 tells us God knows the plans He has for us, plans for good and not evil, to give us hope and a future.

When Bill and I started this journey in January, I never imagined we would still be in the thick of it heading into April. But God did. I hear these words whispered to me this morning, "The Lord is with you, mighty warrior." With my hand in God's hand, I will continue to walk this road and fight these battles regarding Bill's health that still lie ahead of us.

I pray that you, too, will take this commission of the Lord to heart. Whatever you are facing today, know that Lord is with you and you will be victorious in Jesus' name.

Thank you for standing with us. Thank you for rejoicing in yesterday's victory. Let's storm the gates of heaven asking for the completion of Bill's healing in Jesus' name. Hallelujah! #pray4bill #Godisfaithful

Day #79 March 29

Anchor Verse: Hebrews 12:2
Fixing our eyes on Jesus, the author and perfecter of faith, who for the joy set before Him endured the cross, despising the shame, and has sat down at the right hand of the throne of God. (NIV)

Even in the midst of our own healing adventure, it is not lost on me that this is Easter week. Today is Maundy Thursday, the night of the Last Supper, the night Jesus was betrayed and began His walk to the cross, where Jesus would secure eternal life for all those who choose to accept His amazing love gift.

This is a powerful verse, not only in Jesus' life, but for you and me. First, we must fix our eyes on Jesus, not on the problem, other people, or on ourselves, our hope comes from the Lord.

Second, for the JOY that was set before Him, Jesus could endure carrying the weight of the world on His shoulders. Jesus kept His eyes on the glory to come. That's where my eyes are fixed too, on the glory to come when Bill comes out of this time of testing and is healed. Jesus was aware of His surroundings as He walked the path of pain, and encouraged and taught those around Him in the process. God wants to use our trials to bring Him glory – both now and later.

Third, Jesus took the most horrible circumstances and the shame associated with death on a cross and turned it into the hope that we have today. Because Jesus rose from the dead and triumphed over death, we, too, have eternal hope. Early on in this journey, there were prophetic words that came out of Bill's mouth from the Lord, "Satan took me down, but I know that God will raise me up just like He did Jesus."

Easter, Resurrection Sunday, is coming in just a few days. My hands and heart are willing to receive the miracles that God has planned for us this Easter weekend. Invite Jesus into your heart and He will give you eternal life instead of a life in the flesh that is too soon gone.

Thank you for your ceaseless prayers. They are moving the hand of God! With Jesus is our victory. #pray4bill #Godisfaithful

Day #80 March 30

Anchor Verse: Proverbs 3:5-6
Trust in the Lord with all your heart and lean not on your own understanding;
in all your ways submit to him (acknowledge him), and he will make your paths
straight. (NIV)

Today is Good Friday. Today is the day that changed the course of history, literally, our calendars reflect that fact. As I was reflecting on what to share with you, God brought me here to Proverbs, because it's all about trusting God, trusting that His promises are true. We are forgiven. We are loved. We are covered by His grace. We have a second chance.

Good Friday is always a time of reflection for me about the great sacrifice, the high price that Jesus paid for my sins and yours. He died that we might live, not only for eternity, but that we have a new life starting today.

Bill is in a place of new beginnings. You have walked this path with us. You have seen the miracles. You have prayed – day and night. God has been talking to you. He has touched your life in a new way – a new intimacy and you have seen His glory.

But I know that what we have seen so far is not the whole story. Proverbs 3 tells us to trust in Him, with ALL our heart, no room for doubt here, and not to lean on what we know, because it will fall short of what we need. But in ALL our ways acknowledge Him, as King of kings and Lord of lords and He WILL make your paths straight. He will heal and restore. God will do things we cannot comprehend!

This week has been filled with miraculous steps in Bill's recovery. There are still gaps that need to be filled and more healing to come, but I know that God's promises are true.

Earlier this week Bill said to me, "I trust you." I turn my face toward heaven this morning and say, "Lord, I trust you."

Thank you for your faithfulness. Thank you for being our companions on this journey. Be blessed this day! #pray4bill #Godisfaithful

Day #81 March 31

Anchor Verse: 1 Corinthians 15:57
But thanks be to God, who gives us the victory through our Lord Jesus Christ!
(NIV)

Victory in Jesus - that's really what this whole Easter weekend is about, but more than that, it's how we can live each day of our lives as believers. We sing the song, "Because He lives I can face tomorrow, because He lives, all fear is gone." It's true. Those aren't just words in a song. It's the promise we have as God's children. We walk in victory every day.

We have the choice to walk in that victory. Fear might come nipping at our heels. We may face a mountain that we feel ill-equipped to climb. Today may look the same as yesterday, but it's not, it is one step closer to the victory God has planned for you.

Last night, as Bill and I were waiting for the cardiologist to arrive, long past the time of his predicted arrival, it was strange to be at the hospital so late, but I waited in quiet trust. There was a sense of peace. I watched the doctor in the nurse's area as he went through Bill's records, and I prayed that God would show him the way.

Peace filled the room as he entered because the Great Physician was there with us. The Spirit of God is always in Bill's room along with the angelic host that guard him. The doctor spoke of pacemaker surgery - the pathway to victory.

As I remember that first Easter weekend, on that Saturday, the Jewish Sabbath, so many were mourning the death of Jesus, their hope had died the previous day. We know the ending of the story, the resurrection of Jesus on Sunday morning, the path to eternal life. We have victory through Jesus. We have hope. We have joy. We have peace.

Walk in that victory today! Accept the greatest gift of all, Jesus. Your life will never be the same.

Thank you for standing with us as we prepare our hearts and minds for the pacemaker procedure. I am praying for an extra measure of grace for Bill. God is able. #pray4bill #Godisfaithful

Our Walk of Faith

April 2018
New Heart, New Life

Day #82 April 1

⚓ Anchor Verse: Matthew 28: 5-6
The angel said to the women, "Do not be afraid, for I know that you are looking for Jesus, who was crucified. He is not here; he has risen, just as he said. Come and see the place where he lay. (NIV)

It's Resurrection Sunday! He is risen! He is risen indeed! This day commemorates the greatest day of hope we have as human beings. Because Jesus is alive, we can face today and we can face tomorrow with Him at our side.

One of the things I appreciate about this passage is that the first thing the angel said to the women was, "Do not be afraid." That's the same message God has for us today.

You may be facing an uncertain tomorrow or wrapped up in a web of trouble today. Your pillow may be wet this morning from the tears you cried through the night.

This message from the Lord still rings true today, do not be afraid. Jesus is alive. He is risen, just as He said. His promises are true.

There is new life in Christ. All we have to do is say "yes" to Jesus and He will walk with us through the trials and the victories in our lives.

Today as Bill is transferred to the hospital to prepare for his pacemaker procedure tomorrow, I believe it is no accident or coincidence this next step is taking place on Easter Sunday.

I will repeat the words that Bill told me early on in this journey. "Satan took me down, but God is going to raise me up just like He did Jesus." Amen!

Thank you for your faithfulness in prayer. Celebrate with us on this Resurrection Sunday. #pray4bill #Godisfaithful

(And like many things in life, those plans changed. Bill wasn't transferred to the hospital. Instead, Easter Sunday was a roller coaster ride with Bill's heart rate going as low as 12 bpm. Every minute I prayed for his heart to keep beating as it should. Truly, Bill's heart and life were in God's hands.)

Day #83 April 2

Anchor Verse: 2 Corinthians 4: 7-9
But we have this treasure in jars of clay to show that this all-surpassing power is from God and not from us. We are hard pressed on every side, but not crushed; perplexed, but not in despair; persecuted, but not abandoned; struck down, but not destroyed. (NIV)

The all-surpassing power of God is definitely not from us! Through life's trials and even the beautiful days of victory, God is shaping, molding, and making us into the image of Christ.

This morning I woke up, in peace, because I am standing on God's promises and trusting Him with my husband's life. Last night the Lord gave me specific instructions. They are doing remodeling work in our apartment next week. God said to go home make something to eat, pray, pack until 10 pm, and then go to bed, and Bill would be fine. That's what I did. When the devil came trying to make me doubt that Bill was okay or even to call and check on him, I refused to take the bait. I said out loud, "Either I trust you, Lord or I don't. And I trust you, so devil, take a hike." As I lay down to sleep, I spent time praising the Lord for the battle that was already won. I woke up during the night with praise on my lips.

God brought me to this verse, the perfect place. We are hard pressed on every side(amen), but not crushed; perplexed(bewildered, frustrated) but not in despair; persecuted, but not abandoned by You, Lord, and struck down (knocked down) but not destroyed. Hallelujah! This pretty accurately describes the last 83 days of this journey.

Today is the final blow to the enemy's futile attempts to come against God's power and purpose in Bill's body and life. We stand in victory. It's like crossing the Red Sea and the 7th time around Jericho when the walls came tumbling down, and includes what we celebrated yesterday, Resurrection Sunday, Jesus' ultimate victory over sin, death, and the grave.

This is not for us alone, it's God's gift to you. Thank you for being part of the great cloud of witnesses that surround us in heaven and on earth.

Thank you for your prayers throughout this day. All glory and honor go to God! #pray4bill #Godisfaithful #anewheartonEasterMonday

Day #84 April 3

Anchor Verse: Isaiah 55:11
So will My word be which goes out of My mouth; It will not return to Me void (useless, without result), Without accomplishing what I desire, And without succeeding in the matter for which I sent it. (AMP)

God has a plan. Does that encourage you? It does me. As I look at the world around me it seems rather chaotic, even spinning out of control. It may look pretty crazy, but God is not surprised or shaken by it.

This morning as I reflect back over the last few days, really since Friday, when the decision was made that Bill needed a pacemaker (like now!), I am amazed at how quickly things have happened. God moves like that sometimes, and other times, it's like watching a garden grow.

The seed is planted, but it must make its journey up through the soil, and oh, the many days until the harvest comes. A gardener and a farmer understand this concept especially with spring planting near.

This verse in Isaiah reminds us that God's purposes will not fail. They will succeed. They will accomplish what He desires and the matter for which He intended it. That is good news, very good!

My mortal body is feeling the effects of the roller coaster ride of Bill's heart rate this weekend, but my spirit rests in God's truth that His purpose will prevail.

We move forward today on the path God has for us. You can choose to do the same.

Put your hand in His hand and trust that He knows the way, even when your eyes can't see.

Thank you for standing with us and for your many prayers! God has plans for Bill and they are good. #pray4bill #Godisfaithful

Day #85 April 4

Anchor Verse: Revelation 21:5
He who was seated on the throne said, "I am making everything new!" (NIV)

God's mercies are new every morning, GREAT is Your faithfulness, O Lord. Aren't you glad we get a fresh start every day? That's one of the amazing things about God. He is the God of second chances, and third chances, and however many we need. Don't hold on to yesterday's yuck, lay it down at His feet. Put on the cloak of righteousness and the mantle of praise every morning as we lift our voices in prayer and praise to Him.

It's beyond our human understanding how this works, but I am so grateful for this daily gift! This verse from Revelation 21 reminds us that God is making everything new! Hallelujah for that!

When I go to visit Bill every day, I look for the small steps of newness, the little things that are signs of progress – a word spoken, new movement of his body, new strength in his hands, what the tests show, what the medical staff sees, and most of all, what God speaks to me about His transforming power in Bill's life and body.

It's the same in your life. Daily, God is renewing you. You aren't the same person you used to be. He is making everything new! We get to choose if we want to be a part of the renovation process.

As I prepare for the work they will be doing in our apartment next week, packing things up to make room for them to work, I am reminded that there are old things that must go. There is one thing that remains when God is renovating our world, and that is our love for Him.

It is in those renovation seasons, when He is making everything new that we get to know Him more, develop a greater intimacy with Him.

What is God doing in your life? What rooms is He renovating? Step into the newness of His joy this morning. He will bathe you in the streams of living water. God will restore your soul. Sing praises to His name. He is worthy of it all.

Thank you for standing with us as God continues to make everything new in Bill's life. #pray4bill #Godisfaithful

Day #86 April 5

Anchor Verse: Luke 8:39
Return home and tell how much God has done for you. So the man went away and told all over town how much Jesus had done for him. (NIV)

My heart is so full this morning after spending time with God… I could soar like an eagle! There was so much God showed me.

This journey is not just about Bill's daily struggles, about the struggles that have taken place over the 86 days since he first entered the hospital, or about the challenges Bill had before then, it's about what lies ahead.

God is preparing Bill for the future He has for him. In the process, you and I are being transformed into prayer warriors who see God's hand at work. We have a front row seat to God's divine plan, a place of miracles.

In this passage, the story is about a demon-possessed man whose home was the graveyard because he couldn't live around anyone else. Jesus came to deliver him from the torture he lived with every day. I imagine a person with multiple issues - body, mind, and spirit. I pictured Bill and his multiple health issues and God's healing in every part of him.

When the people came to see what happened, they found the man sitting at Jesus' feet, dressed, and in his right mind. They were afraid. The man wanted to follow Jesus. Instead Jesus said to go and tell how much God had done for him. Spread the good news. Let the people see the miracle.

I don't know the plans God has for Bill's life once the healing is completed, but there will be amazing stories to tell – the miracles, the healing, the restoration, the reality of God's amazing grace!

How do we chase away the darkness in the world? We let our light shine. We tell the stories of what Jesus is doing in our lives. We take back the night and we are not afraid. Be strong and courageous.

Thank you for standing with us. I'm looking forward to a great day after yesterday's sleep and restoration in Bill's body. God is good… all the time! #pray4bill#Godisfaithful

Day #87 April 6

__Anchor Verse: Psalm 116:5__
The Lord is gracious and righteous; our God is full of compassion. (NIV)

Compassion moves us from seeing only ourselves and our needs to a place where we see others through God's eyes.

On our journey, we have been so blessed by so many who are filled with compassion, it's the way they live, it's the way they work.

I remember so many in the medical field at Valley Hospital, Deaconess Hospital, Kootenai Hospital, and now at NIACH, who have so tenderly cared for Bill and their compassionate hearts have blessed me as well. It takes a special person to love those who are going through deep waters and who are not their normal selves because of illness.

God gives them eyes to see, and ears to hear. It is the hands of Jesus that touch their patients as they respond in love and speak kindly with respect instead of in frustration. It's a calling to care for others.

You have stood by us during our darkest hours and also rejoiced in our victories. We have done the dance of rejoicing together!

God calls us to be filled with grace and righteousness and with compassion for a broken world filled with broken people.

Yesterday I was really touched by those who tended to Bill. While they were in his room, they spoke with kindness. They tended to him with loving hands. Each action was an encouragement to keep on going and praising him for coming this far. God has given the staff the ability to see Bill as God sees him. We have been blessed to see Bill's sense of humor and personality reappearing. We laugh with Bill and joy fills his room.

May our words and actions light a fire of encouragement and love wherever we go. May God's heart of compassion be alive in you. Thanks for your prayers as Bill works with the therapists. Greater things are yet to come! Love you all! #pray4bill #Godisfaithful

Day #88 April 7

Anchor Verse: Luke 9:23-24
Then he (Jesus) said to them all: "Whoever wants to be my disciple must deny
themselves and take up their cross daily and follow me. For whoever wants to
save their life will lose it, but whoever loses their life for me will save it." (NIV)

There is a price to pay as a believer. There is a price to live in this world, period. As a follower of Jesus, we are guaranteed eternity with Him.

This passage in Luke might sound harsh. They are some pretty tough words. You like the part about love, peace, and joy, but denying yourself, taking up your cross daily, and losing your life sounds difficult. Did you sign up for this when you said "yes" to Jesus? Yes, you did.

Over the course of my life as I have walked with the Lord, my greatest growth came in those moments when I put obedience to the Lord first, when I chose His will, not mine. Following Him means I am not the one creating the plan for my life, I am following His plan.

Over the last three months, many things have been stripped away – our daily "normal" routine, my husband home with me, my work, projects that were planned for 2018, commitments at church, and so much more. In exchange, I have received a greater revelation of who God is, seen mighty miracles, been blessed by an army of prayer warriors, and the privilege of being clay as the Lord, the Potter, remakes me, and molds me, into the vessel of honor He wants to be.

No sacrifice is too great in exchange for the gift of His abiding presence. The things of the world will pass away but eternity with God is ours.

Today God may be calling you to pay the price of being His follower. God may be asking you to lay down your plans so He can give you the bright future God has planned for you along with love, joy, and peace.

As you follow Jesus, He will support you in every way and wrap you in His arms of love. Thank you for your prayers. Daily, they are moving mountains in our lives. #pray4bill #Godisfaithful

Day #89 April 8

Anchor Verse: Hebrews 13:8
Jesus Christ is the same yesterday and today and forever. (NIV)

Hallelujah! That's good news! That Jesus Christ is the same, yesterday, today, and forever! He is the Solid Rock on which we stand. There is no shadow of turning in Him. All we have needed His hand has provided.

On this Sunday morning, I rejoice in the fact that today, one week after Easter Sunday, we can celebrate the risen Christ. We actually celebrate His Resurrection every Sunday! Today it means that my feet are planted on His truth. I see His hand at work because I have chosen to walk with Him. I am loved by Him no matter what others think or even what I might think about myself. I am loved, people, and so are you!

When God looks at you, He sees the beautiful creation that you are. He knows the hopes and dreams planted inside of you. God wants you to know the fullness of His joy. We just have to accept it, no matter what the packaging of the gift might look like.

The other thing that gives me joy is stability, knowing that Jesus is the same yesterday, today, and forever. When it seems like your life is on shifting sand, it's a lie. Your heavenly Father will always fight for you. When our eyes are fixed on Him, we are unshakable, unstoppable, and unmovable.

As I see God at work in Bill's life restoring what the enemy tried to destroy, I see His loving hands. I see the Potter's hand reforming the clay. I am grateful for God's perspective to see beyond today.

Today is my dad's birthday, and from afar, I am celebrating him today and God's work in his life. I am also reminded of not only our heavenly heritage but our earthly heritage. May we continue to sow good seed so that those who come behind us will find us faithful.

Thank you for standing with us. Your prayers are a sweet aroma to the Lord. Be blessed. #Godisfaithful #pray4bill

Day #90 April 9

Anchor Verse: Psalm 77:14
You are the God who performs miracles; you display your power among the peoples. (NIV)

Day #90... three months in ICU units in four different hospitals... wow! It seems there should be some kind of fanfare today or a ticker tape parade. I believe there is a celebration in heaven. I'm celebrating the miracle of 90 days of God's grace, 90 days of God saying, "I'm not finished with you, Bill Hollace. I have plans for you that are good and not evil, to prosper you and not harm you, to give you hope and a future."

The fact that Bill is still alive today and getting better is a testimony to the fact He is the God who performs miracles. God displays His power among us. We just need to keep our eyes focused on Him to see it.

During the last three months, we have faced many challenges. We have faced places that looked like a dead end and instead God opened up a pathway before us, just like He did at the Red Sea for the Israelites.

God has supplied our every need, not only by human hands but supernatural provision. For 90 days, I have spent my days (and the first 5 nights too) inside ICU units and God's hand of protection has been over me to keep me from all manner of sickness and sustain my strength. Ladies and gentleman – that is a miracle in itself!

Today I stand and proclaim that our God is an Awesome God. Our faith has been refined in the fire as our bodies have been buffeted by the storms of life. Our minds have been renewed and transformed while our spirits learned to soar on the winds of adversity pouring forth a spirit of praise. Have we reached our goal? No. However, we rejoice in this moment.

Today Bill will have the opportunity to try some soft foods. Pray for good swallowing. My daily prayer is that Bill would taste and see that the Lord is good. Your prayers have sustained us. Thank you for your faithfulness. Have your own miracle celebration party where you are. #pray4bill #Godisfaithful

Day #91 April 10

Anchor Verse: I Samuel 15:22
But Samuel replied...To obey is better than sacrifice... (NIV)

Obedience - it's at the heart of everything we do. We have a choice at every turn. We can choose to walk with God or to walk away from Him. There are powerful consequences that come with our decision.

In 1 Samuel, as I read about King Saul and his actions when he chose to walk his own way rather than God's way, I was reminded of Moses' same mistake - choosing to disobey instead of doing "only" what God said to do. The Bible says that God regretted He made Saul king. That hurts my heart.

It hurts my heart because it hurts God's heart when you and I disobey Him. Our disobedience may not affect the course of a nation, but it hurts God's heart. We are willing to "settle" for what the world says rather than holding on to God's hand and rising to His best for us. We want to "win" in the world's eyes, when we are losing in God's eyes.

Sometimes we are deceived and believe the lie that being a good person and doing the right thing is enough, it's not - God wants all of you. He wants your heart and your obedience, no matter what the cost.

As we walk into month #4 of this journey, I am reminded more than ever of how important it is to hear God's voice and walk in it. There are competing voices in our ears, but we must listen for His still small voice.

Bill's room is close to the nurse's station and his acute hearing can hear all the conversations and sounds up and down the hallway. Sometimes I sense he is overwhelmed by all the noise. I try and guide his focus back to his room and not what's happening in the hallway.

It's a great reminder to us too. Our ears need to be tuned to God's voice and not listen to all the noise around us in the world. Thanks for your prayers this last day at NIACH and for what will be accomplished today. God has opened the door to the next step in Bill's recovery. Hallelujah!!! God is faithful. #pray4bill #Godisfaithful

Day #92 April 11

Anchor Verse: Deuteronomy 33:25
...Your strength will equal your days. (NIV)

This verse has been floating around in my head for several days. The Word of God contains His truth that is alive and full of power.

We are in another transition place moving from North Idaho Advanced Care Hospital's ICU unit to a skilled nursing facility. Moving from a high intensity, high-ops place to the next step in Bill's recovery. Isn't life like that too? As a baby, all our needs are met by someone else. As we mature and grow, we begin to do more things for ourselves.

It's a new leg of the journey for both of us. That's probably why God has been weaving this verse from Deuteronomy into my spirit – as my days, so shall my strength be. As Bill's days, so shall Bill's strength be.

Yesterday was a challenging day with Bill's heart rate high and blood pressure low. On days like that, I pray a lot more. I stand in the gap for Bill and hold up his arms (not literally). I lay my hands on him and pray. Then God gives both of us strength, courage, peace, and healing.

What are you trying to do on your own? You can't do it in your own strength. Run to the Lord for tasks that might be difficult or those that bring great joy, and He will multiply His blessings in you and through you.

We will move today if it's time for us to go and Bill's heart is back on track. If the Lord has us tarry one more day, I'm good with that. The bottom line – God knows the way. I'm just going to follow Him. He's the best guide I could ever ask for.

Come to the river of life today. Drink deeply and be restored. God will provide all the strength that you need to meet this day's demands.

Thank you for your continued prayers. God will show us the way as we follow Him. #pray4bill #Godisfaithful

Day #93 April 12

Anchor Verse: Matthew 5: 14-16

"You are the light of the world. A town built on a hill cannot be hidden. Neither do people light a lamp and put it under a bowl. Instead they put it on its stand, and it gives light to everyone in the house. In the same way, let your light shine before others, that they may see your good deeds and glorify your Father in heaven." (NIV)

Let your light shine! It is the light in us that eliminates darkness. It is Christ in us - the Hope of Glory!

This morning as I ponder the path ahead of us, I am filled with gratitude for the way God has led us this far. Isn't it comforting to know that God's loving hands hold you up and encircle you? His protective hand has covered us, even in the scary places where life and death were separated by a thin veil.

Our responsibility is to let our light shine before others. There are times when our vessel is dirty and the light is dim, as it is buried under layers of worry and anxiety. Negative darkness threatens to extinguish that flame of hope burning brightly in us.

Today we stand before another open door to the bright future God has for us - the complete restoration He has for Bill. We are committed to choosing the Lord, the light of the love of Jesus at every turn.

As we prepare to leave NIACH, we have heard several say how we will be missed. I believe we have let God's light shine there. We have rekindled the flame of hope in those who needed a lift.

Be that light today. Speak words of life and encouragement. Pray for those you meet – whether in person or online, just one prayer can change a life forever.

Thank you for standing with us. Prayer moves mountains! Be blessed in Jesus' name. #Godisfaithful #pray4bill

Day #94 April 13

Anchor Verse: Luke 12:25-26
Who of you by worrying can add a single hour to your life? Since you cannot do this very little thing, why do you worry about the rest? (NIV)

Life is about change. Many of the changes in our lives we have very little control over, other than the fact we can choose our attitude about them.

Bill and I just went through another change yesterday – the move from an ICU unit in an advanced care hospital to a skilled nursing facility. The distance was only a couple of blocks, but it was a big step for both of us. It is another place to trust God and His plan.

We can trust God with every circumstance and detail or we can choose to worry about it. Trusting God who can do the impossible seems a much better choice.

This passage in Luke brought a smile to my face this morning. I find it interesting that Jesus would classify adding a "single hour to your life" as a "very little thing."

Our human attempt at doing that through Daylight Saving Time hasn't really been that successful.

What are you worried about today?

Instead of worrying, take it to the Lord in prayer. Lay your problems at His feet. Pour out your heart to Him and then take the practical steps that are within your control.

Daily, I am learning to hold things in an open hand, letting God direct my path. It works way better than holding onto everything tightly and stressing out about the little things.

Have a blessed worry-free day in His presence. Thank you for standing with us as God continues to lead us on Bill's healing journey. Great is His faithfulness. #Godisfaithful #pray4bill

Day #95 April 14

Anchor Verse: Matthew 6:21
For where your treasure is, there your heart will be also. (NIV)

Where do you keep your treasures? As a child, we read stories of treasures, precious stones or gold coins, which are stored in treasure chests. Today treasure chests aren't as popular. We don't fill up a box with our treasures and dig a hole, bury it, and then create a map of its location.

But we still store what we treasure in special places. We have competing voices in our heads and our society about what should be treasured. What do you value? Money, possessions, people, your relationship with God, wisdom, honor, courage, etc. Only you can answer that question.

How we spend our time reflects what we find valuable. Looking at your calendar and bank statement, I can tell what is important to you.

During these last 95 days of Bill's health challenges, our lives have been stripped down to what is most valuable to us. When you go through the refining fire of life, when you enter God's classroom and your life is put under the microscope, you get a clearer picture of what really matters.

Daily as I watch Bill's body, mind, and spirit being restored by God's hands, I have seen our lives being rebuilt too. This week as the remodeling work was done in our apartment and I had the opportunity to pack up our belongings, it is with new eyes I look at what we have. What is important? What is just "stuff" that needs to go?

I am doing a heart and mind cleansing. Lord, may I hold on to the gems of truth and wisdom in my life and let go of the things of the past. Let us strip off the old so we can soar with You, Lord. Our heart is set on heaven. That is where our true treasure lies. Our hope of eternity lies with You, Lord. We love you and praise you. Amen.

Thank you for standing with us through the storms of life. May your anchor be Jesus. Be blessed as you are a blessing to so many, especially us. #Godisfaithful #pray4bill

Day #96 April 15

Anchor Verse: 2 Corinthians 3:17-18
The Lord is the Spirit who gives them life, and where he is there is freedom from trying to be saved by keeping the laws of God. But we Christians have no veil over our faces; we can be mirrors that brightly reflect the glory of the Lord. And as the Spirit of the Lord works within us, we become more and more like him. (TLB)

That His glory may be seen, that's what makes life worthwhile. That's what helps us gain perspective as we walk through the valley of the shadow of death, or we are disappointed with how things turned out or when reality falls short of our expectations.

It's been just two weeks since we celebrated Easter – the resurrection of Jesus. Has it been neatly tucked away in a drawer as a page turned on the calendar or is His resurrection power alive in you today?

These verses in 2 Corinthians talk about the freedom we have in Christ and that we are being transformed into His image, that His glory would be seen in us. That has been one of my prayers during Bill's health journey, that the Lord would be honored and glorified.

I have seen the wildfire of God's blessing take hold in your lives and the lives of others. He wants to rekindle the flame of hope in you. Your heavenly Father wants to know you more. God longs to spend time with you just because He loves you.

Take time with God today and come away changed. Just like Moses after being in God's presence, returned to the people and his face was radiant with God's glory, I pray that we, too, would be radiant with His glory.

As Bill is being transformed into the likeness of God and his mortal body is being put back together piece by piece, I see the sweet spirit of the Lord in him.

Thank you for your steadfastness and your numerous prayers. He is worthy of our praise. #Godisfaithful #pray4bill

Day #97 April 16

Anchor Verse: Matthew 20:34
Jesus had compassion on them and touched their eyes. Immediately they received their sight and followed him. (NIV)

Touch is one of the most powerful sensations. God created us to respond to a touch, just like He created us to response to His touch.

When you accepted Jesus into your heart and life, you were touched by God and welcomed into His family. As you encounter others, you have the opportunity to spread the light of the love of Jesus. When we react in anger, fear, or frustration, our touch can be harmful. In that case, we are spreading darkness instead of light.

In this passage, we see the healing power of Jesus' touch. He had compassion on them and touched their eyes so they could see. My prayer is that God would touch your spiritual eyes. Your human eyesight may be 20/20 but God is calling you to see others through His eyes of love.

The power of touch has played a big role in Bill's recovery. When we are touched by hands of love, hands of compassion that are moved by a heart of compassion, seeds of hope are planted in us, even seeds of healing for our mind, body, and spirit.

On some of Bill's darkest days, when he was sedated and signs of life were subtle, I would put my wrist against his, so he could feel my heart beat. His heart would know what life sounded like. His heart would know the rhythm of love, the rhythm of God in me and beat that way too. I would also touch him when I prayed for him from the top of his head to the soles of his feet, I still do.

May your touch bring life to others. May your touch bring hope to the hopeless. May your touch bring joy to one who is weary. Jesus has done that for you and so much more.

Thank you for touching us with your kindness and love. Prayer moves mountains. #pray4bill #Godisfaithful

Day #98 April 17

🜨 *Anchor Verse: Mark 10:9*
Therefore what God has joined together, let no one separate. (NIV)

The blessing of Bill's health journey is that we have been in it together – all the way, every day. There has not been a moment when I was not touched by the trial that was facing him. I believe that's the way God intended it to be between a husband and a wife.

Today is our wedding anniversary, 16 years ago, we said, "I do." And yes, we recited the vows that say for richer, for poorer, in sickness and in health, till death do us part. I meant it then and I mean it today. In fact, I have a greater understanding of what that commitment means.

My heart's desire is for God's best for "us", not just for me. As life has been stripped away in layers, it has been like a whittling knife cutting away the wood to reveal the beautiful creation that was buried inside of it.

God is the master craftsman and we are being transformed into His image every hour of every day. It is beautiful.

Our love for each other and our love for God have been purified in the refining fire. The world and the things of this world, like vendors in an open market, cry out to us to pull our attention away from the most important things in life. However, God is calling us to listen to His still small voice and stay the course with Him.

Are you tucked in with God today? If you are married, are you striving for what's important for only you or are you willing to fight for your marriage and God's best for both of you? What God has joined together, let NO man separate.

As we celebrate our anniversary, my prayer for Bill is not only healing in body, mind, and spirit, but that God would use these days to strengthen our commitment to each other. Join me in rededicating your life and your marriage to the Lord. Thank you for your faithfulness. May the Lord bless you richly. #Godisfaithful #pray4bill

Day #99 April 18

Anchor Verse: Luke 15:4
What man among you, if he has a hundred sheep and loses one of them, does not leave the ninety-nine in the wilderness and go after the one which is lost, [searching] until he finds it? (AMP)

Day 99... who would have thought that a simple case of pneumonia would lead us here 99 days later still in pursuit of complete healing? God did. I find comfort in that this morning.

Today I am reminded of Jesus portrayed as the Good Shepherd who not only tends to the sheep under His care that stay in the fold close to Him, but greater still Jesus' love that will pursue that one sheep that has wandered away and is in danger.

How many times have we been like that one sheep? We may not have run physically away from the Lord into the enemy's camp but our thoughts may have wandered away or our dedication or commitment may have slackened as the things of the world came knocking on our heart's door.

There is safety for the 99 sheep that have chosen to stay together even though they are in the wilderness. They are not safely at "home" in a pen within the confines of a ranch. There are dangers, wolves and the elements are nearby to threaten their safety, yet they are safe. The Good Shepherd knows they are safe or He wouldn't have left them to seek the lost sheep. This is a great illustration of God's love for us.

Whether you are one of the 99 sheep who has listened to the Good Shepherd's directions and is safely tucked in under His care or you are the sheep who has wandered away, Jesus knows where you are.

Let Jesus find you. Enter into that place of rest. Know His peace. Experience His joy. There is rejoicing today in heaven and on earth for the lost sheep that has been found.

Thank you for your countless prayers – day and night. Be blessed this day as you are a blessing to us. #Godisfaithful #pray4bill

Day #100 April 19

Anchor Verse: Psalm 100:4
Enter his gates with thanksgiving and into his courts with praise; give thanks to him and praise his name. (NIV)

Thanksgiving and praise – that's what my heart is filled with this morning. One hundred days of God's faithfulness – hallelujah! He is a good, good Father!

Remembering the journey you have walked can either fill you with great joy or weigh you down as you recount the trials you have encountered. The enemy would have you choose to remember the heaviness; the Lord calls you to soar on eagle's wings as you recount how God has lifted you up during those seasons of adversity.

Today is a day of rejoicing. If the doctor signs the order today, Bill will begin getting unlimited ice chips and water - the first step on the road to food. Today we rejoice because of the amazing progress Bill has made from lying in a bed on a ventilator with few signs of life to a man with bright blue eyes asking questions and making strides daily in every aspect of therapy. That's something to celebrate!

All praise and honor and glory go to God! Bill has done the work. We have prayed the prayers, but it is God's hand of mercy and healing that has reached out and touched Bill. I declare that to be the truth today.

Today, I press in and reiterate my prayers for complete restoration. As Bill described it yesterday, "the invisible wall" that needs to be broken through so that his world would come into complete alignment. That what Bill imagines in his mind would be carried out in his body.

Thank you for your faithfulness. We join hands across the world to form a large prayer circle around Bill. We ask the Lord, the one who created Bill, to complete His healing in Jesus' name.

Thank you for every prayer you have prayed in these 100 days. They have moved the hand of God. #Godisfaithful #pray4bill

Day #101 April 20

Anchor Verse: John 15:4
Abide in me, and I in you. As the branch cannot bear fruit by itself, unless it abides in the vine, neither can you, unless you abide in me. (NKJV)

God is the only reason we have made it this far on our journey. Every morning His mercies are new. We have a fresh start, a new perspective. Every day God's love is abundant and fills us up to full and overflowing. We are not disappointed when we turn our eyes upon Jesus.

My heart is still full of praise and thanksgiving this morning after day 100. All the "heart" posts I did yesterday were a great reminder of all that the Lord has done. I'm sure I could have posted 100 things to be thankful for, that might have been a bit overwhelming for your Facebook newsfeed.

Abiding in the Lord, it's the secret to everything. It's what helps us overcome self-doubt and confusion. The Lord's presence takes us from mourning to dancing. He is our source of wisdom when we don't know which way to go. God doesn't love us because of how we perform or the list of good things we have done, but He loves us because of who we are - His children.

As I review this verse from John 15, I am reminded that there is a season for the vine to bear fruit. As we enter this season of spring (almost for a month now), nature starts coming alive. Step by step, buds, leaves, fruit or flowers, everything comes forth in its time.

There is no magic number to forecast the day of Bill's healing, God knows the details. My job is to trust God and His faithfulness.

Today is Day #101, I don't know what the day will hold, but I know God holds my hand. This morning I go with expectation to see Bill. The night has passed. The dawn is breaking. God's plans for today are good.

Abide in Him, my friends. You will never be disappointed. Great will be the harvest. Thanks for standing with us. Your continued prayers are appreciated. #Godisfaithful #pray4bill

Day #102 April 21

Anchor Verse: Psalm 119:29-32
Keep me from deceitful ways; be gracious to me and teach me your law.
I have chosen the way of faithfulness; I have set my heart on your laws.
I hold fast to your statutes, LORD; do not let me be put to shame. I run in the
path of your commands, for you have broadened my understanding. (NIV)

Every day we walk into new territory. It is a place we have never been. The way before us is often unclear, but as believers, we know that God has already gone before us to make our pathway straight.

I am so grateful that I believe God loves me so much that He wants me to know the path that Bill and I need to take. He has orchestrated every move we have made. It has been done on God's time frame, not mine. Even the specific day and hour of the day that we entered a hospital or were transferred to another facility - the right people at the right place at the right time. Lord, we sing praises to Your name!

Where are you standing? Are you on the road that goes Nowhere? Or have you asked the Lord to barricade that road because you are tired of running in circles as you make poor choices again and again? I pray that you have chosen the path to Somewhere, the path that God has chosen for you. He doesn't want you to miss His best for you. God delights in His children especially when we choose His ways, for our best and His glory.

Bill and I are together walking this path to his healing. God has the road map. I just continue to listen to His still small voice saying, "This is the way walk in it." I pray that is your choice, to listen to His voice and not the multitude of voices around you.

Be still and know that He is God. He will be exalted in the heavens. God will be exalted in the earth.

Thank you for your continued prayers. Pray for wisdom that we would continue to choose God's best path for Bill's healing. Thank you for your faithfulness. #Godisfaithful #pray4bill

Day #103 April 22

Anchor Verse: 1 Corinthians 15:58
Therefore, my dear brothers and sisters, stand firm. Let nothing move you. Always give yourselves fully to the work of the Lord, because you know that your labor in the Lord is not in vain. (NIV)

Stand firm. Let nothing move you. Is that your stance this morning? Or are you weak in the knees and blowing in the wind, following after this person or that person?

This verse reminds us that as a believer we are called to take a stand and to stand strong and ALWAYS give ourselves fully to the work of the Lord. Your labor will not be in vain. Isn't that good news?

There are days when your weariness and fatigue seem overwhelming. Making even one more decision feels like too much. The good news is that the Lord is with you. It is His wisdom that will put your feet on the path of righteousness. His grace is sufficient for this day and every day.

On Bill's health journey, I have learned that this is true. Standing firm when the hurricane force winds were hitting us and the waves of adversity seemed ready to capsize the boat. Jesus spoke to the wind and the waves, and they obeyed. He can do the same in your life today.

The last couple of days Bill has been trying to stand for the first time in over three months. I have seen firsthand what it means to "stand firm." When your muscles have atrophied and your knees are bent from so much time in bed, Bill must stand by faith with help and stretch those muscles and push through the pain, and do a little more each day.

That's what our Christian walk looks like too. When you are headed into new territory, know that the Lord has gone before you and He will make your path straight. Or there may be something from your past that needs to be resolved. Seek His wisdom. Stand firm. Stand on the truth. Don't be moved but step out in faith and let the Lord's strength be yours today.

Thank you for standing firm with us and believing for the miracle of Bill's complete restoration. He is worthy of our praise. Your labor is not in vain. #Godisfaithful #pray4bill #standfirm #yourlaborisnotinvain

Day #104 April 23

Anchor Verse: Exodus 15:2
The Lord is my strength and song, And He has become my salvation; He is my God, and I will praise Him; My father's God, and I will exalt Him. (NKJV)

The power of praise ~ it can lift the weight off your shoulders as you sing and lift your hands and voice toward heaven. God can work through those who praise Him, praise the Lord!

When your heart is filled with love and peace that comes through praising the Lord, there is no room for doubt or fear. Our heart beats with faith, our lungs are filled with hope, our mind is filled with thoughts of the Lord and His ways. We are no longer bound by the cares of this world but we ascend to the heavenly places just as our voices fill the airways.

This morning as I write this the birds are singing outside our bedroom window. They begin their day with songs of praise. There is no more beautiful sound than when heaven and nature sing. Won't you join that symphony of praise this morning?

Praise and worship are two of the most powerful weapons we can use to defeat the enemy. It turns the darkness into light. Fear must flee. It is there where we find strength. He is our salvation, the steady rock on which we stand.

I declare this morning, He is my God and I will praise Him. He is the God of my family, of generations past, and generations yet to come. Lord, You are worthy of our praise.

I challenge you today to sing to the Lord a new song. Sing old hymns or your favorite contemporary song, but get that voice singing. You will find your countenance is lifted and gain a different perspective from the heavenly realm.

Thank you for standing with us. May we flood the throne room of heaven with songs of praise this morning. Great things God has done. Hallelujah! #Godisfaithful #pray4bill

Day #105 April 24

Anchor Verse: Isaiah 43:18-19
Forget the former things; do not dwell on the past. See, I am doing a new thing!
Now it springs up; do you not perceive it? I am making a way in the wilderness
and streams in the wasteland. (NIV)

Don't dwell on the past – what a great reminder from the Lord this morning what matters is where we are and where we are going. It reminds me of the children of Israel when they were going through the wilderness to the Promised Land. When times were tough and it seemed like it was taking "forever" to get there, they remembered all the "great" things about Egypt and not the truth of the bondage and the harsh conditions they lived under during those years.

We are like that sometimes. By default, we revert back to the past. When the way head of us is filled with uncertainty and it's a road we have never walked we start replaying the old script, the way it used to be. STOP!

Don't dwell on the past. God is doing a new thing! He is making a way in the wilderness of your life and bringing forth streams of living water in the wasteland. It won't always be easy. Because our tendency as humans is to "feel" safe, like wearing that old sweatshirt that should be in the rag bag, we run back to the safety of our distorted memories.

Take hold of God's hand and say "yes" to Him. Yes, Lord, I am willing to walk in new places. Yes, I am willing to walk in faith and not in fear. Yes, I believe You are doing a new thing and I embrace it. Yes, I trust You.

We are about to embark on a new path on this journey to Bill's healing. Our days are numbered here at the current facility (due to insurance coverage). God loves Bill even more than I do, so I know that our next destination will be for Bill's best. Please join me in praying that God would close doors that no man can open and open doors that no man can shut. He alone is worthy of our praise.

Thank you for your faithfulness. #Godisfaithful #pray4bill

Day #106 April 25

Anchor Verse: Luke 18:27
Jesus replied, "What is impossible with man is possible with God." (NIV)

Are you facing what seems to be an impossible situation this morning? Finances, relationships, attacks from the enemy, overwhelmed by life, feeling hopeless...you fill in the blank.

The truth is what Jesus said here in Luke 18 to His disciples, "What is impossible with man is possible with God."

As I was reading in the Old Testament this morning in 2 Samuel 22, King David was recounting the many times that God had done impossible things for him. "He rescued me from on high and took hold of me and drew me out of deep waters. He rescued me from my powerful enemy. The Lord was my support."

David said, "You armed me with strength for the battle." Maybe that's what you need this morning – to be armed with strength.

You may have grown weary in the battle when wave after wave of attacks have come. Don't be discouraged, the Lord is lifting you up this morning!

In the last few days, I have seen improvement in Bill but also the reality that the battle is still raging and the enemy is still relentless in this battle for Bill's full recovery.

Just like an army we are advancing, but there are still battles to be won. Stand strong with me.

Thank you for joining me in lifting up your shield of faith over Bill today. Victory belongs to the Lord. We declare that what is impossible with man is possible with God. Hallelujah! #Godisfaithful #pray4bill

Day #107 April 26

Anchor Verse: 2 Corinthians 4:16-17
Therefore we do not lose heart. Though outwardly we are wasting away, yet inwardly we are being renewed day by day. For our light and momentary troubles are achieving for us an eternal glory that far outweighs them all. (NIV)

Our light and momentary troubles - that's really a matter of perspective isn't it? A heavenly perspective changes our outlook from what might seem like a disaster into an opportunity to let God be honored and glorified. Every day, every decision is an opportunity to choose life, to choose God.

On our journey there have been many days, many hours, when the Lord called to us above the raging storm to look to Him and be still, and to know that He is God. With laser focus, we must turn our face to Him and our back to our problems. We must "look full in His wonderful face and the things of earth will grow strangely dim in the light of His glory and grace" is what one of my favorite hymns reminds me.

Today I encourage you with the words of Paul in 2 Corinthians, do not lose heart. Whatever you are facing today, it's not bigger than God. God has not been taken by surprise with the turn in the circumstances you now face. He knows the rest of the story and it is full of glory.

As many of you may have seen last night, Bill was diagnosed with pneumonia...again... we knew something was wrong, but now we know. The doctor started treatment last night, but more than that the Great Physician is already on Bill's case. God is at work to complete Bill's healing. Jehovah Rapha wants us to stand in prayer with Him.

I believe that prayer - that continuous conversation with God when we intercede for others is what helps us to not lose heart when our lives hit a snag. This morning I am ready to do battle for my husband yet again. Thank you for joining me in the fight. The battle belongs to the Lord and we declare victory in Jesus' name. Hallelujah!

Thank you for your prayers, prayers of faith. Your prayers move the hand of God. #Godisfaithful #pray4bill #IwillpraiseHiminthestorm

Day #108 April 27

Anchor Verse: Psalm 119:105
Your word is a lamp to guide my feet and a light for my path. (NLT)

Our life is a journey and God knows the way. I will admit that I am directionally challenged. My husband would tell you that in most cases, if I told you to go right, you should go left. (Although that's not always true.) Please don't add east and west into the directions you give me, I will really be confused!

In my walk with the Lord, I have discovered that when I ask Him for directions, my path is secure. I don't have to worry about taking wrong turns if I listen to Him.

This verse in Psalm 119 reminds us that God's Word will illuminate the place we are right now (lamp to my feet) and also the path ahead of us, what lies ahead in the future (light to my path). Our pastor shared this perspective and it really helped cement the concept in my mind. God has a plan and purpose for you and your life.

Maybe you feel lost today. You can see where your feet are right now but the way ahead of you is murky. That's okay because God is already there. You can trust Him with your family, your home, your job, your health, your present, and your future – all of it is important to Him. God loves you with an everlasting love.

Over the next week, there will be a lot of changes in our lives again as God continues to heal Bill's body and we make a leap to a new location for Bill's continued rehab and restoration.

We trust in the Lord who knows the path we take and that He will make the transition smooth. That God will heal Bill's pneumonia before we leave Post Falls. That God would be honored and glorified as we go to the next place on this faith journey.

Walk with God today. Don't run ahead of Him, walk beside Him and He will illuminate your path. Thank you for your prayers. We are forever grateful. #Godisfaithful #pray4bill

Day #109 April 28

Anchor Verse: Genesis 2:7
Then the Lord formed a man from the dust of the ground and breathed into his nostrils the breath of life, and the man became a living being. (NIV)

The breath of life... it's where mankind started. God breathed into Adam the breath of life and God has done the same for each one of us. Every breath we take is a gift from God.

There are many people who have chronic breathing problems. Every moment of every day they understand the precious gift of oxygen, a deep breath. Over these last three and a half months watching Bill battle pneumonia on several occasions, I have learned to pray for the breath of life. Many times last night, my prayer was for God to fill Bill's lungs with the breath of life.

Bill's sleep has been restless. Sweat was pouring off him as his body fought the infection in his lungs. He was fighting for that precious breath of life. Around 2:00 am, I put one hand on his forehead and the other on his chest and prayed, as I spoke to Bill, "Breathe in through your nose and out through your mouth." I breathed with him. We are called to model right behavior, not just speak it. Bill began to sleep deeply while breathing in through his nose and out through his mouth. Bill is normally a mouth breather; breathing through his nose is not his natural rhythm.

God was breathing into him the breath of life, again and again. His oxygen level was 95%, 96%, or 97%. After I stood that way for an hour praying and speaking these life-affirming directions out loud, I knew it was time to put Bill back into God's capable hands and go to sleep myself.

I slept deeply for an hour as the Lord multiplied its benefit. At 4 am, they came to draw some blood. Bill's oxygen numbers were still good. Yes, Bill's life is in God's hands.

As daylight comes, the battle for Bill's lungs continues but he is sleeping comfortably. God is healing him in Jesus' name. Hallelujah!

Thank you for your prayers. #pray4bill #Godisfaithful

Day #110 April 29

🛟 *Anchor Verse: Psalm 71:20*
You who have shown me many trials and distresses will revive and renew me again, and bring me up again from the depths of the earth. (AMP)

God uses everything for our benefit and for His glory...everything. Nothing is wasted, even our suffering. As many of you know who have followed us from the beginning of this journey, this has not been an easy path. There have been high mountains and deep valleys. There have been places where it looked like a dead end and God made a way. You know exactly what I am talking about.

King David in the book of Psalms experienced times like this too. David knew the depths of despair but also the faithfulness of God as God brought David to a new level of trust and understanding of who God was, and still is today.

We have learned that too. We have learned what it means to go through the refining fire. To watch your plans be stripped away and replaced with walking the tightrope of faith with God's hand as your safety net. By choice, putting on the altar of faith, the one who is dearest to your heart and trusting God with the outcome.

This is God's promise to me and to you, He will revive and renew us again in every facet of our lives. He loves us. Our heavenly Father wants His best for us. Those God has used to the greatest extent throughout history have been tried and tested and not found wanting in any way because our strong foundation is Jesus, the author and perfecter of our faith.

Go forth in peace today. Our God is mighty to save. Thank you for your prayers and faithfulness. #Godisfaithful #pray4bill

Day #111 April 30

Anchor Verse: John 4:14
But whoever drinks the water I give them will never thirst. Indeed, the water I give them will become in them a spring of water welling up to eternal life. (NIV)

Water is necessary for life, in both the physical and the supernatural realm. The balance between enough and too much is a tightrope that is walked every day.

Often the headlines are filled with weather patterns that illustrate the difference - a drought, a flood, and beautiful balance.

Our lives are like that too. We strive for balance but it is not always achieved. Jesus speaks of this living water, water that when we drink it, we will never thirst again; our souls will be satisfied for eternity.

The good news is that begins now when we choose to daily walk with Jesus.

The last few days we have been walking that line between enough fluid and too much fluid, especially in his lungs.

It is the balance between the breath of life and the water of life, in both the natural and supernatural.

We can only achieve that balance as we walk with God. Drink deeply from the water of life this morning and be renewed and refreshed in Jesus' name.

Thank you for your support. Your prayers have brought us refreshing just like a glass of water to a thirsty man. #Godisfaithful #pray4bill

May 2018
Keep the Faith

Day #112 May 1

Anchor Verse: Revelation 3:10
Because you have kept My command to persevere... (NKJV)

It's a brand new month – a month of victory. We have persevered. We have pressed in. Now it is time to declare and see the manifestation of God's victory in Bill's life and body, and in your life.

Did you know that we are "commanded" to persevere? Command is a pretty strong word. Think of the Ten Commandments. As one person put it, it is not the Ten Suggestions. Perseverance is like that. To walk where Jesus walked required His utmost commitment, to walk in places that made no sense to the world, but perfect sense according to God's plan.

Jesus is calling us to do the same. Since January that's where Bill has been, and I have been blessed to walk by his side. We have been called to persevere to the end so that we might see the deliverance of the Lord in the land of the living.

My faith is stronger than ever before. My hope is in the name of the Lord. I will not be moved by what I see but instead I will believe the truth that God, my heavenly Father, speaks to me, and over me, and over Bill.

Are you willing to take a bolder step of faith than you ever have before? Are you willing to persevere to the end and not give up? Are you willing to walk where Jesus walked that we might see the glory of the Lord?

Lord, I am willing to see the greater things of God. In this month of May, show us Your glory. We step into a new realm, a new place of victory in Jesus' name. The things in our life that have been left undone, the relationships that are broken, the dreams that have been crushed by the enemy, we lay them at Your feet this morning and ask for Your healing

Open my eyes to see the hosts of heaven that are fighting for us, as I declare, the battle belongs to the Lord! Thank you for persevering with us. Great will be your reward. #Godisfaithful #pray4bill

Day #113 May 2

Anchor Verse: Isaiah 40:29
He gives strength to the weary and increases the power of the weak. (NIV)

There are many things in life that drain our strength, and illness is one of them. It's like pulling the stopper on a sink full of water; our strength disappears as our bodies are weakened.

I stand in awe of God and His divine plan of creation especially in our bodies. Truly we are fearfully and wonderfully made. Each part of our body is not only designed with a purpose but the intricacy of the design is breathtaking.

As I have walked alongside Bill on this journey and we have overcome one obstacle only to face another, I see the hand of God at work. Not only the amazing healing power seen in Bill's body but when we surrender our lives to the Lord, God lifts our spirit to soar with Him.

This verse in Isaiah reminds me of what I see in Bill every day. He has been knocked down and at death's door more times than I care to remember, but step by step, God gives Bill strength. Isaiah is very specific, strength to the weary. Maybe you are the weary one this morning. God promises to give you strength and power to the weak. I can remember days when Bill couldn't even move. He needed assistance to do anything. Today as I watch him roll over on his own, and with some help, sit up on the edge of the bed and make it to the chair, I am in awe of a God who restores.

Every day someone else is impressed by the depth of Bill's strength, the core that is still strong within him, and his spirit of gratitude. Let's not forget his facial expressions that tell us what is happening inside, but also brings joy to those who serve him. My friends – that is my God at work. That is the resurrection power of Jesus Christ alive in us.

If you feel weak and weary this morning, run to Him and He will lift you up. Our God is an Awesome God!

Thank you for your faithfulness in prayer! #Godisfaithful #pray4bill

Day #114 May 3

Anchor Verse: Psalm 55:22
Cast your burden on the LORD [release it] and He will sustain and uphold you;
He will never allow the righteous to be shaken (slip, fall, fail). (AMP)

What burdens are you carrying today? We all have them – big and small.
From the moment we open our eyes in the morning, the things we need to
do run like a ticker tape across our brain. From meeting our daily needs like
what to wear and what to eat to the bigger questions in life – related to our
jobs, our families, and our future. It's really easy to take on more than we
can handle.

Since the beginning of Bill's hospital stay and recovery, I have carried a
backpack that is filled with a bountiful supply of things that I need on a
daily basis. (I will write an ebook about this one day.) The problem with a
backpack is you continue to throw in one more thing and one more thing,
and eventually it's too heavy to carry - the weight of the load can harm you.

It is the same way with our burdens. As the Amplified translation says it
here, "Cast your burden on the Lord [releasing the weight of it]." There are
times when we don't have the strength to carry the burdens of our lives.
Those burdens and the weight of them will be different for every person.
Lay your burdens at the feet of Jesus. Release the weight of them. You
know they are exhausting you this morning. Jesus promised to sustain you.
He will not let you slip, fall, or fail! What an amazing promise!

As I prepare to go see Bill this morning, I never know what awaits me, the
change in his condition, whether forward, backward, or sideways.

This is what I do know, that God is faithful and He knows the way that we
take. He has seen the end of this story from the beginning. Today, I choose
to trust in and rely on Him. Won't you join me?

Thank you for being our companions and prayer warriors on this journey.
One day closer to Bill's victorious healing. #Godisfaithful #pray4bill

Day #115 May 4

Anchor Verse: Job 42:2
I know that you can do anything, and no one can stop you. (NLT)

God's plans are unstoppable! Did you need to read that this morning? God whispered that in my spirit while I was spending time with Him.

As we go through storms in our lives, the devil uses the weapons of fear and doubt to cloud the truth of God's promises. Satan is a liar and the father of lies. We must cling to the truth that God speaks no matter how hard the winds of life blow.

Job spoke these words after he had gone through unspeakable tragedy – losing everything he had, not only his possessions but those he loved. After this great loss, his "friends" instead of speaking words of life and comfort used words that hurt Job as they sought to find fault in him. Words are powerful; they can build up or cut like a knife.

Through all of that, Job hung on to God and the integrity of God's character. God rewarded Job's obedience.

Yesterday was a tough day in our world when out of the blue confusion struck Bill, something we hadn't seen in weeks. I believe Bill's healing and restoration are near and this was a spiritual attack designed to discourage, when in truth it will be exposed as a futile attempt to steal ground that God has already claimed as His own.

The pain was real yesterday. But just like Job, I declare to God, "I know that You can do everything and that Your plans, O Lord, are unstoppable."

Lord, finish what you have started in Bill's life and his body. We have not come this far to fall short. We still believe the Lord's report of complete restoration. His promises are true. You are worthy of our praise. We love you, Lord!

Walk in God's truth today. Don't fall prey to the snares of the enemy. He is the God of the impossible. Thanks for standing with us. Pray for victory today in Jesus' name. #Godisfaithful #pray4bill

Day #116 May 5

Anchor Verse: James 4:7-8
So then, surrender to God. Stand up to the devil and resist him and he will turn and run away from you. Move your heart closer and closer to God, and he will come even closer to you. (TPT)

What does it mean to give yourselves completely to God? Daily, I am learning to let go of what I thought was "important" in my life and putting each thing in God's hands. When I choose to "surrender" to God, I am strong and can stand against the wiles and strategies of the devil.

On our own, we don't have the strength to withstand the storms of life. We bend and break like branches on a tree during a windstorm. If we ask God to help us, His strength infuses us with His resurrection power. Then we can boldly say "no!" and the devil will run away.

Say no to fear! Say no to sin! Say no to what will harm you and your relationships! Say no to temptation! And say "yes" to God!

Then the payoff comes. When we draw near to God, He will draw near to you. God is always around just waiting for us to talk to Him, to listen to Him, to be in fellowship with Him, but God won't force himself on us. When you take the first step, God will come closer and you will feel His embrace. His arms are strong enough to hold you, yet gentle enough to comfort you.

In these last few days when we encountered a little storm in Bill's recovery, I was taken by surprise. In the flesh, it seemed a little overwhelming until I looked into God's face instead of at the storm. My peace returned and I knew that God would make a way. God will not forsake His children in their hour of need.

Draw near to God today, He wants to draw near to you. Share with Him what's on your heart. Your heavenly Father is ready and willing to listen.

Thank you for your prayers and willingness to hold up our arms. Let's see what God will do today. #Godisfaithful #pray4bill

Day #117 May 6

Anchor Verse: 1 Thessalonians 5:11
Therefore encourage and comfort one another and build up one another, just as you are doing. (AMP)

Encouragement is one of the greatest gifts you can give to anyone – friend or stranger. There is something about a word spoken in love, a positive word that rekindles the fire in our soul. It makes the weary man stand straighter. It gives hope to the one bowed under their burden. It even benefits the one who offers the words of encouragement. As we speak life to another, the fire in our own heart burns more brightly.

On this health journey, God has given me many opportunities to speak an encouraging word to others. In a hospital setting, it truly takes a village to care for people. Doctors and nurses, pharmacists and phlebotomists, x-ray techs and housekeepers, are just a few pieces of the puzzle. God has given me countless opportunities to speak a word of gratitude to them and encourage them as they serve others, often in difficult circumstances. I love to walk down the hospital hallway and thank someone for doing their job and watch the look of surprise on their face that someone noticed.

This morning I want to thank you for all that you have done to encourage us on this journey. You not only have spoken words of encouragement to us directly through your posts but you have come alongside of us through prayer and lifted up our arms when they were heavy with fatigue or overwhelmed by the waters we were walking through.

Paul reminds us to encourage, comfort, and build up one another... just as these believers were already doing. God is stretching us and encouraging His people to go deeper in their relationship with Him. May He lift you up on eagle's wings today that you will run and not be weary and you will walk and not faint. Our God is an Awesome God!

Thank you for your encouraging words day after day. We are blessed by them. #Godisfaithful #pray4bill

Day #118 May 7

Anchor Verse: Luke 24:8
Then they remembered his words. (NIV)

The words of Jesus are still full of power today. Our job is to discover them and remember them. As I child, I grew up memorizing Bible verses that have been tucked into my heart all these years. When trouble comes or in times of thanksgiving and celebration, they spring up in my heart and fill my mind. They are like an ever blooming flower of God's love and grace.

This passage from Luke is from the empty tomb of Jesus when the women were met by two angels that said Jesus was alive, He had risen just as He said. Out of their grief and shock that Jesus' body was gone, they remembered what Jesus told them would happen and they ran to tell His disciples.

What are the words that God has spoken to you? Whether that came by revelation from reading His inspired word, the Bible, or God showed you in a dream or vision, or an audible word. The Lord wants you to know Him more. God wants to comfort you, instruct you, encourage you, and challenge you.

You are not alone. You have a heavenly Father that loves you so much that He wants you to be close to His heart and in His arms every moment.

Today remember God's words above the noise of the world that cries out in chaos. Hear His voice of truth. Stand on His promises. Walk in victory in Jesus' name.

Thank you for your faithfulness. May our prayers move mountains today as God lifts the fog in Bill's life. #Godisfaithful #pray4bill

Day #119 May 8

Anchor Verse: Job 9:10
He (God) performs wonders that cannot be fathomed, miracles that cannot be counted. (NIV)

Wonders and miracles are God's signature of His handiwork in our lives. Daily our lives are touched by the hand of God, but sometimes we do not have eyes to see. Today, live life with your eyes wide open!

Take a moment and consider how God created the whole world as described in Genesis 1. "The earth was formless and empty and darkness was over the surface of the deep." Then God began to breathe new life into the world. He started with light and separated the light from the darkness. That is a miracle that continues today, separating light and darkness, it's the story of the world – order and chaos.

The awe and wonder of creation...every day a new miracle of life. God has never stopped that daily practice of wonders and miracles – wonders that cannot be fathomed and miracles that cannot be counted.

On our journey, I have seen God do amazing miracles. Daily, I stand in awe and wonder. Yesterday was a good example. I came to the hospital wondering how Bill had done during the night hoping that his mental status had improved, and before 10 am, the news was that Bill was headed out of ICU. By afternoon, he was moved and we were discussing Bill's next steps out of the hospital. Wow! When God decides it is time to move in our lives, it happens fast!

The blessing doesn't stop with the wonders and the miracles, the blessing is multiplied as we share it with others and record it so that we may visit it again in a desert season in our lives.

God is faithful. He is a good, good Father. Whatever you are going through right now, you are not alone. God promised that He would never leave you or forsake you. Open your eyes to see His miracles, signs, and wonders today. He alone is worthy of our praise.

Thank you for celebrating the miracles that God has done in our lives. The best is yet to come! Be blessed! #Godisfaithful #pray4bill

Day #120 May 9

Anchor Verse: John 1:5
The light shines in the darkness, and the darkness has not overcome it. (NIV)

The Light of the Love of God never grows dim. The darkness, our circumstances, our trials, our fears cannot extinguish the blazing fire of His love.

The world around us may seem to be in chaos. Your own personal life may be chaotic, too, but the TRUTH is that God still reigns. He is unmovable, unshakable, and unstoppable! Isn't that good news?!?!

When we walk through deep valleys in our lives, even when it seems that the sun has gone behind the clouds, don't let the enemy fool you. Don't believe the lie that God has abandoned you. He will never let go of your hand, never.

God's light shines brightest in the darkness. Your heavenly Father will wrap you in His arms of love and listen to your cries in the night. He will receive your praise and worship as you surrender to Him.

Think about the beauty of the rainbow when the darkness of the storm hits the light of the sun. There is a blossoming of God's glory written across the sky. He is doing that in your life too. Whether you see it or not, God has a plan and it is good.

God has a beautiful ending written about what you are walking through right now. Are you weary? He will give you rest. Are you grieving? He will give you joy. Are you walking in victory? He will multiply your blessings. Lord, be honored and glorified in our lives today.

Thank you for your prayers. We are believing for even greater things in Bill's life today. Lord, open up the pathway of blessing before us for Bill's next steps. In Jesus' name. Amen. #Godisfaithful #pray4bill

Day #121 May 10

Anchor Verse: Philippians 4:6-7

Do not be anxious about anything, but in every situation, by prayer and petition, with thanksgiving, present your requests to God. And the peace of God, which transcends all understanding, will guard your hearts and your minds in Christ Jesus. (NIV)

"Moments of anxiety-free peace" – that was the prayer a business colleague sent to me yesterday. It really struck me as I thought about peace – peace in the midst of the storm. Can anxiety and peace co-exist? I don't think so.

As I thought about peace, this verse in Philippians came to mind, especially that it will guard my heart and mind.

Our heart: God's peace is what guards our heart where our emotions and belief center reside. What is happening in our heart comes out of our mouth – our words testify to that truth. Remember that God is always on duty to protect us and give us peace, no matter our circumstances.

Our mind: the intellectual part of the equation where we reason things out. Sometimes it's also the place where life gets all tangled up! It reminds me of all the cords that Bill was connected to while he was in ICU. All those connections are like a plate of spaghetti and get tangled up so easily. That can happen with our thoughts especially when the battle has been long and brutal.

We are victorious in Jesus' name. No weapon formed against us will prosper... none! Run to the throne of grace today. Join me there where God is waiting to receive us. In exchange for your anxiety, God will grant you His peace that passes all understanding as it guards your heart and mind.

Thank you for standing with us. The battle rages on, but God is leading the charge. He will lead us to victory in Jesus' name. Hallelujah! We praise God for His faithfulness. #Godisfaithful #pray4bill

Day #122 May 11

Anchor Verse: 1 Peter 4:12-13

Beloved, do not be surprised at the fiery ordeal which is taking place to test you [that is, to test the quality of your faith], as though something strange or unusual were happening to you. But insofar as you are sharing Christ's sufferings, keep on rejoicing, so that when His glory [filled with His radiance and splendor] is revealed, you may rejoice with great joy. (AMP)

In this world you will have trouble, but be of good cheer I have overcome the world! Hold on to My peace. Jesus conveyed this message to His disciples and the message is still the same more than 2000 years later. But yet, we are still surprised. Sometimes we think that things should be easy... or at least easier. The truth is that our greatest joy will come when Jesus' glory is revealed.

Until then, we hold on. We walk in victory, the best we can. When we are weak, He is strong. Write down the Bible verses that will get you through the day and read them, even if that is every minute of every hour. Hide them in your heart. Memorize them and use them. In Ephesians, as Paul talks about the armor of God, the last piece is the sword of the Spirit, which is the Word of God. That is what defeats the enemy.

When Jesus was tempted for 40 days in the wilderness, it was the spoken Word that defeated Satan. You can do that too. You have the power and authority in Jesus' name to walk in victory over your circumstances. We have overcome by the blood of the Lamb and the power of our testimony! Amen. Hallelujah!

Peter tells us to strip off the cloak of self-pity, surprise, and outrage because we are going through this trial by fire. Count it all joy that the Lord has entrusted you with this opportunity to shine for His glory. Pieces of broken glass combine to make a beautiful stained glass window to reflect His craftsmanship. You are His masterpiece! Reflect His love and let His light shine through you today.

Thanks for supporting us in our trial by fire. God will reward your faithfulness. #pray4bill #Godisfaithful

Day #123 May 12

Anchor Verse: Exodus 33:14
The Lord replied, "My Presence will go with you, and I will give you rest."
(NIV)

Rest on the journey... what a great promise from the Lord. The Lord's Presence provides us all we need. Hope, love, grace, mercy, and rest... what an amazing God we serve.

When we think about a journey or going on a trip, it can be exhausting. We are drained in the process, not usually rested. Through the supernatural, God gives us rest and we run and are not weary, we walk and do not faint.

This week has been filled with lots of activity. Bill moving out of ICU to the medical floor, and then 48 hours later, the move back to NIACH, and all the while "normal" life going on around us with its responsibilities – bills to pay, groceries to buy, meals to prepare, and cleaning too... and, of course, sleep!

Early in the morning I rise to spend time in God's presence and there I'm renewed and refreshed. There I am filled with His love, His grace, and His resurrection power. My cup is full, more than that, it runs over with joy.

Throughout the day, I sense His presence with us. As Bill and I are in his room and we talk, or I watch him sleep, I can feel the Lord with us. Sometimes His presence is so powerful and His rest so permeates the air that I doze off too.

Do you find yourself in need of rest? Whether you are facing a mountain of adversity or shocking news or you are on Cloud 9, may you find rest in God's presence today as He travels this road with you. You are not alone. He will provide all that you need. God is worthy of our praise.

Thank you for walking this road with us. May today be another day of victory and taking back more ground. Your prayers move mountains. You are loved! #Godisfaithful #pray4bill

Day #124 May 13

Anchor Verse: 2 Kings 18:6
He (King Hezekiah) held fast to the Lord and did not stop following him.
(NIV)

Holding fast, holding on, never letting go of God no matter what happens that is the way we should live. In seasons of adversity, we are prone to hold on to the Lord, sometimes with a "death grip" – holding on so tight it would cut off His circulation if God was a human being. But in times of prosperity and blessings, do you still hold fast to the Lord?

As believers, everything we do should bring honor and glory to God. Every breath we take, every word we speak, every kindness done should cause others to see God's love reflected in us.

We use the phrase "fair weather friends", those who walk with you during times of blessing but run when difficulty comes. This verse in 2 Kings is a good example of being committed to the Lord in every season of our lives, not just "fair weather" believers but those who will continue to follow the Lord until the very end.

In these days of Bill's health challenges, I have held on to the Lord because He was the solid rock, the only solid place some days. God has been unmovable, unshakable, and unstoppable through all of this. Our heavenly Father will bring us into the victory circle as we continue to follow Him.

Where are you? Are you holding on to God's hand or like an independent toddler have you walked away from the only one who can keep you safe through every circumstance? Run to Him today. Hold fast. Your heavenly Father is holding you in His arms of love.

Thank you for your commitment to stand with us. I know the road has been long, but thanks for hanging in there. Be blessed this day and every day! #Godisfaithful #pray4bill

Day #125 May 14

Anchor Verse: Psalm 16:11
You make known to me the path of life; you will fill me with joy in your presence, with eternal pleasures at your right hand. (NIV)

God is so good and delights in His children. He wants us to know the fullness of joy in His presence. His plans for us are amazing! Open the gift of today! God is just waiting for you to open it and receive its blessings.

Have you ever had a gift that you didn't open? It sat around and you just didn't open it – you were too busy or tired or you lost it. I doubt it. As human beings, we LOVE to receive gifts. Often the paper is torn off and boxes ripped open in our zeal to receive what a loved one has given us.

God is offering us the greatest gift of all, why do we delay in receiving it? King David in this psalm tells us that God wants to make known to us the path of life. That's way better than any GPS system. It is the path of life, not the path of regrets or mistakes. In God's presence, there is fullness of joy - it makes my heart happy just to read the verse! Joy is like sunshine on my face – it warms me from the inside out. At His right hand, there are pleasures forever - God's promise for our future is very good!

You may be carrying burdens today that have you weighed down. Your head may be bowed with regret and shame, all you can see is the ground. The Lord is calling you to look up and see your redemption, your salvation, the joy He has set before you – it is found in Him. There you will receive the fullness of His joy.

Today as I prepare to go see Bill, I am asking the Lord to fill up my joy tank to full and overflowing. Carry that joy and share it with everyone you meet today. Let's change the atmosphere wherever we go.

Thank you for your prayers. God hears and answers when we call to Him. Be blessed today. #Godisfaithful #pray4bill

Day #126 May 15

🫀 *Anchor Verse: Psalm 119:147-148*
I rise before dawn and cry for help; I have put my hope in your word. My eyes stay open through the watches of the night, that I may meditate on your promises. (NIV)

Spending time in the Lord's presence is not a luxury, it is a necessity. I don't know about your life, but for me to survive in this world, I need to spend time in God's presence and communicate with Him. I need to hear God's heart beat so that my heart beats with His. I need to read His Word, the Bible, so I will know the way I should go. I need to hear His voice that I might be comforted and grow in my relationship with Him. He brings peace to my soul and chases away any doubt or fear.

Jesus knew that spending time with His Father in heaven was essential. Throughout the New Testament, we read about times in the morning and through the night when Jesus went to a solitary place to pray and commune with God. Here in Psalm 119, King David tells us that he gets up before dawn and cries for help. David sought the Lord, day and night, and found hope in God's Word and His promises.

Through this journey to Bill's healing, many of you have been awakened during the night to pray for Bill and prayed throughout the day. For that I am grateful. We become more sensitive to the Holy Spirit when we make ourselves available to God and are willing to pray, day or night. This is also how we remain strong during the difficult times in our own lives.

God hears our cry for help. He catches our tears. He rejoices in our victories. God loves you so much that He wants to spend time with you.

Make the time to be with God. There are 24 hours a day, 7 days a week. Surely you can find time to spend with your heavenly Father. You will be blessed. God will fill you with His peace and His power. You will be refreshed and renewed and often challenged. Give Him your best. Give God the best part of your day.

Thank you for your faithfulness through prayer – day and night. You are a blessing. #pray4bill #Godisfaithful

Day #127 May 16

Anchor Verse: Hebrews 10:23

Let us seize and hold tightly the confession of our hope without wavering, for He who promised is reliable and trustworthy and faithful [to His word]. (AMP)

Hold on tightly without wavering. Is this the kind of faith you have in God? Are you willing to hold on no matter what your eyes see? Are you willing to stand against the relentless storm because you know that God is reliable, trustworthy, and faithful? I am.

The storms of life come not to destroy us, but to make us stronger. This verse in Hebrews reminds us to seize and hold tightly to the confession of our hope WITHOUT wavering. These words remind me that the storm will be fierce and I must hold on for the ride. The picture of an old wooden ship being tossed about in the storm on a raging sea crosses my mind where the crew would have to tie themselves to something sturdy so they weren't washed overboard. That is the kind of storm I envision.

I believe that you have walked through that kind of storm yourself or you may be in the midst of it right now. Jesus is your anchor. He is all you need. He will supply your every need. God is faithful.

Without our faith in God, I don't know how Bill and I would have survived these last 4+ months without our hope being dashed on the rocks. Because Jesus lives, I know that I can face today and tomorrow. I was talking to a friend last night about Elisha and his commitment when Elijah passed the mantle to him. Elisha burned his plowing equipment and his cattle – he sacrificed all he had, and then followed God without reservation, without looking back.

Does that describe your commitment to the Lord? Are you willing to hold on with Christ as your only safety net? Hold on to the hope you have in God. He will not disappoint you.

Thank you for your prayers. They continue to move mountains in our lives. Be blessed today. #Godisfaithful #pray4bill

Day #128 May 17

Anchor Verse: Acts 2:42
They devoted themselves to the apostles' teaching and to fellowship, to the breaking of bread and to prayer. (NIV)

You don't have to face the difficult times alone. Not only is the Lord with you, but the fellowship of other believers will hold you up.

God has not called us to be Lone Rangers, our strength comes in community. Holding each other up when we are weak, praising the Lord for our victories, and praying, day and night, this is the path to victory.

On this journey through Bill's health battles, we have seen and experienced signs and wonders from God's hand because you have stood with us. We have learned how to use the tools God has given us, as believers, to master the storms of life.

In Acts, we are given a glimpse about how the believers in the early church, not only survived, but thrived. Acts 2:42 says they "devoted" themselves to the apostles' teaching, fellowship with other believers, the breaking of bread (communion), and to prayer.

This is where our strength lies today. Last night I had the opportunity to attend Spokane Dream Center, our home church. It was great to enjoy the fellowship of the saints, to be loved, and hugged, and prayed for. I was refreshed by the Lord in those moments. Thank you to our church family.

Today my strength is renewed like an eagle and I bring that strength with me as I go to see Bill. Where is God calling you to bring that refreshing? Where are you to be devoted to teaching, fellowship, the breaking of bread, and prayer?

Tomorrow (5.18.18) is a Day of Prayer and Fasting for Bill. There is power as we come together with one voice, seeking His face, and believing for a miracle.

Thank you for lifting up our arms. #pray4bill #Godisfaithful

Day #129 May 18

Anchor Verse: James 5:16
The fervent prayer of a righteous person is powerful and effective. (NIV)

Prayer is one of the most powerful weapons (tools) we have to fight the good fight of faith. Prayer is seeking the heart of God. Prayer opens doors to be in God's presence. We can hear God's heart beat as we draw close to Him.

What does "fervent" prayer mean? It is marked by a great intensity of feeling. Does that describe your prayer life?

Prayers that are powerful and effective are not just words mechanically spoken, they touch the heart of God, because they are birthed in the depths of our soul.

As you have walked through the storms of life, God has heard your cry for mercy, your cry for grace.

As Bill and I have walked through this battlefield, it has been the prayers of God's people that have sustained us and brought Bill one step closer to victory each day.

Today (5.18.18) is a day of prayer and fasting for Bill. Your prayers have moved the hand of God. But it's time to press in and seek victory in the areas that have yet to be completed.

Run to Him today. Your heavenly Father longs to hear your prayers. God will collect your tears. He will rejoice in your victories. Lord God Almighty is worthy of our praise.

Thank you for your countless prayers. Join us today as we petition the Lord for the completion of Bill's healing in Jesus' name. #Godisfaithful #pray4bill

Day #130 May 19

Anchor Verse: 1 Corinthians 13:7
It (Love) always protects, always trusts, always hopes, always perseveres. (NIV)

Love is the greatest gift of all. The world was changed because of God's love for us. Every day when love leads the way, lives are still being changed.

1 Corinthians 13 is one of the most quoted chapters about love in the Bible. It is filled with powerful words and imagery. It is filled with challenges and the rewards of love. Most of all, it reminds me of the commitment of love.

Verse seven that I've highlighted today exemplifies the journey Bill and I are walking through right now. "Love always protects, always trusts, always hopes, and always perseveres."

Note the word "always"... not "sometimes", not "when you feel like it", but "always." This is how God loves us and this is the greatest gift we can give to the one we love.

I have been blessed to walk alongside Bill and sit at his bedside, and pray and believe, and yes, protect, trust, hope, and persevere for these 130 days.

God has been faithful to honor that love and to love Bill even more than I do. God has continued to give Bill the gift of life, the breath of life. We are so grateful.

There are many weddings taking place today. Marriages that will step off into the great unknown with love to sustain them and God's hand to guide them.

My prayer for them and for you is that in our lives we would let love lead the way and that we would always protect, always trust, always hope, and always persevere. It is a high calling. It will stretch you and bring you joy and laughter. Faith, hope, and love remain, and yes, the greatest of these is love.

Thank you for your love for us. We are blessed beyond what our words can express. #Godisfaithful #pray4bill

Day #131 May 20

Anchor Verse: Isaiah 55:8-9

"For my thoughts are not your thoughts, neither are your ways my ways," declares the Lord. As the heavens are higher than the earth, so are my ways higher than your ways and my thoughts than your thoughts." (NIV)

Hallelujah that God knows the way that we should take and He is directing our steps! Left to our own ways and thoughts, our lives would be a mess – a gigantic mess!

God is a loving heavenly Father who wants the best for His children. At times, God needs to gently lead us away from the cliff where we are about to fall and leads us beside still waters. Often God must put us back in the "barn" or "corral" where He can watch over us and keep us safe while we heal or finally listen to the voice of reason. And yes, sometimes He takes us to the "woodshed", because God disciplines those He loves.

There are days you may not understand what God is doing – maybe many of your days are like that. You could be working through circumstances that are so painful that it is difficult to bear one more minute of the pain or suffering or loss. Jesus knows about that, too. In the hours before His crucifixion, Jesus asked God to take the cup of suffering away but then said, "Nevertheless, not my will but thine be done."

I am grateful that in those moments of pain, suffering, misunderstanding, or betrayal, (you fill in the blank), by pushing through and letting God have His way, we emerge as new creatures in Christ with a greater understanding of who He is and who we are in Him. We are no longer that fuzzy caterpillar – we have become a brilliant butterfly!

Yesterday as I was watching Bill and listening to him, I see parts of his personality and sense of humor emerging. That's great, but I want all that God has for him, to see the manifestation of the whole miracle – a new man in Christ – body, mind, and spirit. I want to be a new creation, too. That God's thoughts and ways will have done their perfect work in us. We will be beautiful butterflies. We will be soaring on eagle's wings. We will run and not be weary; we will walk and not faint.

Thank you for your commitment to the Lord and to prayer. Lord, have Your way in us today. #Godisfaithful #pray4bill

Day #132 May 21

Anchor Verse: Micah 7:7
But as for me, I watch in hope for the Lord, I wait for God my Savior; my God will hear me. (NIV)

Watching and waiting with expectation for the coming of the Lord, for the answering of your prayers, that is the posture of His children.

When you are waiting for something to happen – your birthday, the birth of a child, waiting for a package to arrive, the arrival of a family member for a visit, it can seem that every minute is like an eternity, because excitement is stirring in us. We live with anticipation, a burning in our heart and soul. That's how our relationship with God should be, when every moment of every day we look for the manifestation of God's presence.

We may see it in the smile on someone's face, a kind word spoken, a butterfly, a child's laughter, a hug, or a gift placed in our hands.

Whether you are standing on the mountaintop of victory this morning or going through the valley of the shadow of death, know that God is with you. He hears the cries of your heart. You are wrapped in His arms of love. Walk in hope. Don't let fear have any ground. Keep your armor in place day and night. Put on the belt of truth, the breastplate of righteousness. May your feet be fitted with the gospel of peace. Put on the helmet of salvation, lift the shield of faith to deflect the fiery arrows of the enemy, and wield the sword of the spirit which is the Word of God to take him down.

We wait in expectation just like the watchman on the wall. We know that the day of His appearing is near. May God reveal Himself to you today – through the moving of the Holy Spirit in your life or the comfort of Jesus' words in the Bible or God's mighty hand as Your Creator and Deliverer. He is your refuge and strength, an ever-present help in time of trouble.

You are loved and appreciated. Thank you for standing with us and holding up our arms with your prayers. #Godisfaithful #pray4bill

Day #133 May 22

Anchor Verse: 1 Chronicles 16: 25, 29
For great is the Lord and most worthy of praise...Ascribe to the Lord the glory due his name; bring an offering and come before him. Worship the Lord in the splendor of his holiness. (NIV)

God is worthy of our praise and thanksgiving and worship for what He has done and has yet to do in our lives. Is your heart full of thanksgiving this morning? Did your mouth speak forth words of praise to your heavenly Father as you woke up? Come before Lord God Almighty and worship Him in the spirit of holiness for He is worthy of our praise.

I'm not sure that in today's world we honor the Lord as much as we should. When He has done great things for us, do we run to Him with hearts filled with thanksgiving and praise? I am reminded of when Jesus walked the earth and the times that He healed others. Some came back to Him with words of thanksgiving and praise, and others just ran on their way to live their lives. Where do you stand today?

On this journey through Bill's health challenges, we have experienced moments of great victory and times when we laid still in God's arms of love when the days were dark and we needed to trust God because the storm was intense. Through it all, I have learned to trust Him more and more. Before I run to others via text or phone or Facebook, I run to Him with my heart full of thanksgiving and praise. Sometimes with tears of joy running down my face, because I have seen God's hand move in a mighty way. God has done great things for us.

I never want to lose that sense of awe and wonder – not just when God does big things - like Bill's first meal of "real" food, but even in the little things, when a thumbs up or the next breath was a victory in itself.

Today my prayer for you – my prayer for us is that we would ascribe to the Lord the glory due His name, and that we would give Him all our praise, for He has done great things for us. Hallelujah!

Thank you for your faithfulness in prayer. #pray4bill #Godisfaithful

Day #134 May 23

Anchor Verse: John 8:12
When Jesus spoke again to the people, he said, "I am the light of the world. Whoever follows me will never walk in darkness, but will have the light of life." (NIV)

The light of life, the gift of life... what a blessing! Do you really understand how amazing life is? How amazing it is that you woke up this morning and that your heart was beating all night to distribute your blood throughout your body and your lungs gave you oxygen to provide the breath of life? Lord, you are worthy of our praise.

In these last months, I have learned so much about the human body and the wonderful way that God made us and put us together. I stand in awe and wonder. Not just about the body God made, but about the way He designed our bodies to be repaired. Thank you, Lord, that You are the Great Physician.

Jesus is the light of the world and when we walk with Him we walk in the light not in the darkness.

Are you walking in the light this morning? We walk in the light when we walk in obedience to His commands. We walk in the light when we love and encourage rather than hate and destroy. We walk in the light when we choose to believe the truth that is found in Jesus rather than the lies of the world.

Hold on to hope today even when your eyes cannot see the manifestation of it... yet. Jesus is calling you out of your fear and frustration and your unbelief.

Listen to the voice of truth. Stand in the light of His love. Worship Him in the spirit of holiness. He alone is worthy of our praise.

Thank you for the gift of your prayers. They are lighting our way to victory. #Godisfaithful #pray4bill

Day #135 May 24

Anchor Verse: Isaiah 64:4
For from of old no one has heard nor perceived by the ear, nor has the eye seen a God besides You, Who works and shows Himself active on behalf of him who [earnestly] waits for Him. (AMP)

God is working on your behalf as you wait for Him. It may seem like the light of day is long in coming, but even in the night season He is with you.

As this verse in Isaiah describes, not only is He working for you and not against you, but what God is actively doing is greater than what anyone that has ever lived on earth has heard or perceived or seen... wow! I don't think we can comprehend that.

We have a responsibility. We must earnestly wait for Him. We need to be faithful. We need to seek His face. We need to trust Him even when we don't understand. We must listen for His still small voice directing our path.

My friend, He is your heavenly Father and God loves you with an everlasting love. Many of you are walking through times that are testing your soul and stretching your endurance.

God has not left you alone. He is active. God has a plan and purpose for your life and it is good. Put your hand in His hand and never let go.

As I see Bill emerging from the fog, I can see new light and life in his eyes. I can see our God who has been actively working on Bill's behalf. The best is yet to come.

Thank you for your prayers. Together with God's intervention, they have changed the course of our lives. #Godisfaithful #pray4bill

Day #136 May 25

Anchor Verse: Psalm 90:12
  Teach us to number our days, that we may gain a heart of wisdom. (NIV)

Every day is a gift. Will it be an offering of praise to the Lord or a day wasted frivolously or recklessly? You get to decide.

God is showing me that every detail of every day matters. There are no accidents in God's Kingdom. It is no coincidence about the people who cross your path, those you encounter in the grocery store or your workplace to those you interact with on social media.

Every day is filled with the miraculous. Look at God's handiwork. Listen to the sounds of life – the birds singing, the freight train's whistle, or the sound of children playing; all of these and more make up the gift of a day.

On this journey, daily I learn something new. Daily, I have the opportunity to reflect God's love and speak words of life over others and myself. Daily, I see God's miracles in my husband as my mouth speaks praises to the Lord, my Healer, and the Lifter of my head.

As I read this verse, I was convicted by the Holy Spirit to not forget the lessons I have learned on Bill's health journey. He reminded me that our lives would forever be impacted by them and that these 136 days have changed the course of our lives – and yours too.

Once you have seen the hand of God at work, don't forget it, turn it into wisdom – a lesson learned, a miracle lived. The greatest tragedy of our lives is when we see the face of God and are touched by His love – and walk away unchanged. I'm sure that breaks His heart.

Be like a sponge. Soak up everything God has for you – let it soften your heart with His love and then share that love with others.

We have been blessed by God's presence and your faithfulness on this journey. Thank you for your prayers. They have moved the hand of God. Have a blessed day! #Godisfaithful #pray4bill

Day #137 May 26

Anchor Verse: 1 Chronicles 29:5b
Now, who is willing to consecrate themselves to the Lord today? (NIV)

Good morning! Today is a new day, a gift from God. If you are reading this, you are blessed indeed with the breath of life, the blessings of life, and God's love enveloping you wherever you are right now.

Daily, God gives us the opportunity to choose where we will walk and how we will walk. The context of this verse was in relation to the building of the temple, but I believe God's call is still the same today.

The Lord's call to us in 2018 is: Are you willing to serve, to dedicate, to consecrate yourself to the Lord?

Consecration is about holiness and choosing God's way instead of the world's way. Are we willing to put God's desires for us before the desires of our flesh? To stand apart with God rather than follow the crowd like sheep?

It may mean you need to sacrifice some of the things you hold dear, even the desires of your heart, your plans. In exchange for what you willingly lay down, God will give you so much more – more than you can ever imagine!

God rewards those who diligently seek Him. Are you willing to do that today and every day? The choice is yours. The choice is mine.

As Bill continues to awaken and heal, the choice is his too. God has given him a second chance at life, an opportunity to truly understand what it means to be a new man in Christ.

My hope and prayer is that it won't take a near-death experience for God to get your attention. Choose this day whom you will serve, as for me and my house, we will serve the Lord.

Thank you for your faithfulness. Keep praying! God hears and answers. #Godisfaithful #pray4bill

Day #138 May 27

Anchor Verse: John 10:10
The thief comes only to steal and kill and destroy; I have come that they may have life, and have it to the full. (NIV)

Life lived to the full can only be found in the Lord. Walking with Jesus, the Good Shepherd, we are protected from the thief, the enemy that comes to steal, kill, and destroy the plans and the life God has for us.

What is our responsibility? If we wander away into the world, the wilderness, the arms of temptation, and seek to satisfy the desires of our flesh and believe the lies of the enemy, then we break God's heart and our lives are easily broken, dashed upon the rocks. Jesus calls out to us to return home to be with Him where it is safe. If we ignore His call, we are lost and can easily be hurt. Yes, many are even destroyed.

The good news is you don't have to run away from Jesus. Even if you have, He is waiting with arms open wide to receive you – right now. Just call out His name, "Jesus" and run back to Him. Jesus will receive you and restore you. God loves you with an everlasting love. The thief (the enemy, Satan) comes only to steal, kill, and destroy. That's his sole purpose.

God's desire is that you would have life to the full with Him, in daily fellowship, being loved, and loving others. There you will find the fullness of His joy.

As we have walked through Bill's health challenges, I have never been more aware of this truth. Many times on our journey the enemy has come to steal, kill, and destroy Bill and the promises and plans God has for him, for us. We have stood on God's promises, we have run to the throne of grace, and we have been held in His arms of love. Every day we experience that life to the full God has for Bill.

Our prayer is that God has touched your life. Thank you for leaning in and staying in the fold. There you will find the fullness of His joy. #Godisfaithful #pray4bill

Day #139 May 28

Anchor Verse: Matthew 11:28-29
Come to me, all you who are weary and burdened, and I will give you rest. Take my yoke upon you and learn from me, for I am gentle and humble in heart, and you will find rest for your souls. (NIV)

Are you weary and carrying heavy burdens this morning? Run to Jesus – crawl if you must. You will find rest for your soul. Jesus will exchange your burdens for His peace.

Every time I read this verse in Matthew, I am reminded of the gentleness and strength of our Savior and Lord. He can handle whatever you face, but more than that, Jesus doesn't want you to face life's difficulties alone.

Not only does Jesus say take my yoke which is lighter than the one you have been carrying, but He tells us to learn from Him. If we choose to learn lessons on our journey through our trials, then the next time we face a challenge, we are better equipped to handle it with Jesus' help. It's time to grow up and stop being whining, weak children. We must mature and grow so we are equipped for Kingdom work.

Many of you are facing life-changing challenges today. Whether you are walking through the valley of grief, being stretched in your relationships or facing illness – in your own life or that of a loved one, or just trying to finish school and graduate, Jesus is there for you.

Whatever your trial, whatever your challenge, Jesus' message is the same, "Come to me, all of you (that includes you too) that are weary and carrying heavy burdens and I will give you rest (that's a promise). Take my yoke upon you and learn from me, for I am gentle and humble in heart, and you will find rest for your souls." He will hear the cry of your heart and answer... every time.

Thank you for your continued prayers for Bill. They are moving mountains. Our God reigns! #Godisfaithful #pray4bill

Day #140 May 29

⚓ ***Anchor Verse: Colossians 2:6-7***
So then, just as you received Christ Jesus as Lord, continue to live your lives in him, rooted and built up in him, strengthened in the faith as you were taught, and overflowing with thankfulness. (NIV)

Living in Christ is an amazing adventure when we keep eternity in view. When we take our eyes off ourselves and look around to see the glory of God everywhere and in everyone we meet. May your heart be filled with awe and wonder today!

Receiving a new life in Christ is not just for that one moment when we say "yes" to Him and turn our back on the old life of sin.

Our walk is a daily walk. It is a moment by moment choice – choosing to walk in faith when our eyes can't see, choosing to trust when the circumstances seem overwhelming, and rejoicing with every breath.

In these verses in Colossians, Paul tells us to be rooted and built up in Christ, strengthened in the faith as you were taught, and overflowing with thankfulness. It makes me stand straighter and fills me with confidence.

Are you rooted in Christ Jesus? When your roots go deep, you will continue to be built up in Him because you have a strong foundation. As we are strengthened by faith, our Christian walk and witness reflect His power and glory.

Choosing faith and not fear as we walk through life's difficulties will magnify the impact of our testimony.

Overflowing with thankfulness, we are like the well that never runs dry. Our cups are not just filled with gratitude, but they are overflowing!!!

My brothers and sisters, this is how we are called to live. We are called to live triumphantly in Him. Not in our strength but in His strength.

Thank you for holding up our arms on the challenging days/nights and rejoicing with us in our moments of triumph. Keep on praying for the complete victory that is yet to come. #Godisfaithful #pray4bill

Day #141 May 30

Anchor Verse: John 11:40
Then Jesus said, "Did I not tell you that if you believe, you will see the glory of God?" (NIV)

All we need to do is believe. Believe in Jesus. Believe in the resurrection power of Jesus. Believe that He overcame death and the grave. Believe that He loves you with an everlasting love. Believe that your past does not dictate your future. Just believe...

This passage from the gospel of John is about Lazarus's death. Jesus is at Lazarus's tomb and has just asked for the stone to be removed. And Martha (the practical one) says to Jesus, "It's been four days. It's going to smell really bad!!!"

Jesus knew that God's might and power and glory were about to be revealed. How long Lazarus had been dead was not the issue.

Many times in the Bible when a miracle happened, when God moved in a mighty way, it was because people believed in what their eyes couldn't see. Their spirit touched heaven as it reached out in faith and God rewarded their faithfulness.

On our journey, there were moments when I chose to believe that God would reveal His glory, that healing would come in Jesus' name. In the flesh, things looked pretty bad, at times, really bad. Some people, some medical professionals could only see what was happening in the flesh, not what God was showing me in the spirit.

I saw life, I saw hope. I saw my husband walking in his healing – yes, like half the length of a football field as he did yesterday. They saw the end, I saw a new beginning.

Whatever you face today, take Jesus' words to heart, "Did I not tell you that if you believe, you will see the glory of God?" Look for that hope today. Be willing to receive the miracle.

Thank you for standing with us in prayer. Together we will see the complete manifestation of Bill's healing. #Godisfaithful #pray4bill

Day #142 May 31

Anchor Verse: Psalm 91:11
For he will command his angels concerning you to guard you in all your ways.
(NIV)

You are not alone. As you walk through this life, God has His eyes on you. He loves you. Your heavenly Father desires the best for you. He is not just a "fair weather" friend. God is by your side as you go through the storm, the fire, and the flood – He will never leave you or forsake you.

Psalm 91 is a rich chapter filled with so much imagery and so many promises. In verse 11, I can imagine the God of the universe gathering His angels around Him and assigning them people and places to be present to protect you and me.

Nothing happens outside of His will or His way. May this truth bring you comfort and joy.

This morning, on this last day of May, I am reflecting on the goodness of the Lord.

On the first day of May, Bill was in ICU with double pneumonia and sepsis – a very scary place in the flesh, but in the spirit, Bill was surrounded by angels that were guarding him in all his ways and blessing me.

On this last day of May, Bill's progress has been exponential! There is a day and night difference from the first day of the month and the last day – all according to God's plan.

I am grateful that the Lord is the one who numbers our days. His ways prevail, not ours. God has your best interests in mind. Whether you are in the fire of adversity or walking on the mountain of triumph, the Lord is with you. His angels guard you in all your ways.

Thank you for your faithfulness through this season. We are blessed. Please keep praying for the complete manifestation of the miracle. #Godisfaithful #pray4bill

June 2018
Count it All Joy

Day #143 June 1

⚓ *Anchor Verse: 2 Chronicles 16:9*
For the eyes of the Lord range throughout the earth to strengthen (and encourage) those whose hearts are fully committed to him. (NIV)

God's promises are powerful and filled with truth and strength. They will give you courage when you are scared, hope when you feel hope slipping away, and empower you to take the next leap of faith with Jesus.

This morning God is looking to see if your heart is fully committed to Him. Do you know why? Because He wants to strengthen you.

You have demonstrated that you are faithful to walk with Him in the darkness and the light, through the good times and the bad. You have held on to His hand when there was nothing else left to support you.

When faith was all you had, God showed Himself faithful. Just like Job, you cried out to the Lord and said, "Though He slay me, yet will I trust Him."

As we walk into this new month, God wants to do a new thing in you. He loves you so much. God wants to strengthen and encourage you.

Think of the times in your life when a word of encouragement was the spark that rekindled the fire in you. You were motivated to take the next step, to finish a course in school, to tie another knot in the rope and hold on one more day. God's strength will carry you through every trial.

As I see Bill doing his workouts in physical therapy, I stand in awe as he takes one step and then another, or lift weights, or uses the NuStep machine, or masters getting dressed. As I see the fog lift and mental clarity return, I know God is restoring Bill's mental strength. I hear the scripture verse, "I can do all things through Christ who strengthens me."

May this month be a month of new beginnings. Renew your commitment to God. He will strengthen you to finish the race and win the prize.

Thank you for encouraging us on this journey. A new month & new miracles. Your prayers have strengthened us. #Godisfaithful #pray4bill

Day #144 June 2

Anchor Verse: Psalm 118:24
This is the day the Lord has made; We will rejoice and be glad in it. (NKJV)

Every day is a day of rejoicing! My prayer first thing in the morning is, "Thank you, Lord, for the breath of life."

As we have gone through Bill's recent health challenges with pneumonia, I more thoroughly understand the complexity of our lungs and the value of oxygen to our bodies.

Every day should be a day that we are filled with joy. Life with God is a roaring adventure. When we face our challenges and our triumphs with rejoicing, God does amazing things, in us, and through us.

Today is a special day for Bill and me because he is finally making the long awaited step into rehab where there will be intense therapy to prepare him (and me) for his return home. Bill at home...wow... that seems like a dream come true.

As you have followed us, you have seen many of the challenges we have faced to get here – the U-turns and the deep dives where it looked like the plane would crash into the ground.

But God in His faithfulness has heard the prayers of His people and delivered Bill from destruction more times than I can count – or may even know.

My challenge to you today is to rejoice in this day because God is in control. Even when you don't have all the answers, God does. He will save your life from destruction and meet your every need. We know that all things work together for good to those who love Him and are called according to His purpose.

God has plans for you today... enter into His courts with praise. Open your eyes and your heart to receive the gift of this day. You are loved and appreciated.

Thank you for standing with us. Rejoice! #Godisfaithful #pray4bill

Day #145 June 3

Anchor Verse: John 9:25
All I know is that I was blind and now I can see for the first time in my life!
(TPT)

When the Lord opens our eyes, we can see like never before. Once He touches and heals us, there is no turning back.

In this passage from the gospel of John, we are talking about a blind man that had his physical eyesight returned. God can restore our emotional and mental and spiritual eyesight.

When you encounter the Lord, old thoughts, prejudices, lies from the enemy, and even self-doubt, guilt, and shame can be washed away by the blood of Jesus, with a touch from the Lord our Healer.

Yesterday in our quiet moments after dinner, Bill and I had time to talk. I had the opportunity to listen as Bill shared some of the things he has gone through on this journey, some of his conversations with God. They were sacred moments.

Last night Bill's room was turned into holy ground. Honestly, every room, every facility where we have been has been transformed into holy ground. Many other lives have been transformed through Bill's miracles.

How is your eyesight today?

Do you need to be touched and healed?

Run to Jesus.

Just as Jesus touched and healed the blind man, He wants to heal your brokenness, your fear and anxiety, and break the chains that bind you. He is the Lord your Healer.

Thank you for your prayers. They have brought new life to Bill and our household. We are blessed. #Godisfaithful #Hallelujah #pray4bill

Day #146 June 4

Anchor Verse: James 4:10
Humble yourself in the sight of the Lord and He will lift you up. (NKJV)

It is not in our own strength that we are mighty. By acknowledging our dependence on God, we acknowledge His glory, His majesty, and His authority. Without Him, we can do nothing, but with Him, God will move the mountains in our lives.

Our life as a believer is often filled with truths that seem contrary to the rational reasoning of the world. Think about scripture verses like, "When I am weak, then I am strong." (2 Corinthians 12:10); "In quietness and confidence shall be your strength." (Isaiah 30:15); "For whoever wants to save their life will lose it, but whoever loses their life for me will find it." (Matthew 16:25)

It is only with our hearts and minds submitted to God that we can understand that we are living an extraordinary life; we are in this world but not of this world.

Practically, what does it mean? It means running to my heavenly Father and confessing that my way is not the best way. My heart's desire is to live for Him alone. I am choosing Jesus over the things of the world and I am willing to receive God's best for me even when the gift is not what I expected.

As we approach five months on this journey to Bill's healing, together Bill and I would agree that this is nothing we would have asked for but everything we needed. Our love for God and our trust in Him has grown exponentially while our love for each other grows stronger every minute.

We are being transformed into the likeness of Christ as we are refined in the fire of adversity. More of Him, less of me – all for His honor and glory.

Thank you for your prayers that have lifted us up through the challenges and magnified our praise through Bill's victories. Blessed be the name of the Lord. #Godisfaithful #pray4bill

Day #147 June 5

Anchor Verse: Psalm 34:6-7
In my desperation I prayed, and the Lord listened; he saved me from all my troubles. For the angel of the Lord is a guard; he surrounds and defends all who fear him. (NLT)

When trouble comes, where do you run? I run to the Lord. Crying out from the depths of my soul, my heavenly Father hears the cry of His child's heart.

He is a good, good Father and our distress does not go unnoticed. He feels our pain. God sees our tears and He calms our fears. The angel of the Lord encamps around us and we are not afraid.

Yesterday we hit another rough patch. When trouble came and Bill's speech was slurred, it stopped us in our tracks. Quickly we responded in the natural to get help, and more quickly, our prayers ascended to heaven.

As we walked through those next hours, even before we got to the ER, Bill's response was, "It's going to be okay. God has work for me to do, for us to do."

We saw God stand up to the enemy of our souls and say, "He is mine. No harm will befall him." I have never seen Bill so alert and healthy as he was in the ER last night.

God's grace and power were evident. What a great reminder that this war is not finished. We must stand strong to the end and cover Bill in prayer.

Whatever you face today, in your desperation cry out to God and He will hear and answer. His children will lack no good thing.

Thank you for standing with us. Together we will see the victory of the Lord. Hallelujah! #Godisfaithful #pray4bill

Day #148 June 6

Anchor Verse: John 16:31
"Do you now believe?" Jesus replied. (NIV)

How many miracles in your life does it take before you believe in God? Before you believe that Jesus loves you?

We are a fickle people. We more quickly believe the commercials we see on television for products or programs that will change our lives than we believe God's promises in the Bible. What's wrong with this picture?

Looking back over our own lives we can see the hand of God at work, countless times that are not "coincidences" when God intervened and our lives or the lives of those we love were forever changed. Miracles are happening in the lives of others. We hear their testimonies and rejoice.

I hear the words of Jesus echoing down through time, "Do you now believe?"

In John 16, Jesus is talking to His disciples, men who had witnessed the many miracles Jesus had performed. They even had private lessons with Jesus where He shared teachings and truth that were not shared with the masses that came to see Jesus.

As Jesus is nearing the end of His time on earth, He is sharing more of what is to come with His disciples. Was Jesus hoping that finally they "got it"?

The question is, do you "get it" today? Have you seen the miracles? Have you heard His truth countless times? Today is the day I pray you answer, "Yes, Lord, I believe."

Through Bill's health journey, you have heard of countless times when God showed up and did what was impossible. Praise the Lord with me and shout with a voice of triumph for what He has done. Greater things are yet to come. #Godisfaithful #Hallelujah #pray4bill

Day #149 June 7

Anchor Verse: John 17:20
My prayer is not for them alone. I pray also for those who will believe in me through their message. (NIV)

Our lives are lived not only for the present but for generations yet to come. What is the message your life is speaking today?

What is the legacy you will leave behind?

When Jesus prayed this prayer to His heavenly Father in John 17, He was not only praying for His disciples, but for us, those who would believe in the message of Jesus Christ, as Savior and Lord.

It is reassuring to me that Jesus knows me, cares for me, and stands in the gap for me. What I am going through does not catch Him by surprise. Jesus not only knows about our trials but He knows the victory story.

As Bill and I have walked through his health challenges, I have become more aware of the power there is in unity, especially among believers. God's glory is magnified in us and through us. It is important that we build each other up and not tear each other down.

Today, my prayers are not just for me and my family, or even for you alone, but for those who will come behind us – generations yet unborn. May they find us faithful. They will look back at how we walked our walk and lived our lives. My prayer is that my legacy will lead them to believe and boldly approach the throne room of grace in their time of need.

Thank you for your prayers. Thank you for your faithfulness. You have planted a seed of faith that will bear much fruit beyond your lifetime. Today is a new day. May God's glory and grace be multiplied in you. #Godisfaithful #pray4bill

Day #150 June 8

Anchor Verse: Psalm 146:2
I will praise the Lord all my life; I will sing praise to my God as long as I live.
(NIV)

Life is like a roller coaster ride – you never know what is going to happen next. At the same time, there is excitement and anticipation for what is yet to come.

Our walk with Christ is like that, too, but the best part is that Jesus is always holding our hand. He is the author and perfecter of our faith and we can sing praises to Him even in the storm.

Today is my birthday. Five months ago, we started this roller coaster ride. It has been a road filled with many emotions but there has been one constant – keeping our eyes on Jesus with hearts filled with praise.

I have learned so much about faith and trusting God when my eyes couldn't see the way ahead. Walking by faith and not by sight took on a whole new meaning. More than that, I have learned that praising God for all things and through all things brings me closer to His heart and the peace that passes all understanding resides there.

Today I enter the 59th year of life, the last year of my 5th decade on earth. I remember when I turned 50 and the freedom that I felt to be all that God created me to be. I am certain this year will continue that transformation.

With my mouth, I will make known His faithfulness to all generations. Join with me in celebrating God's faithfulness and mercy and grace.

As I woke up this morning and heard Bill breathing, I received the greatest birthday gift of all.

Fill your heart and mouth and mind with praise today. He is great and greatly to be praised. Thank you for your prayers for us. We go forth expecting miracles. #Godisfaithful #pray4bill #Hallelujah

Day #151 June 9

Anchor Verse: 2 Chronicles 32:8
With him is only the arm of flesh, but with us is the Lord our God to help us and to fight our battles. (NIV)

Be strong and courageous...

Courage helps us face the unknown with faith in God and a heart filled with hope. It takes more than physical strength to make it through this world, victory can only be found in God.

I am so grateful that I don't have to face life's challenges alone. How about you? The truth is, I couldn't do it alone. Our battle is not just a battle of the flesh, but a spiritual battle. Sometimes we need to be reminded that God is fighting our battles for us.

As my husband continues to move forward on this healing journey, we are reminded that we must fight to regain the territory that illness temporarily claimed in Bill's body, mind, and spirit. The great wars in history have been stories of battlefields that were won and then lost, and then retaken again.

Are you ready to reclaim the territory the enemy has taken from you? God may be calling you to actively fight in the battle through prayer and being vigilant that you are not leaving the gate open through sin and disobedience. You may be called up to "active duty" and fight on the frontlines with the armor of God in place.

In other seasons, God and God alone will fight for you. He will cover you under the shadow of His wings as God himself, Lord God Almighty, and the heavenly host fight for you when your strength is gone.

God sees you this morning. He knows your pain. He knows your despair. Your heavenly Father knows your fears and sees your tears. He will fight for you. There is healing for every wound in the name of Jesus.

Rest in Him today. God is faithful. Thank you for your prayers. Keep praying. Bill is making progress. #Godisfaithful #pray4bill

Day #152 June 10

Anchor Verse: Revelation 3:20
Here I am! I stand at the door and knock. If anyone hears my voice and opens the door, I will come in and eat with that person, and they with me. (NIV)

Before the days of doorbell and electronic gadgets, a friend or neighbor would knock on your door if they wanted to visit or be invited in. They came with a purpose and took the initiative to come to you, often bearing gifts or a homemade treat to share.

We speak of that time as the good old days when there was time for coffee and a visit at the kitchen table or in the backyard on a summer evening.

Oftentimes today our lives are too full of running here and there or involved with other means of social interaction that we miss the blessings right in front of us.

In this verse in Revelation, Jesus is the one knocking at the door of your heart asking to come in and sit with you and get to know you and instruct and comfort you.

Whether believer or unbeliever, fellowship with Jesus is crucial. He is the source of life and without Him our well soon runs dry.

Even more so through these days of Bill's health journey, I have found that time with Jesus is as important as food and sleep.

My soul must be fed as well as my body. My mind is at rest when it abides in the presence of the Lord.

What about you? Is Jesus knocking at your door this morning? He wants to come in and sit awhile with you. Let Him in. You will be blessed.

Thank you for standing with us. God is faithful. He is the source of life. #Godisfaithful #pray4bill

Day #153 June 11

Anchor Verse: Isaiah 12:2
Behold—God is my salvation! I am confident, unafraid, and I will trust in you.' Yes! The Lord Yah is my might and my melody; he has become my salvation! (TPT)

I will trust and not be afraid. When we trust in God, we exchange our fears and anxiety and worry for faith, peace, and joy. What a great exchange! The best part is that the Lord helps us walk through that valley to the mountaintop of victory! We never walk alone.

God puts a song in our hearts as we walk in fellowship with Him. It is a song that no recording artist can capture because it is a heavenly melody that encourages, heals, and delivers us.

It is our refuge in the storm. It is our battle cry. It is a song of celebration.

The enemy whispers seeds of doubt and fear. He sows weeds in the beautiful garden of praise and thanksgiving that is blossoming in you. It is your job and mine to cast them aside, to refuse to let them take root.

Listen to the voice of God. Sing songs of praise and thanks, worship Him in the spirit of holiness. You will transform your mind.

These last few days as I have seen Bill struggle with this battle of his mind, I have observed two things. One, the influence we have as believers to come alongside another to pray and speak words of life. God can use you to help another to fight their battle and win.

Two, the peace we have when we choose God, believe Him, and trust Him. We are safe on solid ground once again. God's promises are true.

Thank you for your prayers and faithfulness. May God be your strength and song this day. #Godisfaithful #pray4bill #Hallelujah

Day #154 June 12

Anchor Verse: Zechariah 4:6
Not by might nor by power, but by my Spirit, says the LORD Almighty.
(NIV)

There will be times in our lives when we can't will ourselves through a situation. Moments when we don't have enough resources - physically, mentally, emotionally, or spiritually.

We have two choices. We can either quit and throw in the towel or we can look to Jesus, whose resources never end.

Where are you today? What are you facing?

It is the Spirit of the Living God in us that gives us victory. It is the Spirit of the Living God that gives us strength, hope, and instruction. You don't have to do life alone and neither do I. Hallelujah for that!

Often the biggest obstacle in our way is ourselves. We are too proud or too embarrassed to ask for help. It's time to put our ego aside and run to God, and sometimes to others, to receive the help we need. God is faithful. He will supply our needs – all of them.

On this long health journey to Bill's healing, there have been countless times when my tank was empty or the mountain was too big to conquer alone. I ran to God first and then often I ran to all of you to stand with us. Your faithfulness has not gone unnoticed by us or by God. Today I run to God again.

As we move forward on the path to going home, I pray for no more ambushes from the enemy, for strength for the path that lies ahead, and God's help. God is faithful. He will provide. We are blessed.

Thank you for your prayers. God hears and answers. #Godisfaithful #pray4bill

Day #155 June 13

Anchor Verse: John 21:17
The third time he said to him, "Simon son of John, do you love me?" (NIV)

Jesus is our Comforter, our Savior, our Friend, but also our Protector, Defender, our Lord and Savior who demands our obedience. He is gentle in His restoration to a lost soul, a lost sheep, but is not hesitant to ask the hard questions.

He is the Good Shepherd who is willing to lay down His life for His sheep, but God is also willing to discipline us to save our lives.

In this passage in John, Jesus is speaking to Peter who three times denied he knew Jesus on the night Jesus was betrayed. Yet, in this passage beside the Sea of Galilee, his fishermen disciples' home turf, Jesus gently restores Peter. "Do you love me?"

It is not lost on Peter that the question is asked three times. Peter chooses to follow Jesus' path of restoration.

In the process, Jesus has a new task for him, "Feed my sheep." Just as Peter was called to be his disciple the first time, Jesus again says, "Follow Me."

This morning I believe that Jesus is asking us the same question. Fill in the blank with your name. "_____, do you love Me?"

You may have walked away from Jesus. You may have never chosen to invite Jesus into your heart, into your life, but today is that day.

Say yes to Jesus and then follow Him. He has a plan and purpose for your life and it is good.

Thank you for your love and prayers for us. We are blessed and we look forward to the plans God has for us. God is good, all the time. #Godisfaithful #pray4bill

Day #156 June 14

Anchor Verse: Jeremiah 31:3
I have loved you with an everlasting love; I have drawn you with unfailing kindness. (NIV)

Everlasting love...it's difficult to wrap our mind around because in our humanity we often fall short of that goal. Only God loves us with an everlasting love. In the process, He empowers us to love others and ourselves.

Unfailing kindness and everlasting love are attributes of God but also the fruit that comes from the lives of His children. Kindness and love are what take the rough edges off a world steeped in chaos and confusion. When kindness and love are part of daily living, they bring us joy not only as we give but as we receive.

Even when we read about acts of kindness and love, it rekindles hope in us. When another's dream comes true or there is healing, we, too, are encouraged and believe that miracles still happen.

As Bill and I see others at the rehab hospital get better and go home, we know that one day we will be the ones leaving with smiles on our faces.

Until that day comes, we find comfort in His love for us. We find peace in God's presence and we spread His love and kindness to all that we meet.

Are you aware of God's love and kindness this morning?

God is calling you to come and rest in His everlasting arms of love. Be comforted. Be encouraged. Feel His love. He will make you whole in Jesus' name.

Thank you for your faithfulness. You are loved and appreciated. God is love. #Godisfaithful #pray4bill

Day #157 June 15

Anchor Verse: Joel 2:28b
your old men will dream dreams, Your young men will see visions. (NIV)

God has a plan and purpose for each one of us. He often uses the unlikely to accomplish His purposes. God takes the ordinary and makes it extraordinary. You are never beyond God's reach. You are never too old or too young... no matter what others might say.

Have you ever entered seasons of frustration, doubt, and fear? Has the enemy attempted to snuff out your candle to prevent you from letting your light shine brightly for the Lord? We all have been in those places.

This verse from the book of Joel reminds me that God has plans for each one of us. "Old men will dream dreams and your young men will see visions." God has a message to share. Are we willing to receive it and share it?

On Bill's health journey, we know that there have been moments when life and death were only a heartbeat away from each other. When Bill wasn't able to communicate with me, I could sense that Bill and God were having conversations of their own.

In these last weeks as more healing has occurred, Bill has shared some of what happened, and it is powerful. That is a story to share at a later time. But today, Bill has a new zeal for life. God has given Bill new dreams. Bill's heart is filled with a new love for God, a new appreciation for life.

Many younger men and women have crossed our path and I have seen God at work in them. It takes both young and old alike and all of us in between, to carry out God's purpose here on earth.

Be attentive to His voice. God has something to share with you today.

Thank you for your prayers. As the enemy attacks continue, God is using what the enemy meant for evil for Bill's good. #Godisfaithful #pray4bill

Day #158 June 16

Anchor Verse: Acts 2:25-26
King David said this about him [Jesus]: I see that the LORD is always with me. I will not be shaken, for he is right beside me. No wonder my heart is glad, and my tongue shouts his praises! My body rests in hope.

Resting in hope. That's where we find power. That's where we find peace.

Is your heart glad this morning? Is your tongue filled with rejoicing? During my darkest hours and greatest challenges, when I turned my questions, my fears, my tears into songs of praise and worship, my heart was lifted high because God could fill it.

He works through those who praise Him. Praise the Lord!

As you walk through life's challenges, there may not be time to pull out your hymnal or even your Bible or pull up the app on your phone. It is in those seasons that the passages of Scripture you have memorized and entwined in the beats of your heart will sustain you. The name of "Jesus" is powerful medicine.

David says that he saw the Lord always before him. And because of that fact, that truth – David was not shaken. David went through some pretty deep valleys and rough places.

David went through seasons of loss and sorrow. His life was in danger countless times. The Lord was always with him. When David kept his eyes on God rather than his circumstances, David moved on triumphantly.

Today you can walk in victory. It won't always be easy. You may skin your knees. You may get frustrated and cry but God will never leave you or forsake you. Accept His peace.

Jesus is waiting to comfort you today and empower your mind and body for the next step on your journey.

Thank you for caring and holding up our arms. You are appreciated and loved. #Godisfaithful #pray4bill

Day #159 June 17

Anchor Verse: Proverbs 17:22
A happy heart is good medicine and *a joyful mind causes healing, But a broken*
spirit dries up the bones. (AMP)

Laughter is good medicine. One of the therapists here at the rehab hospital reminded me of that just a couple of days ago. There is so much in the world to be so serious about that sometimes we just need to take a break and turn to joy and laughter. Whether it is a TV show, a movie, a person with whom you can share memories and just laugh, but truly it fills our heart with joy and lifts the mantle of heaviness draped over our shoulders.

Physically, endorphins are released when we laugh and have a merry heart. Isn't God amazing that when He created us He made sure there was an antidote to our burdens?

Some of you today may be walking through deep valleys, day and night the weight of it never leaves you. Grief can be like that. This verse in Proverbs reminds us that a happy heart brings healing.

I encourage you to spend time with someone today or participate in a healthy activity that makes you happy. It's Sunday...go to church and spend time with the family of God, we were meant to ease each other's burdens.

May your heart find healing today and your dry soul be watered with God's healing rain. There is hope in the name of the Lord.

Thank you for your prayers. He is our ever-present help in time of trouble. #Godisfaithful #pray4bill #Hallelujah

Day #160 June 18

Anchor Verse: Psalm 124:8
Our help is in the name of the Lord, the Maker of heaven and earth. (NIV)

Our only solid foundation in the storms of life is Lord God Almighty, Maker of heaven and earth. Just like a child runs to his parent during times of trouble and distress, God beckons us to come when life is tough.

Not only when life is tough, but when life is good. Your heavenly Father wants to share all of your life and emotions, your triumphs and your challenges.

As we have walked through this valley of Bill's health challenges, I have learned what it means to listen for God's voice when the world is loud and chaotic. His voice can only be heard when I quiet myself before Him in His presence. It is there, and only there, that I find the fullness of His joy.

It is in the name of the Lord we have prayed together and asked for God's healing touch upon Bill's body, mind, and spirit. There is power in the name of the Lord.

As Bill and I look forward to when he is released from the hospital and we are "on our own", our help will still come in the name of the Lord.

Today He is your shelter in the storm. God will never leave you or forsake you. Jesus came that you might have life abundantly and the Holy Spirit comforts and directs you in the path you should take.

Be encouraged, my friend. You do not walk alone. Praising the Lord for you and His faithfulness. Be blessed today. #Godisfaithful #pray4bill

Day #161 June 19

Anchor Verse: Nehemiah 13:31
Remember me with favor, my God. (NIV)

There are times in our lives when our prayers turn from tears and cries for mercy to confidently asking the Lord for favor.

Today's passage comes at the end of the book of Nehemiah when Nehemiah has left his position as cupbearer to the king and in the face of great opposition has led the people to rebuild the wall around Jerusalem. Nehemiah now asks the Lord to remember him with favor.

At the end of this long battle where the people worked using one hand and carried a weapon in the other, while tuning out the naysayers that mocked them, Nehemiah lays his completed work at the Lord's feet.

There comes a time in our lives when we must do the same thing. We work hard at the tasks, the mission God has placed in our hands and heart, and at its completion, we offer it as a sacrifice of praise to the glory of God.

God has been so faithful to Bill and me on this journey. I pray that just like Nehemiah we are faithful to Him. God rewards our obedience.

Others may not understand the path that you are walking, that God has chosen for you, but do not be discouraged, your heart's desire should be to hear God's approval not the praises of men.

Today I challenge you to offer God the fruits of your labor. May His praise be continually on your lips.

Do the work and the Lord will reward you because He loves you and He rewards those who diligently seek Him.

Thank you for your faithfulness to us through prayer. May you be blessed this day. #Godisfaithful #pray4bill

Day #162 June 20

🜨 *Anchor Verse: Micah 6:8*
He has shown you, O mortal, what is good. And what does the LORD require of you? To act justly and to love mercy and to walk humbly[a] with your God. (NIV)

There are many things I love about God, my heavenly Father. One of them is that I am grateful for the Bible, His instruction manual, to show us how we should live.

In our education system, we have discovered that people learn differently. Just as God made each of us unique, you may learn best by verbal instruction or reading directions or maybe hands on, by touch, works best for you. All of these methods are a reflection of God's wonder – there is no one like you. Whatever your learning style, there are foundational truths, instructions that are the same.

In Micah 6:8, we find such a list. The Lord requires that we do justly – seek justice, God's justice, not any personal vendettas. We are to love kindness and mercy – that is a two-way street. It is something we may desire for ourselves, but are to offer others in our daily interactions. And then, humble ourselves and walk humbly with God. The proud fall and it is not pretty. When we walk in humility, we are teachable. God will lead us to places we can't even imagine.

When I read this list, I am grateful I don't have to live out this mission on my own. God will give me the strength. God will give me the wisdom. He will lead me and direct me. My heavenly Father will make His face to shine upon me as I walk in obedience.

As Bill and I have walked this path to his healing, the Lord has shown us His faithfulness day after day, time after time. As we prepare for the next chapter, I know He will guide and protect us there.

Trust Him today with your present and your future. God loves you with an everlasting love.

Thank you for your fervent prayers in these remaining days of June as our next steps are made clear and transitions are made. He is worthy of our praise. #Godisfaithful #pray4bill

Day #163 June 21

⚓ *Anchor Verse: Proverbs 24:16*
For the lovers of God may suffer adversity and stumble seven times, but they will continue to rise over and over again. But the unrighteous are brought down by just one calamity and will never be able to rise again. (TPT)

Today is the longest day of the year. As I was reflecting about time, it reminded me of what God can do when we walk with Him and dwell in His presence. God lives outside of time, and in those moments when we spend time with Him, we too are suspended there.

As my mind moved from the timelessness of God, I thought about what God had done in these last 163 days. Many times God carried Bill away from the brink of death and helped him rise again and again. Each time Bill has risen higher and reclaimed more ground.

This verse in Proverbs describes the life of a believer so well. The lovers of God will suffer adversity – yes, we will and yes, you have... all of you have suffered adversity of some kind. Some of you multiple times and you have stumbled BUT you and I continue to rise and rise again.

Why? Because God's hand is upon us and He helps us get up again.

This is a beautiful illustration of Bill's journey. You have witnessed the many times he has been taken down by one kind of illness or another. And yet, because of God's faithfulness, Bill gets up again to fight another day. His sweet spirit is evidence of God's restoration.

Each time God picks you up, a little more of God's goodness and grace is left behind. Hold on to hope, my friends. Hold on to God's hand. He will never leave you or forsake you.

Thank you for your faithfulness. We are blessed by your partnership and prayers. #Godisfaithful #pray4bill #Hallelujah

Day #164 June 22

Anchor Verse: Psalm 34:1
Lord! I'm bursting with joy over what you've done for me! My lips are full of perpetual praise. (TPT)

Honoring the Lord through our trials and our victories is the way that God has called us to live. It is in obedience to our loving heavenly Father that we fill our mouth with praise even when life's circumstances threaten to overwhelm us. I will praise Him in the storm.

Whether your night was filled with blissful sleep or your pillow is wet with tears this morning, offer the Lord your sacrifice of praise. We have talked about this before, about the power of our words, it affects our heart and our attitude, in fact, the course of our lives!

Praise can be our best defense, not only from internal enemies – like doubt and fear, but external battles. As we walked through Bill's health challenges, there were times I stood alone in front of the Lord as He asked me to trust Him when my eyes couldn't see. God was asking me to trust Him, His perfect will and perfect plans when medically the situation looked hopeless.

When we honor the Lord and seek His glory, the Lord can carry out His best plans for us. It won't always be easy, but I can promise you it will be worth it.

What are you walking through right now that the Lord is asking you to lay on the altar of praise? You know what it is. Just like Abraham was asked by God to sacrifice his only son Isaac, God is asking you to give Him what you are clenching in your hands. God is not a cruel God. He will fill you with the fullness of His joy when we offer our very lives to Him. Just like Abraham, the Lord will reward your obedience.

Today is a new day, a new season. God can work through those who praise Him! Thanks for your faithfulness. #Godisfaithful #pray4bill

Day #165 June 23

Anchor Verse: Acts 7:5b
But God promised him that he and his descendants after him would possess the land, even though at that time Abraham had no child. (NIV)

Faith means walking into a place where we cannot see the outcome and often we do not know the way. As we walk in obedience without a road map, several things happen.

One, we grow in our relationship with God, our heavenly Father. We learn to hear His voice and tune out the world because He is the only one who knows the way. It's like driving your car up a steep mountain with a plunging ravine over the side and no guardrail. (My fingers and toes are clenched as I type this.) We slow down and proceed with caution. The risk of getting hurt is so great that our instincts are to be cautious.

Two, we learn to rely on God's promises. It's all we have. Abraham who was given the promise to become a great nation when he was old and didn't even have a child had two choices, either to doubt or to believe God. You have the same choice today. There may be no solid ground under your feet anymore. Yet God is holding you in His arms of love. The prayers of God's people are keeping your head above water. Day and night, God's promises fill you with hope.

"But God promised..." These words jumped off the page this morning. They give me reassurance that in the days to come, even this day, I can trust Him because His promises are true.

What are you facing today? You do not face it alone. The Lord is with you. Jesus is holding your hand and the Holy Spirit is directing your steps. Always remember, greater is He that is in you than he that is in the world.

Thank you for your many prayers that have flooded the throne room of grace. Our victory is shared with you. It is your victory too. Be blessed today. #Godisfaithful #pray4bill #Hallelujah

Day #166 June 24

Anchor Verse: Job 2:10
He replied, "You are talking like a foolish woman. Shall we accept good from God, and not trouble?" (NIV)

Have you ever walked through circumstances when you felt like Job? When it seemed like the world was crashing down around you and everything you held dear was being taken away from you? I believe most, if not all of us, would answer yes. It may not be the exact script as Job's story but tragedy strikes each life.

The point of this story is not so much the tragedy but Job's reaction to it. Because of his relationship with God, Job could walk in integrity and see the bigger picture. Job recognized that tragedy comes in this life but God is faithful even in our darkest night.

Job's relationship with God was so powerful and Job trusted God so much that even when his "friends" and his wife were offering less than helpful advice, Job stood strong with the Lord. There will be times in your life when you will need to take your stand with God. Sometimes God will take you to a place where you can only go alone.

Bill and I have walked through some deep waters these last six months but God has been faithful. He hasn't given us more than we could bear with His help. Just as Job fell to his knees in worship when tragedy struck, I encourage you to go to your knees this morning and thank God for His love for you. Thank the Lord that He sees something in you worth refining that God would be honored and glorified.

Our life is a reflection of God's light in us. Reflect His light and love today. Trouble will come and trouble will go but God will never leave you or forsake you. You are loved.

Thank you for standing with us through the storm and bringing the light of the love of Jesus into our lives. #Godisfaithful #Hallelujah #pray4bill

Day #167 June 25

Anchor Verse: Job 4:12
A word was secretly brought to me, my ears caught a whisper of it. (NIV)

God is invested in your life. He knows the way that you take. Just like a good parent who loves their child, God loves you and rejoices in your victories and His heart hurts as you walk through tragedy.

Just as your best friend communicates with you, so does the God who created the universe and knows every hair on your head. He wants to talk with you. From the moment your eyes open in the morning until you fall asleep at night, God is sending you love notes.

In the last few days as we had thunderstorms in the area, the skies and all of nature, spoke loudly with God's many voices. From the rushing wind, booming thunder, crack of the lightning strike that lit up the sky, even the silence when the power went off, all of these are the voice of God.

Many people walk through life unaware of God's daily visitation. Do you ignore His voice or did you hear His whisper when God asked you to pray for Bill in the middle of the night? Many of you have heard His voice and prayed, oh so many times. Thank you.

If your ears are open to hear and your heart is willing to receive it, you will catch the sound of His voice. He will calm your heart. The Holy Spirit will comfort you and guide you. Then you must walk by faith.

As we stand on the threshold of a change in direction as we head back home tomorrow, we walk with God. There is a new path of healing ahead of us. There will be challenges. There will be victories. But we will hold on to God's Word and trust Him with our very lives. Hold on to hope today. God is faithful.

Thank you for your continued prayers especially in the next 48 hours as we transition home and learn to live life outside the hospital. All things are possible with God. #Godisfaithful #pray4bill

Day #168 June 26

Anchor Verse: Job 5:9
He performs wonders that cannot be fathomed, miracles that cannot be counted.
(NIV)

My heart is filled with gratitude and praise this morning. God has done great things for us, God has done great things.

This verse from Job describes the moments in our life when God's glory shines so brightly that we stand speechless in His presence. Have you ever prayed and hoped for a healing miracle, a restored relationship, forgiveness, and a fresh start free of the burden of guilt and shame?

That is what God offers His children. That is what God is offering you today. Jesus paid the price on the cross more than 2000 years ago that we might experience abundant life to the full. What is stopping you from saying yes to this priceless gift? Don't delay any longer. The time is now.

Today is a day of victory in our lives. Today we will leave the rehab hospital. Bill will return home to our apartment and sleep in his own bed – something he hasn't done in 168 days. Today we start a new chapter in our lives.

Our hearts are filled with praise this morning. We will continue to need your prayers as we take the next steps on this healing path. We look forward to seeing the completion of Bill's healing – body, mind, and spirit. Without a doubt we know, all things are possible with God. Just as Job said, "He performs wonders that cannot be fathomed, miracles that cannot be counted" – we echo his words this morning and praise God.

Thank you for your faithfulness. God's mercies are new every morning. Hallelujah! #Godisfaithful #pray4bill

Day #169 June 27

Anchor Verse: Psalm 143:8
Let the morning bring me word of your unfailing love, for I have put my trust in you. Show me the way I should go, for to you I entrust my life. (NIV)

The dawning of a new day, there is peace in His presence as the cool air filters in the window. The gift of life, the glory of the Lord, they are intricately intertwined together. It is in these quiet moments that the Lord touches earth with His presence. It is here that my body and spirit find hope, power, and purpose. I sense His love for me and I hear direction for the day. Without Him I am nothing, with Him all things are possible.

In quietness and confidence shall be my strength. Show me the way that I should go, it's all that I really want. I am tired of running in circles, Lord. I am tired of hitting walls when You have windows that open up to the best plans You have for me.

This morning I am blessed. I woke up with my husband next to me after months of illness and often difficult nights wondering what would happen next.

As he still sleeps, I run into the Lord's presence grateful with a heart filled with joy and thanksgiving. I trust God for this day and the days ahead. As I listen to Bill's deep gentle breathing, I hear life, I hear hope.

I encourage you my friends to pay attention to the "little things" in your life, the precious moments that can easily slip away. Capture those God moments and treasure them in your heart.

Thank you for standing in the gap with us. Rejoice with us even though there is still healing work to be done. #Godisfaithful #pray4bill

Day #170 June 28

Anchor Verse: Romans 12:13
When God's people are in need, be ready to help them. Always be eager to practice hospitality. (NLT)

Our heavenly Father has a generous heart and He challenges us as His children to live the same way. Growing up I can remember countless times when we would have guests in our home, whether exchange students visiting for a weekend or pastors and missionaries visiting our church, or our school friends. Mom's kitchen was a favorite destination for many.

Our parents taught us by example how to reach out to others in need through words and actions. In times of need and celebration, our joy is multiplied and our burdens are not quite so heavy when others come alongside us.

This has been the story of Bill's health journey. Your encouraging words, your actions, and your prayers have renewed our strength, increased our joy, and helped us carry our burdens. You have no idea how much this has meant to us unless you have experienced similar circumstances in your own life and been blessed in this way.

I encourage you today to take Paul's advice in this verse from Romans. Whether you are the person doing the blessing or you are the recipient of this outpouring of generosity, you will be blessed.

Always be eager to practice hospitality. Note: Paul doesn't say fulfill your obligation or do it because it is expected of you, but "be eager!"

Thank you for the many ways you have impacted our lives. We are grateful. #Godisfaithful #pray4bill

Day #171 June 29

Anchor Verse: Psalm 5:3

In the morning, Lord, you hear my voice; in the morning I lay my requests before you and wait expectantly. (NIV)

Do you face the day with expectation or dread? You have the opportunity each day to face life with the God of the universe acting on your behalf. Wow!

The same God who created the majestic mountains, the beautiful blue ocean, painted every detail on the butterfly's wings and gave the birds a new song – that is the God who will direct your steps today!

Life is an adventure if you entrust God with your day. Whether you face joy or sorrow, turn it over to God and watch His miracles unfold.

My time together with God in the morning is where I find my strength. It is where I feel His presence. It is where I hear His voice, urging me forward or cautioning me to slow down and rest in Him.

When I live life this way, I have eyes to see God at work. What may seem to be coincidence to some, I know is a miracle.

What a better way to live expecting God to show up in the details of your life rather than be overwhelmed by doubt and fear.

Today I encourage you to start this day with expectation. As the scripture says, "This is the day the Lord has made, I will rejoice and be glad in it." Hallelujah.

Thank you for praying with expectation on our behalf. We stand with you this morning expecting to see the miracles of God's hand in our lives. #Godisfaithful #pray4bill #Hallelujah

Day #172 June 30

Anchor Verse: Revelation 22:13
I am the Alpha and the Omega, the First and the Last, the Beginning and the End. (NIV)

Today is the last day of June and what a month it has been! Each month is a reminder to me that God is in control of my life. In small segments of time, 28 - 31 days, He not only shows His faithfulness, but He unveils His plan and purpose for my life. In Philippians 2:13 it says, "Yes, it is God who is working in you. He helps you want to do what pleases him, and he gives you the power to do it."

Isn't that good news? It's not all about you or your strength or your power or your will or your ego. It's about God's perfect will for you.

We are halfway through the year of 2018. It doesn't matter what happened in the past, what matters is what lies ahead.

This morning as I was spending time with the Lord and He was bringing verses to mind to share with you, out of the depths of my spirit came this verse from Revelation. I could hear the voices of the Trinity emphasizing the words of Jesus. There was the voice of the God of creation, the one who created us. Then the voice of Jesus, the one who loves us, died for us and will stand and defend us. It was the quiet whisper of the Holy Spirit, reassuring me that He would guide and direct me this day and the days ahead. Hear His words again: "I am the Alpha and the Omega, the First and the Last, the Beginning and the End."

For us, this month started at NIACH, with the hope of moving to the rehab hospital to strengthen Bill for the next phase of his journey. This morning, he is home waking up in bed beside me.

Go in God's peace today and celebrate this last day of June. He will never leave you or forsake you...never.

Thank you for your continued prayers. There is still more healing to come but nothing is impossible with God. #Godisfaithful #pray4bill

July 2018
Walking the Tightrope
of Trust

Day #173 July 1

Anchor Verse: Acts 10:9, Mark 1:35
About noon ...Peter went up on the roof to pray...Very early in the morning, while it was still dark, Jesus got up, left the house and went off to a solitary place, where he prayed. (NIV)

"Be willing to fight for this precious time with Me." These were the words that popped off the page of my devotional book this morning.

The battle is real, my friends. Time spent with God is our lifeline. Prayer is the key to overcome the challenges that we face. Through prayer, the hand of God is moved. God moves through the whole earth looking for those who are dedicated to Him. Are you one of them that He finds faithful?

As we stand on this first day of July, my heart is full. It is like standing on the mountaintop and surveying the valley below. The path is filled with winding roads, storms, sunny places, beautiful spaces, and dark wooded areas too. Ultimately it is always a place of victory because God is there!

What I have learned in the first six months of the year is that God is faithful and He calls us to live the same way. Lord God Almighty calls us out of the pit of mediocrity to soar in heavenly places with Him.

The only way to be like Him is to spend time with Him. Just like any other precious relationship, it's going to take effort on my part. There will be those who don't understand the way that you take or your willingness to sacrifice time and sleep to bask in the sweet peace of His presence. But that is not your worry. Your concern is to be obedient to the Lord and learn from Him.

As to the way Bill and I take on his healing journey, God alone knows the path. I know that the enemy will not relent until the victory is completed in Jesus's name. I will stand and fight from a place of victory until we see the manifestation of God's best for Bill.

Thank you for your countless prayers. Choose to rest in His love. #Godisfaithful #pray4bill

Day #174 July 2

Anchor Verse: Deuteronomy 33:27a
The eternal God is your refuge, and underneath are the everlasting arms. (NIV)

Earth is not our home. The four walls in which you live, whether it is a mansion, one room or a tent, none of these are your home either. The Bible says that the eternal God is your dwelling place. There and there alone you will find refuge and strength.

More than a dwelling place, God's arms of love are wrapped around you – He will never let you go – never! Practically, what does this mean? It tells me that no matter where life takes me – the winding roads, the places of despair, or the mountains of hope – God is there. He is my unshakable, unmovable foundation.

Today as we leave behind our apartment where we have lived for 10 years and almost 10 months, we walk into a new place of God's blessings. With our possessions stuffed into boxes and containers that will be moved by the hands of those who love us, Bill and I embrace this fresh start that God has miraculously provided. Who knew that our dream of moving to a two-bedroom apartment would come at the end of this life and death journey with Bill's health? God did.

He rewards those who diligently seek Him. But remember, God is not like a vending machine where we put in our good deeds and His blessings are dispensed. In my daily Bible reading, I find myself in the book of Job. God used Job's difficult circumstances to draw him into a deeper relationship, a deeper understanding of God, and a greater appreciation for life. Bill and I would testify that we, too, have been taken to a deeper place with God through Bill's health challenges.

As we make our move today from one place in our apartment complex to another, we will finish our walk out of the wilderness to the Promised Land. This will not be the end of our challenges but it will indeed be a place of blessing.

Thank you for your faithfulness all these months. Please pray for a smooth move today. You are loved and appreciated. #Godisfaithful #pray4bill

Day #175 July 3

Anchor Verse: Job 27:11
I will teach you about the power of God; the ways of the Almighty I will not conceal. (NIV)

Sharing what God has done in your life – His power, His majesty, His love and His grace, there is no greater testimony; there is no more powerful story.

During parts of this journey where we faced what looked like a brick wall or the end of the road, you have witnessed the healing power of God.

You have learned to pray without ceasing and how to wage war against spiritual forces. Victory comes when we truly believe when we pray.

There is no greater love than God's love. There is no greater power than God's power. There is no greater peace than God's peace. And there is only God's will – that's all that matters. "Not my will, my God but yours."

Now we enter a new chapter in our lives. Just a week ago Bill came home from the hospital after 168 days. Yesterday we moved into a two-bedroom ground floor apartment where we not only have space for Bill to continue his recovery, but God's peace is here. We had the best night's sleep we have had in days, weeks, maybe even months. (Being exhausted from moving probably helped the sleep.)

Most of all we want to declare God's faithfulness in this season of our lives. Today marks 175 days we have been on this journey. We have entered the second half of 2018 and we believe God's plans for us will continue to accelerate. Thank you for your faithfulness and prayers. The floodgates of heaven will continue to open for those who have walked in obedience to God. May your lives be forever changed by what has happened in ours.

Thank you, Lord, for the great things You have done. All glory and honor belong to God. #Godisfaithful #pray4bill

Day #176 July 4

Anchor Verse: Galatians 5:1

Let me be clear, the Anointed One has set us free—not partially, but completely and wonderfully free! We must always cherish this truth and stubbornly refuse to go back into the bondage of our past. (TPT)

We live in a country where we enjoy freedom to live and pursue our dreams. Often we take those freedoms for granted as they are the invisible safety net that guards us each day. Nonetheless, they are the bedrock, the foundation of this nation.

As believers, we experience an even greater freedom in Christ. We live life with eternity in view. We are free not only to walk in freedom but to leave our past behind and pursue God's best for us each day.

This passage tells us that "the Anointed One has set us free." Truly free! Not just partially, but completely and wonderfully free. That's something to be celebrated every day of our lives. We must cherish it and guard that freedom. Most of all, you and I must "stubbornly refuse to go back to the bondage of our past" as we choose to walk in freedom with Christ.

Today we celebrate Independence Day in the United States, freedom that was bought and paid for by the lives of many in the past and still is today.

What will you do with that freedom? Is it an opportunity for selfish pursuit alone or an opportunity to grow and use your other hand to lift up others?

Today Bill and I will be celebrating not only our country's independence but the freedom we have in Christ and what an amazing gift these freedoms are to us. Whom the Son sets free is free indeed!

Enjoy your celebration. Thank you for your faithfulness in prayer. #Godisfaithful #pray4bill

Day #177 July 5

Anchor Verse: Job 33:14
For God may speak in one way, or in another, Yet man does not perceive it. (NKJV)

I believe that all of us want to stay on track in our lives. Our heart's desire isn't to end up in the weeds, off the road, in the middle of a mud pit. Sometimes that is where we find ourselves.

God speaks to us in many ways. We don't always recognize His voice, that's what the passage in Job tells us today. This morning as I was hanging out with the Lord, I was thinking about the new place God had provided for us and the differences between our new apartment and our old one. From the kitchen sink in our old apartment, I could look out the window and often see eagles riding the wind currents. They always appeared when I needed to know that God was near, and right on cue, God "spoke" to me. Yes, a bird in flight can be a way that God speaks.

In our new apartment, I will be looking at the wall when I do the dishes. What can I put there as a reminder of God's presence with me?

In these months of Bill's health challenges, I have sought to hear God's voice like a thirsty man in the desert. During the times of chaos and confusion when there were many voices speaking or total silence, my heavenly Father knew the way through this valley of the shadow of death, all I needed to do was to follow His voice.

Do you recognize His voice? Sometimes He speaks to us through the Bible, a message from our pastor, or the words of a good friend. Other times, it's that inner voice in our spirit that speaks peace in the midst of the raging storm.

My prayer for you today is that you would silence all the other voices and listen for God's voice alone. He is always the voice of truth.

Thank you for standing on the wall with us for Bill's complete healing. The Lord is good. #Godisfaithful #pray4bill

Day #178 July 6

Anchor Verse: Jeremiah 9:23-24
This is what the LORD says: "Don't let the wise boast in their wisdom, or the powerful boast in their power, or the rich boast in their riches. But those who wish to boast should boast in this alone: that they truly know me and understand that I am the LORD who demonstrates unfailing love and who brings justice and righteousness to the earth, and that I delight in these things. I, the LORD, have spoken! (NLT)

My strength is not in my own flesh, it comes from God. How many of you would raise your hands and say amen? If you haven't discovered that lesson already, trust me that lesson is still in God's curriculum for you.

Our perspective changes when life moves from what we consider "normal" to a different playing field. Those circumstances may be a promotion at work, moving to a new location, or even a tragedy.

Human beings are resilient, God made us that way. We usually adapt to our new circumstances and make our way through them. That's a good thing. Where we can get off track is when we take credit for our wisdom, our power, or our riches. The truth is that every good and perfect gift comes from God not because we are so stunning, as our pastor often says, but because God loves us so much.

If you really want to boast, then boast in the fact that you know and understand God and His attributes and have chosen to see life from His perspective.

Through Bill's health journey, as "normal" was stripped away, God has shown me the joy that comes from understanding Him and His ways. His peace passes all understanding, and yes, His strength sustains me, no matter the challenges that face me day and night.

Today I encourage you to boast in what God has done, not the size of your bottom line, your advanced degrees, or how much power you have in the business world. In God alone, we will be satisfied.

Thank you for your ongoing prayers. We continue to move forward but every day we need God's grace. #Godisfaithful #pray4bill

Day #179 July 7

Anchor Verse: Job 36:26
How great is God — beyond our understanding! (NIV)

Have you made God too small? Is He so small that He fits on your smartphone as a quick inspiration? Is God confined to one hour of Sunday worship? Or have you reduced Him to the limits of what your mind can comprehend? If you have, then your understanding of God is too small.

When was the last time you looked at nature with awe and wonder? As I type this, I am looking out the window at the morning sky and see His handiwork in the clouds backlit with sunlight against a beautiful blue backdrop. My heart is filled with praise and thanksgiving. God the Creator of the universe is my heavenly Father and He cares about every detail of my life... everything!

On this journey we have walked, and are still walking, God's hand has been evident at every turn. His ways have often been beyond understanding but most of all I see evidence of His love for Bill and me; people at the right place at the right time, even physical needs being met after only whispering them in my heart.

Today I will choose to follow the God that is beyond my understanding. I chose to trust Him when my eyes can't see. I will sing of the God of my salvation and the wonder of His ways. Hallelujah!

What will you choose? Will you choose to trust in the God of miracles even when your eyes can't see beyond the next bend in the road? Take a leap of faith. Trust Him with all your cares, your hopes, and dreams. God is faithful – oh, yes, He is faithful!

Thank you for your faithfulness. Thank you for standing with us in our hour of need. Thank you for rejoicing in our victories. Our God is an Awesome God! #Godisfaithful #pray4bill

Day #180 July 8

Anchor Verse: Acts 17:28
For in him we live and move and have our being...we are his offspring. (NIV)

God is our Father. He is the Creator of all mankind and the entire universe. He loves you with an everlasting love and nothing can separate you from the Love of God that is in Christ Jesus. Now that's good news!

This verse from Acts as the apostle Paul is addressing the people in Athens at a meeting in the Areopagus, was to remind them, as well as us, that there is only one true God and our lives are lived in His presence and for His pleasure every day.

We are His offspring. You are His child! As I read this verse with a fresh perspective this morning, I thought of how so many people are having their DNA tested to determine their lineage, their ancestral background. Acts 17:28 will save you the money – you belong to God – first, last, and always. Nothing else matters.

Laid over the top of that foundation is that fact that daily, we live and move and have our being in Him. I find great comfort in the truth that He is always with me.

Just like a shepherd keeps an eye on His sheep, so God tends to you. He is the Good Shepherd and Jesus will go to any length to keep you safe.

As Bill and I have walked this journey of his health challenges, and today we continue to walk on that healing path, I am comforted to know that God is with us. Even when caregivers and therapists are not yet lined up in the flesh, God is in charge of Bill's healing and recovery, just as He has been from the moment we entered the ER on January 10, 2018.

My friends, remember where you belong today, to whom you belong. We thank God for your presence in our lives. #Godisfaithful #pray4bill

Day #181 July 9

Anchor Verse: Acts 18:9-10a
One night the Lord spoke to Paul in a vision: "Do not be afraid; keep on speaking, do not be silent. For I am with you..." (NIV)

Social media is filled with the details of our daily lives for all the world to see. Where do we tell the stories about the miracles God has done in our lives? Where do we help another without considering the cost?

As we began this journey, I started sharing with just a small group of individuals – family and friends. Facebook touches many lives but honestly I wasn't sure I wanted to expose such a personal and private journey with so many that I only knew online. If I was going to share, God would have me be real and not hide the difficult places.

Somehow He would use our difficult circumstances to touch the lives of others – we are just two ordinary people.

Paul may have felt the same way. God wanted to touch people's lives through the telling of Paul's story as he shared about the God who had transformed his life. Paul needed to be reminded, just like you and me, to not be afraid and keep on speaking the truth about what God had done in his life. Saul, a man who had been persecuting Christians, had an encounter with God that totally changed his life. His name was changed to Paul and now he shared what God had done wherever he went.

I will continue to share our story until God's work through our story is finished. Be strong and courageous. You do not need afraid about whatever you are facing for the Lord is with you.

Let your light shine today. May the Lord be honored and glorified in your life. Thank you for being a part of our story. Your prayers are woven throughout the tapestry of our victory. #Godisfaithful #pray4bill

Day #182 July 10

Anchor Verse: Psalm 116:7
Return to your rest, my soul, for the Lord has been good to you. (NIV)

Being at rest in the midst of adversity and hardship is a gift from God. Our instincts are to be on edge when we are in unfamiliar places. We walk cautiously and often fear tries to creep in and steal our joy.

As believers, children of God, we are privileged to walk with Jesus through every day, every circumstance. We can talk with Him. We can let Him speak words of peace to us and comfort our souls. Entering into a place of rest is still a choice that we make daily, in fact, every moment of every day.

Yesterday Bill and I were talking about this path we have been walking. He has no memory of most of it, it's a black hole. About six weeks ago is when Bill started remembering things again. We both shared about what God was doing and how it had changed our lives. Bill and God had some interesting conversations, as Bill described it, when he was in a place between life and death.

The rest and peace that I felt and walked in during those days when Bill was "here but not here" were truly a gift from God. Now we find ourselves in a new place – a new apartment, new expectations, and new people on our team with new responsibilities. None of it is beyond what we can handle with God's help.

Finding rest in Him is even more crucial these days because we are back in the world. We were in a protected place for a season but the time has come to be in the world but not of the world. God continues to write the pages of our future. It's very exciting. For today, my soul rests in the Lord and I am at peace.

I pray that your soul finds rest in the Lord this day. The Lord is good and His love endures forever.

Thank you for standing in the gap with us. Your prayers matter and have resulted in much good fruit. Be blessed today! #Godisfaithful #pray4bill

Day #183 July 11

Anchor Verse: Acts 20:35b
Remembering the words the Lord Jesus himself said: 'It is more blessed to give than to receive.' (NIV)

There is a blessing that comes from giving without counting the cost.

When I think of Jesus and many other heroes of the faith who have gone before us and those serving Him today, this is how they live their lives. They seek the Lord first and when He says go, they go to bless others and give of their time, their money, and their efforts.

Is this how you live your life? Do you truly believe that it is more blessed to give than to receive?

Do you ask "what's in it for me?" or do you trust the Lord to bring the blessing?

I have learned that it's not about keeping score. When we give something away, we don't look for the blessing to immediately follow. It's not like having a chalkboard, one for you, now a blessing for me.

Living with a selfless heart means that we walk by faith, sowing seeds of kindness, delivering a meal to a family walking through hard times, dropping off groceries, having a cup of tea/coffee with a friend who is grieving. The opportunities are endless!

Today I encourage you to listen to that still small voice within you as the Holy Spirit guides you to opportunities to give and receive the blessing purely in the act of giving.

Sowing seeds of kindness, speaking words of encouragement, these are the actions that will change the world around us.

Thank you to each one of you who has lived this out in our lives and blessed us so much on Bill's health journey. Great will be your reward in heaven. #Godisfaithful #pray4bill

Day #184 July 12

Anchor Verse: Psalm 3:5
I lie down and sleep; I wake again, because the Lord sustains me. (NIV)

Sleep is a gift from God. I am so grateful that we are not created like machines that never need to rest, that can go on and on and on, 24 hours a day, 7 days a week year after year after year.

Instead God created us with the ability to work and then rest. We all know what it feels like to be worn out by the end of the day. After a good restful night's sleep, we awaken refreshed ready to take on the challenges of a new day.

Have you ever stopped to think about this gift from God? Not only the gift of sleep, but the fact that God sustains us, cares for us, rebuilds us at a cellular level as we sleep.

I heard a TED talk about the need for sleep. If you try to operate on less than five hours of sleep for a sustained time, your body suffers. Sleep isn't a luxury, it's a necessity.

There is also the sleep of the righteous, those who know God, love Him, and have a relationship with Him. As we lie down and sleep, we are not only restored but often God speaks to us through dreams and visions. It is while we are sleeping that He quiets our fears and restores our strength. What a blessing that comes from our heavenly Father's hands.

There are some nights when Bill doesn't sleep very well, neither do I. After one of those nights of interrupted sleep, I find myself in God's presence in the early morning hours and He speaks peace to me there. God renews my strength. Just like mothers who tend to their children or those who tend to family members who are sick, I believe there is an extra measure of grace given by the Lord.

Thank you to those of you who have sacrificed your sleep to pray for Bill, for both of us. May the Lord richly bless you as you lie down and sleep for He is with you. #Godisfaithful #pray4bill

Day #185 July 13

Anchor Verse: Psalm 34:5
Those who look to him are radiant; their faces are never covered with shame. (NIV)

Being in the presence of God makes you radiant with His love and His light. Have you ever been walking down the street and seen someone who is radiant with God's love? They just light up the sidewalk around them.

On our journey this year, I have seen people like that. The song, "They will Know We are Christians by Our Love" I believe can be revised to "They will know we are Christians as we are radiant with God's love."

Someone commented that God's grace was visible in my appearance. That's how I want to live all the time! I don't want to be mud-stained by the world. I want to be a lighthouse of hope.

Just like the early disciples when they walked by those who were sick and their shadow fell on them, the power of Jesus within them healed the sick and lame. Why don't we live in that power and that place today? We should. We can. Let's do it!

Be that light in the darkness. Be the one who has faith when those around you are swimming in doubt. May the peace that passes all understanding not only guard your heart and mind, but may it still the stormy waters around you.

My brothers and sisters, let's ignite the fire of His love in those around us. May a tsunami of God's blessings flow in us, through us, and from us.

Having walked through these deep waters by God's grace alone, I know that God has plans for Bill and for me. We don't know what they are but we are willing to find out. We have shared God's love and light in our lives with you and our prayer is that you will pass along that flame, that hope to others.

May you be radiant today. Let your light shine. Help a friend. Speak words of life to yourself and others.

Thank you for your faithfulness. We are blessed. #Godisfaithful #pray4bill

Day #186 July 14

Anchor Verse: Psalm 37:23-24
The steps of good men are directed by the Lord. He delights in each step they take. If they fall, it isn't fatal, for the Lord holds them with his hand. (TLB)

Walking through life isn't always easy, even Jesus wasn't immune from difficult times. Jesus promised that as children of God we would have tribulation but He has overcome the world. Now that's good news!

You may be walking through deep waters this morning or a dry desert where everything seems barren and dusty. Maybe you woke up this morning with a tear-stained pillow or shouts of hallelujah. No matter your condition or feelings know that God is with you always.

Bill and I have been walking a pretty rough road since January. There are times when people hear what has happened and they shake their heads and look very troubled. A doctor made the comment that Bill had been a very sick man "but you seem to be handling it quite well."

Why? Because I have hope that comes in the name of the Lord. Bill's recovery to date is miraculous – without dispute. And God isn't finished with him yet.

Verse 24 really hit me this morning, "Though he falls, he will not stay down, because the Lord holds him by his hand."

Bill has "fallen" countless times on this journey from a medical standpoint, every time the Lord has lifted him up. The loving hand of Jesus filled with resurrection power gives Bill strength when in his humanity Bill has none.

Our prayer for you today is that you would follow the Lord. That your steps are pleasing to the Lord and though you fall, you won't stay down. It's time to get back up because God has plans for you.

Thank you for your faithfulness in prayer. May the Lord's hand sustain you today in whatever you face. You are loved. #Godisfaithful #pray4bill

Day #187 July 15

Anchor Verse: Psalm 9:10
And those who know Your name [who have experienced Your precious mercy]
will put their confident trust in You, For You, O Lord, have not abandoned
those who seek You. (AMP)

God's promises are true and they are your anchor in the storms of life. The book of Psalms is filled with King David's beautiful words to the Lord that describe not only his victories, but his times of doubt and challenge. It's a great place to find refuge and strength no matter your circumstances.

This verse really struck me. "Those who know your name, who have experienced Your precious mercy, will put their confident trust in You."

I was just talking with someone yesterday about putting my confident trust in the Lord. It was because of my intimate relationship with God that I could stand on the truth of His promises that He was going to save Bill's life and walk with us on this road to recovery.

"Confident trust" to me means more than just trusting, it means I have confidence in the one making the promise. God has proven Himself to be faithful over and over again through these 187 days, actually all the days of my life. How can I do anything less than believe His promises are true and that He loves me and the man He called to be my husband?

God will not abandon you. Your enemies will abandon you and sometimes even your friends will abandon you when they have crises that top your immediate need. But God will never, I mean never, abandon you. Don't rely on your feelings but stand on the truth and character of God.

I love the Lord even more than I did when we started this journey. And yes, I love Bill even more too. Having confident trust in God will change your life. Come and join us on the journey.

Thank you for your prayers day and night. Be blessed! #Godisfaithful #Hallelujah #pray4bill

Day #188 July 16

Anchor Verse: Psalm 16:7
The way you counsel and correct me makes me praise you more, for your whispers in the night give me wisdom, showing me what to do next. (TPT)

I am so grateful that God is a 24/7 God. He doesn't sleep when we sleep. God is always active tending to our best interests. The other cool thing is that He wants us to bloom and grow in our knowledge of Him and His ways.

We have the freedom to choose the way we will walk and if we will decide to walk in obedience to His ways. We are not robots where God has the master control. Oh the joy that comes when we make good choices! How do you know the way to take?

Spending time in the Bible, reading His instructions, listening to wise counsel as He speaks to me day and night, and praying for wisdom and revelation have kept me on course.

Nighttime is designated for sleep, but that's not always true for those who suffer from insomnia. Others have been led by the Lord to watch and pray during the night hours and sometimes God instructs us while we sleep in the depths of our mind and heart. When we wake up we know exactly what we need to do, the course of action we need to take.

During Bill's health journey, I have come to know God in a new way. I have a more intimate relationship with Him. I have sought His face, and in His presence, I have not only experienced the fullness of His joy but my strength has been renewed like an eagle in flight. Not every night do we get a good night's sleep, even then God is there.

I am grateful for God's wise counsel as He shows me what to do next. His peace has been a blanket to comfort me in the night seasons. His joy has given me strength when in my humanity I had an empty gas tank.

May you be led by His grace. Thank you for your prayers during the night, they have keep us afloat. #Godisfaithful #Hallelujah #pray4bill

Day #189 July 17

Anchor Verse: Psalm 18:16
He then reached down from heaven, all the way from the sky to the sea. He reached down into my darkness to rescue me! He took me out of my calamity and chaos and drew me to himself, taking me from the depths of my despair! (TPT)

God is so faithful! He doesn't see you from afar and leave you alone. He is with you in your pain and your sorrow. God dances with you when you are filled with joy.

The Prince of Peace anoints you with His blessings. God is a proud Father when you walk the path of obedience.

God is a very protective heavenly Father. No one messes with His kids. If you think you are alone in life's struggles, then you are wrong. His eyes never leave you.

Your heavenly Father will meet your every need, even giving you extraordinary strength when you are dead on your feet.

There have been times in this six-month journey when many were on the path beside me, and other seasons where God and I were in that solitary place alone.

Maybe you're weary this morning and covered with muck from going through deep waters, as this verse in Psalm 18 says, "He reached down into my darkness to rescue me and... He drew me to himself, taking me from the depths of my despair."

My brother and sister, trust Him even when you cannot understand the way He is leading you. Trust Him in the chaos. Trust Him in the darkness. Rejoice with Him when victory comes. He is worthy of our praise.

Thank you for walking with us when you could. Thank you for your prayers. May the Lord bless you. #Godisfaithful #Hallelujah #pray4bill

Day #190 July 18

Anchor Verse: Psalm 22:30
Our children too shall serve him, for they shall hear from us about the wonders of the Lord. (TLB)

Sharing our stories with the next generation – the miracles and challenges and victories about what God has done in our lives – this is our legacy.

Our legacy is not the size of our bank account, our possessions, or even what we have given away, it's the seed that we have sown in generations yet to come.

In our lives, and especially in our church, we are seeing young people turn their lives over to the Lord and leave the messiness of their past behind. Out of that renewed commitment to God, they are coming together in marriage and putting God first in their lives – a strand of three cords is not easily broken.

Even more beautiful are the children of this union – another generation that speaks of God's faithfulness. They are committed to sowing seeds of goodness and kindness and speaking of God's faithfulness. At a young age, they are being taught to pray and believe that God will move, and He does. God answers the prayers of our children and grandchildren.

Our legacy is beautiful when it is built on Jesus Christ. When our stories inspire hope in those who are going through deep waters. It is not just for our benefit that we go through the refining fire. We are being pruned because God knows the plans He has for us and that is to be a beacon of hope for those who will come behind us.

The Bible is filled with stories of ordinary people, just like you and me, who are used to show His might, His power, and His faithfulness.

How will the Lord use your life? What are the wonders of the Lord you need to share today? Go and do it. Do not delay.

Thank you for your faithfulness. Our victory is your victory. Be blessed today! #Godisfaithful #pray4bill

Day #191 July 19

Anchor Verse: Psalm 25:5
Guide me in Your truth and teach me, For You are the God of my salvation;
For You [and only You] I wait [expectantly] all the day long. (AMP)

The strong foundation of learning is truth... God's truth. If we believe things that are lies, we will fall and find ourselves in the pit of fear and despair.

I have learned so much since the beginning of this year and have so much more to learn. God created us with the capacity to learn new things and not be overwhelmed because He is right there beside us coaching us along the way.

Who do you believe? Where do you get your instruction? You need to make sure it is God's truth found in His Word, not just a good idea or passing fad.

When I read this passage this morning, it reminded me of the path we have been walking. While Bill was in the hospital there was a "village" of people to monitor his every step, and now it's God and me. Yes, there are others to help us but the dynamics have changed. Truly, my hope is in God all day long.

For example, this week we have extreme heat here in Spokane and the first wildfire of the season. Bill has never done well in the heat even prior to this illness. Now with lungs that have had pneumonia three times, smoke in the air is not our friend.

Yesterday I realized that I could choose to live in the camp of fear and apprehension or I could trust God to navigate us through the wildfire season. I chose to trust God. My heavenly Father reminded me that nothing was too hard for Him, nothing. So I took a deep breath and moved on knowing that He will "teach me" to walk this path.

Where does your hope lie this morning? Is your hope in God or are you living in fear? Fear not. He promised to be with you every step along the way. Thank you for your prayers. #Godisfaithful #pray4bill

Day #192 July 20

Anchor Verse: Psalm 27:13-14
I remain confident of this: I will see the goodness of the Lord in the land of the living. Wait for the Lord; be strong and take heart and wait for the Lord. (NIV)

Confidence in the Lord, His timing, and His ways, that's the place where my soul has found peace, my heart finds solace.

Waiting for the Lord is different than waiting for people or for services to fall into place or for prescriptions to arrive. Waiting for the Lord is a place of peace in the midst of chaos. It's the place that David talks about in Psalm 23. "He makes me lie down in green pastures, He leads me beside still waters. He restores my soul."

We can't always go to that place in our natural environment but when we spend time with the Lord, we can certainly go to that place in our spirit.

My strength is found in His presence. He raises me up when I am weak. He gives me the mind of Christ when decisions and circumstances are coming at me at lightning speed and I need to be wise. God is there in the quietness when my dear husband is sleeping and I can hear the breath of life being inhaled and exhaled from his lungs.

Our heavenly Father is there when Bill smiles and laughs and jokes around. He is there when Bill eats and grows stronger. God is there when we pray and seek His face for what lies ahead of us – for it is good.

As you wait on the Lord this morning, know without a doubt that God loves you and that He will never leave you or forsake you. Find new strength in Him today.

Soar on eagle's wings above your circumstances for God is in control and you will see the goodness of the Lord in the land of the living.

Thank you for your continued prayers. God is in charge of Bill's recovery. Every day we are one step closer. #Godisfaithful #Hallelujah #pray4bill

Day #193 July 21

Anchor Verse: Isaiah 30:15
For the Lord God, the Holy One of Israel, says: Only in returning to me and waiting for me will you be saved; in quietness and confidence is your strength; but you'll have none of this. (TLB)

God alone is the way to peace. He is our strength in every season, for every reason. We know that in our heads. We know that in our hearts. Why do we refuse to be comforted in His presence? All we need to do is stop and be still with Him.

It is a sad commentary on our society that we are driven to stay on the move all the time. Sitting still, spending time with others in quiet conversation or just being alone with the television, internet, and Facebook turned off is so foreign to us. We have been conditioned to always have our airspace filled with "stuff."

God is patient. He is a good, good Father and hovers around us – even when we ignore Him.

I so love my time with the Lord in the morning. In the quietness of the day, no matter what had happened during the night – a night of rest or a night of restlessness, I find joy and strength in His presence.

Truly I will testify that in quietness and confidence is my strength! There is no way I could have made it through these last months of Bill's illness without God, not only the God who is Healer and Provider, but the one who loves me and spends time in that intimate relationship with me. Without the sound of His voice to reassure me, give me wisdom, to be my strength, surely I would have perished on my own.

My friend, I encourage you today to return to the Lord, to wait on Him, and be saved. It breaks my heart to think of the millions in the world who refuse God's open arms of love and the offer of sweet peace. Please don't refuse His gift any longer. God loves you with an everlasting love.

Thank you for your prayers. They have been our lifeline. May you be blessed today. #Godisfaithful #pray4bill

Day #194 July 22

Anchor Verse: Psalm 31:24
Be strong and let your hearts take courage, All you who wait for and confidently expect the Lord. (AMP)

As this new day dawns, be strong in the Lord and let your heart take courage. You know what it feels like to be weak and filled with fear. In fact, that might be where you are this morning.

Jesus said, "Be of good cheer, I have overcome the world!" If Jesus has overcome the world then surely He can help you through the problems you face today.

This message is addressed to those of you who are waiting and have been waiting for a long time for something you desperately need. That might be a financial blessing – a job, increase in pay, because there are unpaid bills with a collection agency breathing down your neck. Or it might be the restoration of your health or that of a loved one, or peace of mind in the midst of chaos. King David who wrote this psalm goes one step further and says, "Confidently expect the Lord."

Wow! There's a big difference between a hopeful wish and believing that God will deliver you. You wait in expectation for the knock on the door, the phone call, the healing – and when it comes, God gets all the glory.

I have been blessed on Bill's health journey to stand in that place of confident expectation. Knowing in my heart and believing that God would save Bill from what seemed to be certain death.

Today as Bill continues to heal at home and we face the attacks of the enemy, I still choose to wait in expectation and trust the Lord. I will trust Him when the medication hasn't arrived. I will trust Him when the nurse and therapists still haven't shown up. I will trust Him when I don't always know the way to go, but I will listen for His still small voice saying, "This is the way, walk in it."

Thank you for standing on the wall with us and fighting alongside me for Bill's complete recovery. May God be glorified. #Godisfaithful #pray4bill

Day #195 July 23

Anchor Verse: Psalm 34:14
Turn from evil and do good; seek peace and pursue it. (NIV)

Your role in life is not passive, it is active. We must be engaged if we are going to stay on track with God's plans for us. The expression "go with the flow" is often spoken but when it comes to God and His ways, that's not the way it works.

This verse in Psalm 34 gives us clear marching orders. We are to turn away from evil and do what is good. I really like the imagery here. "Turn away" because we know that if temptation is kept right in front of our eyes, it is easy to be sucked in. We must turn away, go another direction, fix our eyes on God and what is good and holy – what we look at, what we read, what we listen to – all of those things matter because they shape who we are and how we speak and think and what we believe. It's time to wake up from our sleep and stand up for what is right – to do what is good!

The second part of the verse reminds us that we will need to pursue peace – it can be elusive when we are in the midst of difficult circumstances. First of all our hearts must be set on desiring peace of heart and peace of mind. Some people love to live in chaos and constantly be putting out fires – you get exhausted that way and the enemy comes rushing in and fills you with bitterness, anger, resentment, etc.

There is nothing like the peace of God that passes all understanding. Rest in His presence. Do good. Seek peace. Not only will it transform your life, it will change the world.

Thank you for your faithfulness. Be blessed as you are a blessing to so many. #Godisfaithful #pray4bill

Day #196 July 24

Anchor Verse: Psalm 36:5
Your love, Lord, reaches to the heavens, your faithfulness to the skies. (NIV)

When we shift our focus from our earthly troubles to our amazing, Awesome God, our heavenly Father who loves us so much, how can you not praise Him?

As I read Psalm 36, I could picture a summer day where the blue skies are like an artist's canvas and God paints a panoramic view of His creation. All of it is signed with His signature of love. God wrote you a love letter this morning with your name on it, with every detail designed to bring about His best for you.

God's love and faithfulness are two constants in our lives. If anything, they grow sweeter and stronger as the days go by, as our eyes are opened to the revelation of who He is as we spend time with Him.

There were moments when we walked on paths that goats could barely navigate, through swampland and quicksand, through dry deserts where we became parched. The Good Shepherd led us beside still waters and made us lie down in green pastures and there refreshed our souls.

I have learned to praise Him when my eyes couldn't see the path ahead, even praise Him in the storm. I praised Him with tears of joy running down my cheeks as Bill broke through the victor's tape as he conquered another portion of the race called rehab and recovery.

I sing this morning, not because things are perfect, but because I know God is faithful. His love will lead us to our destination. I thank God for the honor and privilege of being Bill's wife through this storm and the path where God is leading us because He loves us.

God is faithful, my friends. Never doubt it. Always trust Him. He will not fail you. Thank you for standing with us. #Godisfaithful #pray4bill

Day #197 July 25

Anchor Verse: Jeremiah 29:13
You will seek me and find me when you seek me with all your heart. (NIV)

We used to play the game of Hide and Seek when we were children. One person would hide and the rest of us would go looking for them. When you are really little, sometimes your hiding place was really obvious, but honestly, the thrill was in being "found."

I believe that is still true today as adults. The "fun" does not lie in the hiding as it did when were children, but the greater need, the greater joy lies in being found. God has planted that desire in our hearts to be found by Him, to be in relationship with Him.

The enemy will have us believing the lies that God doesn't care about us, that we are alone in the battles that we face. But that's what they are – lies.

The choice is ours. God reminds us that if we search for Him, we will find Him, but our attempt must be wholehearted. A double-minded mind will fail to get anywhere.

It's like that fictional animal from Doctor Doolittle "pushmi pullyu" (Push Me-Pull You). That creature didn't get anywhere when it was being pulled two different directions!

This may be what you are struggling with this morning – the Lord is calling to you to follow Him, to be in relationship with Him, while the world is calling you to pursue things that will only last for a moment. What will you seek? To whom will you be faithful?

Through each step of Bill's healing journey, I have had the choice to listen to the world or listen to the Lord. I chose to walk on His path of peace even in the midst of the storm.

Today I will choose to search for Him and find Him as I seek God with all my heart. Won't you please join me?

Thank you for your continued prayers. We have not attained complete victory yet... but the battle belongs to the Lord. We are more than conquerors. #Godisfaithful #pray4bill #Hallelujah

Day #198 July 26

Anchor Verse: Psalm 40:5
Many, LORD my God, are the wonders you have done, the things you planned for us. None can compare with you; were I to speak and tell of your deeds, they would be too many to declare. (NIV)

Today is a day of celebration. I am celebrating the gift of life, the gift of God's hand ever-present in my life. I am celebrating the gift of my husband, Bill. Why you might ask? Today is one month since his release from Rehabilitation Hospital of the Northwest, which marked 168 days of hospitalization, 168 days away from home on his path to healing.

This is the journey of miracles that I am celebrating today. This morning I join with King David who wrote Psalm 40 so long ago, who also knew what God's faithfulness looked like. David knew what it meant to be in despair, to look death in the face, and to have God deliver him from it all and be filled with so much joy that he danced before the Lord.

That's the God I know and serve. That's the God who loves me with an everlasting love. That's the God who sustained Bill when he was in "that dark place between life and death" but God appeared to him in the light and spoke words of life to him.

God has commissioned us to tell our stories, the stories of His faithfulness. We must share the miracles because others need to have their faith ignited. The flame may be growing dim in your heart this morning and the reflection of Christ's love and light in us can help you through your own struggles.

Whatever you are facing today, you are not alone. Today we celebrate the power of prayer and what God can do when together we storm the throne room of grace.

Nothing is impossible with God. Bill is still a miracle in the making. This month has stretched me to a whole new level as full-time caregiver without the support we anticipated, but God has met our every need.

Let our praise rise as a sweet aroma to heaven. Thank you, Lord, for Your faithfulness. Bill and I thank you for your faithfulness through prayer. #Godisfaithful #Hallelujah #pray4bill

Day #199 July 27

🜨 *Anchor Verse: Hebrews 6:18*
He has given us both his promise and his oath, two things we can completely count on, for it is impossible for God to tell a lie. Now all those who flee to him to save them can take new courage when they hear such assurances from God; now they can know without doubt that he will give them the salvation he has promised them. (TLB)

There are some of you this morning who are thinking about giving up. You think it is too hard. You can't see the end in sight. It seems that every direction you turn there is another problem, or worse yet, you are standing still and you get run over by more problems. The words in your head have turned negative and the enemy of our souls, the devil himself, is fueling the fire of discouragement. Does this sound like you?

We must run to the Lord and take hold of the hope that He promises. It doesn't say walk or saunter or dilly dally or I'll think about it tomorrow when I don't have any other options left, it says RUN!!!

Why? Because when you are nested in that hope, when you are tucked in with God, the storm may be raging around you but you can look into God's face. You can hear the words of Jesus, you can feel peace as the Holy Spirit leads you and speaks to you, and you can rest secure.

It doesn't mean that your problems will change instantly but your perspective has changed. You are holding on to hope. In the devotional I was reading this morning it said, "Hope is a golden cord connecting you to heaven."

We lose hope when we cut God out of the equation. On this journey, my hope has been secure in God, the anchor of my soul. There have been moments when it looked really bad, but I chose to believe God's truth.

Bail that water out of your boat and ask Jesus to come and pilot your lifeboat. All you have to do is ask. He'll come running to help you.

Thank you for your faithfulness in prayer. Greater things are yet to come. #Godisfaithful #Hallelujah #pray4bill

Day #200 July 28

Anchor Verse: Psalm 46:7

The Commander of the armies of heaven is here among us. He, the God of Jacob, has come to rescue us. (TLB)

Our lives are not lived alone. The Lord Almighty is by our side through the blessings and the trials.

Today is an important day, a significant day. Two hundred days ago Bill went into the hospital with pneumonia. We had no idea that 200 days later we would still be fighting the battle that began that day.

Many of you have been with us these 200 days, you have held up our arms, you have prayed day and night, you have spoken encouraging words and been Jesus' hands and feet.

How can you choose a Bible verse to sum up the circumstances and emotions that surround this event? The Lord led me to Psalm 46. "The Commander of the armies of heaven is here among us. He, the God of Jacob, has come to rescue us."

We serve a big, big God who put the sun, moon, and stars in the sky and He cares about me and you. God wrote a book about our lives before we were even born. He knew the path that Bill and I would take these 200 days. God has tested us and tried us. The Prince of Peace has been with us through the refining fire. The Commander of the angel armies has dispatched the armies of heaven to carry out His wishes as we were protected from the fiery darts of the enemy of our souls.

In the heavenly realm, we have already attained the victory. In the flesh, it may seem that we have a ways to go, we do. It is nothing compared to the battles that have already been won.

We are excited. We are encouraged. Our hearts are burning brightly with God's love and His hope.

Watch what the Lord will do this day and the days to come. Great is His Faithfulness! Hallelujah! Amen! #Godisfaithful #pray4bill

Day #201 July 29

Anchor Verse: 2 Thessalonians 3:3
But the Lord is faithful, and he will strengthen you and protect you from the evil one. (NIV)

Good news! The Lord is on your side. He knows every battle you face. God knows your trials and your victories. The Lord sees you this morning – those who are discouraged and feeling hopeless. He will not leave you alone. Your heavenly Father will strengthen you and protect you from the evil one.

Faithfulness – it is a trait that is not always seen in the world. Too often people give up when the going gets tough. They walk away. God never walks away from you. If you close your eyes and quiet all the noise around you, you can feel the power of His presence; you can hear His still small voice speaking words of encouragement.

As we enter this next phase of Bill's recovery with the entrance of nursing and therapists to help him get stronger and progress, I am so grateful for God's faithfulness. We will be stretched. Bill's brain will be taken to a new level. We have developed a routine, a pace that is comfortable. Now we will be called to push past that.

The enemy will come knocking at the door once again trying to discourage Bill that this part is too hard, but Jesus will answer the door and will kick the enemy to the curb. We believe in the victory God has for Bill. We believe that God is faithful and His protection, His guarantee for safe passage out of this illness has not expired.

Lord, we praise and thank you for Your faithfulness. We thank you for Your hedge of protection around us. We thank you for the opportunity to stretch our faith and let our prayers arise to heaven's throne room. Thank you for those who stand with us, who are on their knees on our behalf. May the blessings of heaven flow upon them this day. In Jesus' name we pray, amen.

Thank you for your faithfulness in prayer. We are blessed. #Godisfaithful #Hallelujah #pray4bill

Day #202 July 30

Anchor Verse: Psalm 52:9

For what you have done I will always praise you in the presence of your faithful people. And I will hope in your name, for your name is good. (NIV)

We praise You, Lord, this morning for the great things You have done and the greater things that are yet to come. I will praise you with every breath I breathe, every word I speak. I take every thought captive in Jesus' name. Hallelujah!

God has done great things for us and we know that it is only by His grace, by His hand that we are saved. Praise and hope – they are inseparable – one fuels the other.

When we worship the Lord, we take our eyes off ourselves and our circumstances. As we look into His face, we see His love, His steadfastness, His grace, and we feel His peace. Nothing else matters when we are in His presence.

As July comes to an end, I was just reflecting this morning on what God has done, just this month. From the move from our old apartment to helping us get settled and follow-up medical appointments, and new strength and healing for Bill, and watching my husband bloom and grow under God's direction. Hearing the stories of what God has done not only in our lives but in yours. I will praise Him forever for what He has done.

Let us join together our hearts and hands and lift our praise to heaven. Yes, we still have challenges – we will as long as we are present in this sinful world. As believers, we are in the world, but it's not our forever home.

Sing Hallelujah to the Lord this morning! Open your eyes to see what He will do this day.

Don't miss an opportunity to share what God has done in your life. He is worthy of our praise. Hallelujah!

Thank you for your continued prayers. #Godisfaithful #pray4bill

Day #203 July 31

Anchor Verse: Proverbs 17:17
A friend loves at all times, and a brother is born for adversity. (NIV)

This life is not meant to be lived alone. When I say "alone", I am not equating it with marital status. In the book of Proverbs, it reminds us that friends and family are part of the community that surround us to support us on this adventure called life.

On this last day of July as I reflect on another month of 2018 that is now history, I am drawn to this verse, to you and so many others that have surrounded us on our journey.

There are times when you must face things with only you and God. I am so grateful that this experience has been deep and wide with the love and support, and especially the prayers of those around us. I know that you have shared our needs with others, and literally people all over the United States and the world have been praying for Bill, and me, too.

It is an honor and privilege to "love at all times" – the good times and the challenges. When you are willing to walk through the fires of adversity with someone, God forms a bond that is imprinted on your heart forever.

As I think about the extraordinary ways that people have shown us their love and support, it doesn't take long before my eyes are filled with tears of joy and thanksgiving. They are leaking the gratitude that fills my heart.

We are about to embark on the next phase of this journey, with a nurse checking on Bill's physical status and therapists working with him at home to help him excel to the next level. We need your arms of love around us again. Bill's body and mind will be stretched. It is by God's grace Bill will climb the next rungs of the ladder of success on his health journey.

Thank you for your continued prayers. Truly they elevate us and encourage us on this daily trek to the Promised Land of God's healing. #Godisfaithful

Our Walk of Faith

August 2018
Prayer Changes Us

Day #204 August 1

Anchor Verse: Romans 4:20-21
But he [Abraham] did not doubt or waver in unbelief concerning the promise of God, but he grew strong and empowered by faith, giving glory to God, being fully convinced that God had the power to do what He had promised. (AMP)

The faith of Abraham stands like a lighthouse through the centuries. I wonder if he knew that thousands of years later people would marvel at his faith and belief in God even when his eyes couldn't see the way ahead.

Somehow I don't think that Abraham was concerned about being "popular" years down the road. I believe that his eyes were fixed on God, trusting Him to do what He promised.

Even so, Abraham made some mistakes, he stumbled in the flesh but then made it right with God by asking for forgiveness and kept on walking that road of faith.

Verse 20 tells us that Abraham "did not doubt or waver in unbelief concerning the promise of God." He trusted God with the outcome. In fact, his faith grew stronger and Abraham was empowered as he gave glory to God.

That's the kind of faith we need to strive for today. When the circumstances we are walking through are difficult and in the present moment we are not seeing the manifestation of the promise, we know God is faithful and the answer is coming.

We have been blessed during Bill's health journey with that kind of faith. In these past weeks as Bill is able to communicate, he speaks of that faith as well. We have no doubt that God will complete Bill's healing and the people who surround us are speaking that same confidence into our lives.

Whatever you are facing, ask God to give you faith like Abraham, who did not doubt or waver in unbelief concerning the promise of God. God is faithful. He doesn't lie. His promises are true. Trust God today even when your eyes can't see the outcome. You are loved with an everlasting love.

Thank you for your continued prayers. We are walking to the Promised Land of healing. #Godisfaithful #pray4bill

Day #205 August 2

⚓ *Anchor Verse: Psalm 62:7*
My victory and honor come from God alone. He is my refuge, a rock where no enemy can reach me. (NLT)

In a world where we applaud achievement and success, it is refreshing to remember that my victory and honor come from God.

Victory and honor originating from God, according to His standards – I can think of no greater achievement. On my life's journey, I have learned the things that delight God are often not what we would read in a newspaper headline or make the top story on the internet.

Many stories in the Bible about people doing things that delighted God's heart were carried out without the applause of men.

In fact, in Matthew 6:3, when Jesus talks about giving to the needy, He says do it in secret and God who sees what is done in secret will reward you.

In these months since January when we were in the fight for Bill's life and we were "removed" from the "rat race" of life, I have gained much wisdom.

I have seen the weariness of the "rat race" of life. I have seen with a new set of eyes the success that so many are chasing. Frankly, it makes me tired. I don't want to go back there again.

God is choosing a new place, a new purpose for both of us.

God is our refuge. He is protecting us from our enemies and that includes pursuing things that really don't matter to Him. On this path to healing as God brings us to a new place, my hope and prayer is that all that we say and do will bring honor and glory to Him.

Please join us as we seek His face, His victory, and honor. God will protect you as you seek His best. May you walk in victory today in Jesus' name. Hallelujah! #Godisfaithful #pray4bill

Day #206 August 3

Anchor Verse: Psalm 63:7
For You have been my help, And in the shadow of Your wings [where I am always protected] I sing for joy. (AMP)

I don't know how people make it through life without God. I can't imagine facing life without His peace and His presence. Being in a relationship with God brings new enjoyment to life because we can see the world through His eyes of love. It makes my heart sing.

During Bill's health challenges, I have often sung songs of joy in my spirit and in the quietness of my heart (especially in those ICU days), and out loud when I was at home.

When I think about being under the shadow of His wings, the image I see is standing in the rain under an umbrella. Maybe it's all this heat that is causing my mind to think about the refreshing nature of rain, but God's blessings fall on us from heaven every day. They refresh our spirit. They feed our souls.

When was the last time you had the urge to sing for joy?

Over the last few years, the Lord has been teaching me to play instrumental praise music while I work. It sows goodness and light into my body and mind and creates a positive atmosphere.

There are other songs that are my battle cry when I am storming the gates of heaven in intercessory prayer. And the old sacred hymns testify to God's faithfulness. Sometimes we need music to soothe our souls and refresh our spirit.

Rejoice in Him. Thank God for what He has done. He is your hope and salvation. Sing a new song today.

Thank you for your prayers. Thank you for the times you have sown joy and hope into our lives. #Godisfaithful #Hallelujah #pray4bill

Day #207 August 4

Anchor Verse: Psalm 139:16

Your eyes saw my unformed body; all the days ordained for me were written in your book before one of them came to be. (NIV)

There is great comfort in knowing that God has everything under control in our lives when it becomes chaotic to the human eye. When the storms in our lives arrive, it's a good time to ask the question, "What is God up to? What am I supposed to be learning right now?" There is always a lesson to be learned.

It may not be something you need to do, but something you need to surrender and lay down. We have been through many twists and turns on Bill's journey of healing. Most of the time we couldn't see the path ahead of us, daily each step was a walk of faith. I believe God ordained it that way.

This morning in my quiet time with God, He reminded me of this verse in Psalm 139. It was a call to remember that even though there are days when we hit warp speed and other days that are slow and steady, all of them were written in the book about our lives before we were born.

God showed me the book about my life... there were pages that were tear-stained, those that were muddy, those whose words jumped off the page with happiness and victory. It is a beautiful tapestry that He designed uniquely for me. God wrote a book about your life, too, custom designed for your good and His glory.

Today is a day of rest for us. It has to be. It's time to put away the Welcome mat outside the door of our lives and be tucked in with God. As we rest in His presence, feast on His faithfulness, and sleep, we will rest under the shadow of His wings.

If possible, take some time away from the rat race of life and rest in Him. Allow God to send angels to minister to you. You are tired, weak, and worn and yet you fight on. Even Jesus stopped to rest.

Thank you for your relentless prayers. We need to rest and renew our strength today. Our God is truly an Awesome God! He is your God too. #Godisfaithful #pray4bill

Day #208 August 5

⚓ *Anchor Verse: Romans 8:11*
The Spirit of God, who raised Jesus from the dead, lives in you. And just as God raised Christ Jesus from the dead, he will give life to your mortal bodies by this same Spirit living within you. (NLT)

This morning I stand in awe of the God who created us. Not only the beauty of all that surrounds us but the complexity, yet the simplicity of our bodies. It is impossible to say there is no God after seeing what I have seen these last 208 days.

There have been many life-changing moments. One of them happened just days after Bill was admitted to the hospital with pneumonia. We prayed and God began the series of miracles that you have read about through today.

About three days after Bill was admitted to the hospital I remember him saying to me that just as God raised Jesus from the dead and brought him back to life, God would do the same for Bill. Wow! I almost started crying right there. What a profound declaration. It could only have come with an encounter with God.

As I read Romans 8:11, God reminded me of His promise to Bill. "The Spirit of God, who raised Jesus from the dead, lives in you. And just as God raised Christ Jesus from the dead, he will give life to your mortal bodies by this same Spirit living within you."

We have eternal hope this morning! As a believer, the Spirit of God lives in you. That means you have resurrection power in your mortal body. If you woke up this morning feeling a little weary or out of sorts, read this truth and tap into His resurrection power. Strip off the cloak of heaviness that has you burdened down. Put on His robe of righteousness and put your hand in His hand. Jesus saved you. God delights in you. Trust Him with your life and your dreams. You are loved!

Thank you for your faithfulness. Our gift is to remind you that God loves you and lives in you. Be filled with His joy today. There is hope in the name of the Lord. #Godisfaithful #pray4bill #Hallelujah

Day #209 August 6

Anchor Verse: Psalm 71:14
But as for me, I will wait and hope continually, And will praise You yet more and more. (AMP)

There is often one thread that holds a tattered cloth together. God has created hope to be that thread that keeps us connected to Him. We have hope because Jesus was born, lived, died, and rose from the dead.

Are you holding on to hope this morning? The psalmist didn't stop there. I believe that hope is what we carry on the inside. It's our internal fuel that keeps us going. But more than that, we need to declare, sing, and praise the Lord! It's an external manifestation of our hope.

Sing – make a joyful noise if you have to! Praise Him – with your words. Rejoice in the God of your salvation.

If your attitude of gratitude has slipped, start with the fact that your heart pumps on its own and your lungs breathe in and out. Praise the Lord!

Thank you, Lord, for the parts of our body that are on auto-pilot. If it were up to me to make sure that my heart beat the right amount of times per minute, I would have been dead a long time ago.

On this journey, there were days when the list of things that were going our way was pretty short. However, we only needed one thing on the list, and that was God. Our hope is in Him.

Every day I see a little progress. I see more light in Bill's eyes. He can communicate better. I see his desire to walk and to resume a more "normal" life returning every day.

We wait patiently for the full transformation, the full manifestation of God's healing glory in Bill. As I have used the caterpillar to butterfly illustration many times, we have not traveled this far to cut short the process and have a "crippled" butterfly that can't soar for God's glory.

Thank you for standing in that hope with us. You have held up our arms when we were weak. Great will be your reward. #Godisfaithful #pray4bill

Day #210 August 7

Anchor Verse: Ephesians 4:29
And never let ugly or hateful words come from your mouth, but instead let your words become beautiful gifts that encourage others; do this by speaking words of grace to help them. (TPT)

Words are so powerful. Every word that you have spoken to yourself or others has left an imprint – to build up or to harm.

Are your words beautiful gifts that encourage others? They don't have to be eloquent words or a long speech. The words "I love you" or "I appreciate you" or "You are loved" build a fire of hope in the soul of another.

In the early days of Bill's illness when he was in really tough shape, I was very careful of the words that were spoken around him. I spoke words of life to him.

I spoke the Word of God over him, Bible verses that I had memorized in my youth became seeds of hope planted in Bill. God's Word became our best defense, greater than the doctor's medicine.

On some of the darkest days when the doctors, nurses, and others couldn't see what I was seeing, I laid my shield of faith over him to deflect those words, those fiery arrows from the enemy.

Use your shield to deflect negative words, wounding words over your children, your spouse, your friends, family members, or even strangers who God brings across your path. There is so much power when our shield of faith is used to its greatest potential!

Let your words be a beautiful gift today. Do not resort to ugly or hateful words. May the light of the love of Jesus fuel the words that you speak and cover others with His grace.

Thank you for the encouraging words you have spoken to us and over us and on our behalf to our heavenly Father. Great will be your reward. Be blessed this day! #Godisfaithful #pray4bill

Day #211 August 8

Anchor Verse: Titus 2:7
Above all, set yourself apart as a model of a life nobly lived. With dignity, demonstrate integrity in all that you teach. (TPT)

In the quietness of the night, God spoke to me, "Be an example. Be holy as I am holy."

This message wasn't just for me, it's for you too. As believers, we are called to reflect the light and love of Jesus. Our actions are being watched by others. We are a mirror. Our lives reflect what is happening in our hearts. The words of our mouth speak forth what our mind is focused on. What kind of example are you?

In our Bible verse today, Paul is speaking to Titus and tells him to "show yourself in all respects to be a model of good works, and in your teaching show integrity, dignity." Wow.... if all of us followed Paul's teaching consistently, what would the world be like today?

Today, our challenge is to walk that path. Be an example to your children, even when you're tired. Be an example to strangers as they observe you in the grocery store or at social events. Be an example to your co-workers about having joy in the workplace, no matter the conditions. Be an example to your church family that you are not just a Sunday Christian.

This year God has walked with us through some difficult circumstances. It has been a great opportunity and privilege to be an example of hope, integrity, dignity, and love. We were called to trust Him even when the results weren't visible. Today as God continues to "polish" the work that He started, we are called to teach in a new way, a new arena.

I stand in awe of God this morning. God doesn't waste anything that we walk through – it's all for His glory! In your joy or your adversity, praise the Lord. May you be an example of what a child of God does and says to bring honor and glory to their heavenly Father.

Thank you for being an example of faithful prayer warriors. We are blessed. The best is yet to come! Hallelujah! #Godisfaithful #pray4bill

Day #212 August 9

Anchor Verse: Psalm 78:70-72
He chose his servant David, taking him from feeding sheep and from following the ewes with lambs; God presented David to his people as their shepherd, and he cared for them with a true heart and skillful hands. (TLB)

God is preparing you right now for the future He has for you. You might feel like you are on the backside of the desert, unnoticed, abandoned, even feeling sorry for yourself that your dreams will never come true (the enemy likes to lie to us like that), but the story's not over yet.

What a great reminder this morning as I read these verses in Psalm 78. King David who became the leader of Israel was once the younger brother that was sent out to tend the sheep while his older brothers went off to war. It was on those lonesome trails and dark starry nights that God was training David for his leadership role. God was training David to be an example that we are still learning lessons from today.

As a leader, David learned how to be strong, yet gentle. As verse 72 says, "He cared for them with a true heart and skillful hands." David was being trained internally and externally for the position God had for him.

Often our lives may be filled with chaos, demands on our time, our children growing up, an unexpected health crisis, even death and life. God uses all of them to shape us and mold for His use to reflect His love, His light, and His glory.

On January 1, 2018, I never expected that 10 days later Bill and I would be thrown into this health crisis and that 212 days down the road I would still be sharing the lessons God was teaching me.

What's your story? Take a moment to reflect about how God has been directing you to the place you are today. Know that you are surrounded by people who love you. Remember that God is fighting for you; even this chapter is part of His plan.

Thank you for sharing this journey with us. We have been blessed more than you know. You are loved. #Godisfaithful #pray4bill

Day #213 August 10

⚓ *Anchor Verse: John 15:2*
Every branch in Me that does not bear fruit, He takes away; and every branch that continues to bear fruit, He [repeatedly] prunes, so that it will bear more fruit [even richer and finer fruit]. (AMP)

Growth does not happen in a vacuum. It is a process, sometimes a painful one. God created four seasons and within those a growth pattern – a time to plant, a time to cultivate, a time to harvest and a time for the land to rest. It is much like that in our lives.

God desires me to grow – to become stronger in Him, to bear much fruit. Anything that doesn't bear fruit He cuts away. Ouch! I think we are all familiar with that place, but only a loving heavenly Father will take away that which is useless, and doesn't serve His purpose anymore. God wants us to thrive and grow, not become dead wood.

And then the pruning process... I have talked about this on our journey. In this translation it says, "He cleanses and repeatedly prunes every branch that continues to bear fruit." So, if you've been pruned in your life once, it's not over yet! As long as there is life in that branch, God will continue to prune it so that it will bear much fruit – richer and more excellent fruit.

Now that's good news. It reminds us that the pruning process has a purpose – it's to make us better that we might bear more fruit. God doesn't prune us to inflict pain. Our heavenly Father doesn't do it to harm us; it is done for our good and for His glory.

This morning I have a different perspective on the pruning process. I am grateful that God continues to prune me; it means there is hope, life, and potential in me. God knows the bountiful harvest that is coming in my life, and in yours, if we abide in Him.

Stay the course. Submit to His loving hands and thank God that He is not only cutting away the dead wood, but the Gardener of our Souls tenderly trims the living vines that they will bear more fruit.

Thank you for your faithfulness. Your prayers have borne much fruit. #Godisfaithful #pray4bill #prunedforHisglory

Day #214 August 11

Anchor Verse: Romans 11:36
For everything comes from him and exists by his power and is intended for his glory. All glory to him forever! Amen. (NLT)

The world does not revolve around you. Sometimes we need that reality check especially when the devil has us spinning in circles. When things get chaotic in our lives, it is easy to fall into a place of introspection where all we can see is ourselves and our needs and problems.

Romans 11:33 reminds us of the bigger picture. It reminds us that God created the whole universe and every day is a new gift from Him. God keeps everything going – the sun rises at His command. Our heart beats, our lungs take our next breath because of His power and His plan. And all of it is for His glory – our victories and our challenges when given to God bring honor and glory to Him.

It's really all about Him... our lives are all about Him too. When I live my life according to God's best for me, I am a fragrant aroma rising to the throne room of grace. I shine for His glory. I am a light to others because Jesus is shining through me.

In these months of Bill's health journey, I have received a greater revelation of who God is and how great His desire is to be a part of our lives. He is not an absentee parent. God loves to talk with you and walk with you. Your heavenly Father delights in your victories, and yes, He mourns with you in your loss.

I encourage you to take some time to reflect today. Sit down and listen. Be quiet before the Lord and listen to what He has to say. Look out the window and stand in awe of His glory and majesty. Praise His name!

Thank you for your faithfulness on our journey. We have traveled in the company of the faithful. We are blessed. #Godisfaithful #pray4bill

Day #215 August 12

Anchor Verse: Psalm 86:11
Teach me more about you, how you work and how you move, so that I can walk onward in your truth until everything within me brings honor to your name. (TPT)

An undivided heart – it's a lofty goal. It seems in this world that we are pulled from every direction. There are demands on our time, our energy, our finances, and yes, our soul.

Honestly, there is only one anchor and that is the Lord. There is only one truth and that is found in the Bible. There is only one hope and that is Jesus. Only one Spirit that will direct your life in the plans God has for you, the Holy Spirit.

It's really quite simple when you look at it from God's perspective but we have to be taught those ways. As our heart's desire is to walk in God's truth, we need to not only desire it, but we need to learn how to walk in God's truth. We need to hunger and thirst for righteousness. As a deer pants for water, so my soul pants for you, Lord.

As I have walked with Bill on this health journey, I have learned more and more about having an undivided heart. No matter how dark the night or how bright the day, God has been my anchor. As He stripped away so many things in our lives, things we thought were essential, God was teaching me what was most important in my life.

As we walk out the other side of this miraculous journey, and continue to walk in God's miracles every day, Bill and I are both more committed than ever to the Lord, to each other and our marriage. With joy, we look forward to the plans God has for us. We know that it is His strength and power that will lead us onward, not our own.

Our prayer for you today is that you would have an undivided heart. That you would be sold out to God 100% and that nothing is more important than your relationship with Him.

Thank you for your continued faithfulness in prayer. We are blessed by your encouraging words. #Godisfaithful #pray4bill

Day #216 August 13

Anchor Verse: Acts 20:24
But life is worth nothing unless I use it for doing the work assigned me by the Lord Jesus (to finish the race and complete the task)—the work of telling others the Good News about God's mighty kindness and love. (TLB)

The last few days Bill and I have been talking about running the race God has for us. As Bill continues to move along this healing spectrum from the place he was – flat on his back in a hospital bed to a wheelchair to walking with a walker toward his goal to walk with a cane, and who knows what lies beyond that – maybe walking and running without having to use oxygen, we walk in expectation. We are listening for the voice of God. We pray for guidance because we don't want to miss the opportunities He has for us.

The life we live is not just for ourselves. God has put us here because He has a plan and purpose for our lives. As an author and editor, I know the power of stories. I know that words can evoke emotion and can be used to teach and encourage. I also believe that when God gives you a story, it is yours alone to tell. Please don't deprive us of the gift of that story.

In Acts 20:24, it reminds us that the work assigned to us is the work of telling others the Good News about God's mighty kindness and love... and I would add… His great faithfulness.

What is the story that you have to share? What is the race that God is calling you to run? The good news... you will never have to do it alone. He will supply your every need as you walk in obedience.

Use your life for His glory. Use your life to tell your story of God's faithfulness. It will encourage others and give you strength to face the next mountain ahead of you.

Thank you for your countless prayers. We still need them. The battle has entered a new arena, the war is not over. God is so good. #Godisfaithful #pray4bill

Day #217 August 14

🜲 *Anchor Verse: Psalm 90:4*
A thousand years in your sight are like a day that has just gone by, or like a watch in the night. (NIV)

Time... it is so much greater than the hours on a clock or the minutes that pass by. For a student in the classroom, an hour of class might seem like it takes forever to pass while an hour spent with the one you love isn't nearly long enough.

This year I have learned so much about time and God's perspective. Appreciating time is a gift from God. When I survey the last 217 days, I think about moments when a second seemed like an eternity and days flew by like a single breath.

I have learned not to be a slave to time or the clock or my list of things to be done in a 24-hour period. Psalm 90:4 reminds us that God lives outside of time. What do I mean by that? He is not bound by minutes and hours and seconds, or even weeks and years. God wrote a book about your life before you were even born. He knew that some course changes would happen in a split second while others would take years to put in motion.

In the past, I never valued sleep as much as I do now. There are many new moms reading this today that know what I mean. Especially in those first weeks after Bill came home from the hospital and we were trying to get used to life on "our own" where I was the nurse, respiratory therapist, cook, housekeeper, physical therapist, occupational therapist, speech therapist, appointment scheduler, encourager, prayer warrior, and wife, just to name a few hats, I learned that every minute of sleep was precious.

In these last few days we have entered a new place, a new season, a new transition, and it fills me with awe and wonder all over again. God is giving Bill dreams and visions of his healing and running the race God has for him. Others are being given visions of complete restoration. Our sleep has been deep and wide the last few days. Hallelujah!

Thank you for the gift of your time. We are blessed by your commitment to pray. Have a blessed day! #Godisfaithful #pray4bill

Day #218 August 15

Anchor Verse: Psalm 92:1-2
It is good to give thanks to the LORD, And to sing praises to Your name, O Most High; To declare Your lovingkindness in the morning, And Your faithfulness every night. (NKJV)

Good morning! As this day begins, we have a blank slate before us. We may have plans but they don't always come to fruition. One thing we can always count on is God's love and faithfulness.

As I read Psalm 92 this morning, it reminded me that at the beginning of the day as we proclaim God's steadfast love, it's because we know we can trust Him. He has a great track record. God has never let us down. As we take our first step out of bed, we know that God is already there waiting for us. Our heavenly Father promised He would never leave us and His promises are true.

As you walk through this day, continue that praise song in your heart. No matter the circumstances that arise, praise the Lord. Whether they are victories or challenges, God will use each one for your good and His glory.

And at the end of the day, remember His faithfulness. Share God's faithfulness with those you know and love. Fill your Facebook newsfeed with good things, the God things that have happened today.

Your story is a testimony of God's steadfast love and faithfulness. Sing praises to His name this morning. Praise God from whom all blessings flow!

No matter what your night was like, you have a fresh start. His mercies are new every morning. Great is your faithfulness, O Lord.

Thank you for your faithfulness to us. Your prayers continue to move mountains in our lives. #Godisfaithful #pray4bill

Day #219 August 16

⚓ *Anchor Verse: Philippians 4:8*
Finally, brethren, whatever things are true, whatever things are noble, whatever things are just, whatever things are pure, whatever things are lovely, whatever things are of good report, ij there is any virtue and ij there is anything praiseworthy—meditate on these things. (NKJV)

Where we focus our thoughts often determines our destination. If you woke up filled with expectation of what God had in store for you in the day ahead, there's likely a smile on your face. If you woke up this morning all grumbly and cranky and you couldn't think of one good thing, my friend, you are going to have a rough day.

The Bible shows us in this morning's verse what to think on, to focus on, to meditate on throughout day – actually our whole lifetime! Whatever is true, honest, just, pure, lovely, of good report, if there is ANY virtue, and any praise, think on these things.

This list eliminates a lot of the "junk" that surrounds us. You may be wondering how you avoid all the negativity and unwholesome words and thoughts and ideas in the world. It's what we take in and hold on to that becomes the problem. If you take in negative thoughts and dwell there, the light inside you will grow dim.

Think of it like a buffet restaurant where you have dozens of choices. In your thought life, choose those that will build you up, not tear you down.

Focusing on what God has told us through His Word and also direct revelation or words of encouragement from others has been so important rather than jumping off the cliff into the abyss of worry or the countless horrific things that could have happened.

Even when "bad things" happen and we are focused on the Lord and His Word, mighty miracles are manifested because we are ready to receive them.

Thank you for lifting us up with your encouraging words, especially the prayers prayed on our behalf. #Godisfaithful #pray4bill

Day #220 August 17

Anchor Verse: Romans 16:10
Greet Apelles, whose fidelity to Christ has stood the test. (NIV)

Today many of you are going through deep waters. You are being tested. You are being refined. Yes, God is asking this question, "Will your fidelity, allegiance, faithfulness, loyalty to Christ stand the test?" It's not easy. Jesus told us while He was here on earth that it wouldn't be easy. He said that daily we would have to take up our cross and follow Him. Jesus was serious.

The good news, you don't have to do it alone. All you have to do is speak the name of Jesus and help is by your side. God has angels watching over you, every move you make. They will keep your feet from falling. The Holy Spirit was given as our Comforter and Guide to help direct our path. God, our heavenly Father, Lord God Almighty, will move heaven and earth to protect His children and help you fulfill the calling He has on your life.

As Bill and I have walked through these months of testing since January, I have learned how deep my roots are in the Lord. A tree that has shallow roots will easily fall over when the winds of adversity blow. We have seen examples of that in our own lives and broadcast throughout the media.

My encouragement to you today is to get firmly rooted in the Word of God. Surround yourself with those who will pray for you and hold up your arms when you are too weak to stand on your own. Always remember you are child of the King of kings and the Lord of lords. As a believer, the resurrection power of Jesus Christ lives in you and mighty miracles are manifested in your life.

My prayer for you today is that your name can be written in this empty blank. "Greet _____ whose fidelity to Christ has stood the test." Whether Jane or Bob or Bill or Robin or Dave or Jennifer... my prayer is that God will give you the strength so that your fidelity, your faithfulness to Christ will stand the test.

Thank you for your faithful prayers. We are so grateful. #Godisfaithful #pray4bill

Day #221 August 18

Anchor Verse: Psalm 91:1
He who dwells in the shelter of the Most High Will remain secure and rest in the shadow of the Almighty [whose power no enemy can withstand]. (AMP)

Sometimes we just need to know that everything is going to be alright. There is security that comes when we know that God has us covered as we go through the storms of life. We may face disappointments or pain or betrayal or loneliness, but through it all, God never changes. He is the solid rock on which we stand. A mighty fortress is our God – our refuge and strength in time of trouble.

Psalm 91 is filled with great imagery and promises. In verse 1, there are two important parts. First, we dwell in the shelter of the Most High. To dwell means to stay there, reside, be settled there. It's a commitment we make not just to run there in our time of need but it's where we live with the Lord. When we do that, the Bible says we will remain secure.

Security is a big thing in the world today. We all want to feel safe. God promises that as we dwell with Him, we will remain secure. Hallelujah!

The second part is that we will rest in the shadow of the Almighty, whose power no enemy can withstand! Did you catch that part about "resting" in the shadow of the Almighty? Rest while God fights for you.

As we dwell in the shelter of the Most High, we will remain secure AND we will rest in the shadow of the Almighty who will fight for us and defeat our enemy. That's God's promise to you today and to me.

My friend, it's time to stop blaming God for what's not going right in your life. It's time to run to God and dwell (stay put, stop running) in His shelter where your heavenly Father will supply all your needs. Then rest in Him, in His promises, and trust Him, your Shield and Defender, to fight for you.

Your weariness will be exchanged for His strength. Your weakness will be replaced by His power. Victory can be yours if you will accept His gift of love. Do it today. Don't wait any longer.

Thank you for your continued prayers. Every day is a step closer to Bill's complete restoration in Jesus' name. #Godisfaithful #pray4bill

Day #222 August 19

Anchor Verse: Psalm 104:13-14
He waters the mountains from his upper chambers; the land is satisfied by the fruit of his work. He makes grass grow for the cattle, and plants for people to cultivate— bringing forth food from the earth. (NIV)

God is a God of order, not chaos. He offers comfort in contrast to the world in which we live today. If you are caught up in the confusion and chaos of the world and daily living, it's easy to lose sight of the majesty of God's creation.

This year I have learned about the simplicity yet the complexity of the human body through Bill's illness and recovery. In these two verses, it gives us a glimpse of God's handiwork.

God waters the mountains from His upper chambers and the land is satisfied. This is a sharp contrast to the smoke and wildfires that seem to be burning out of control across America.

In verse 14, it reminds us that the earth was designed for food for the cattle but also for us to grow crops to eat. This summer many of you have grown produce from your own gardens, you know the pleasure that comes from home-grown food.

Read all of Psalm 104, as a reminder that when the world was created God brought order out of the chaos. He desires order in your life today.

It hurts His heart when your life is spinning out of control because of the choices you have made.

It's not too late to know His peace. His arms are always open wide to receive you. Run to Him today and exchange your weariness for renewed strength. He loves you with an everlasting love.

Thank you for holding up our arms when we are weak. Your prayers have borne much fruit. #Godisfaithful #pray4bill

Day #223 August 20

Anchor Verse: 1 Corinthians 3:6

My work was to plant the seed in your hearts, and Apollos' work was to water it, but it was God, not we, who made the garden grow in your hearts. (TLB)

We work together to accomplish God's purposes here on earth. It's like running a relay race. We each run our leg of the race using the gifts that God has given us to do good in the world.

As today's scripture reminds us, Paul said that his job was to plant the seed in the hearts of the Corinthian church, Apollos watered the seed, helped tend to the needs of the congregation but it was God, who brought the increase, and caused them to grow in grace and love and a deeper relationship with Him.

It's a great reminder that we need to check our ego at the door. We are not so important that great things happen because of us. God invites us to be part of His grand design – to help build the Kingdom of God on earth.

Every kindness you show, every encouraging word, every cup of cold water given in Jesus' name is a seed planted that God will use to bring a great harvest.

What a privilege we have to touch people's lives, to be part of something so much bigger than us! It reminds me of our journey to this place. How through these many months of Bill's illness it took a team with each person's expertise to bring Bill to where he is today. Ultimately, it was the hand of God who brought about Bill's healing.

Embrace the gifts you have today. Rejoice that the God who created the universe has a plan and purpose for your life. Do not be envious or jealous of another person's gift, but with gratitude sow the seed you have in your hand. Great will be the harvest in Jesus' name.

Thank you for your faithfulness in prayer. Prayers today for clean air would be greatly appreciated. #Godisfaithful #pray4bill

Day #224 August 21

Anchor Verse: Job 33:4
For the spirit of God made me, the breath of the Almighty keeps me alive.
(NLT)

He is the breath of life. Our bodies are the most powerful testimony to Almighty God who created the universe who cares about every detail of our lives. There were no parts left over when God put you together.

Today as so many are fighting adverse weather conditions especially smoke from wildfires that are blazing across the United States and Canada, breathing comfortably can be a challenge. Protecting our lungs from the harmful atmosphere is a place God invites us to the table to be a part of the solution. Being wise, sheltering in place, and taking precautions – these are ways we can honor the Lord who created our bodies.

On this journey, Bill has had pneumonia three times since the beginning of the year. His lungs are healing but we need to protect them as best we can. The days when he was on the ventilator and a machine was breathing for him, I was praying that God would restore Bill and fill him with resurrection power and the breath of life.

We often take breathing for granted until you face external circumstances that compromise your breathing. As this verse in Job reminds us, the Spirit of God created us and the breath of the Almighty keeps us alive.

My prayers go out to you this morning if your air quality has been compromised. We need to pray for those facing fires and smoke and compromised breathing.

Breathe in deeply of His spirit this morning. May it not only fill your lungs but your soul with life.

Thank you for your faithfulness to pray for Bill. God is the breath of life. May the Lord fill you with joy and peace. #pray4bill #Godisfaithful

Day #225 August 22

⚓ *Anchor Verse: Psalm 112:4-5*
Even in darkness light dawns for the upright, for those who are gracious and compassionate and righteous. Good will come to those who are generous and lend freely, who conduct their affairs with justice. (NIV)

There are blessings for those who walk according to the Lord's way. The Bible is filled with instructions about how to live a holy life, a life pleasing to the Lord. It reminds us of the benefits that come when we follow Him and walk in faith and not fear.

These are not just lessons in a book, they will reap great rewards. This verse from the book of Psalms reminds us that "even in darkness light dawns for the upright." That, my friend, is good news! Even when you are walking through the valley of the shadow of death, the Lord is with you. When everyone has counted you out and your circumstances look too grim, know that the Lord has not given up on you. This will be your finest hour because God will shine more brightly against the darkness.

In these verses, we see the characteristics of those who walk uprightly (do the right thing, live a life pleasing to the Lord.) They are gracious, compassionate, righteous. Good will come to those who are generous, lend freely, and conduct their affairs with justice.

This sounds like the person that we, as believers, strive to be. You may be looking at that list thinking there is no way I can do that on my own. You are absolutely correct! That is why Jesus sent the Holy Spirit to help us. We have the example of Jesus and His walk in this world to guide us and a heavenly Father that loves us so much that He wrote a book about our life before we were born – that includes our challenges and our victories.

As I read today's verses, I remember the path we have taken with Bill's health, the dark nights, and the days when even the doctor had a worried look on his face. I remember when God showed us His power and Bill turned the corner. When his lungs got stronger, and his heart responded to the medication, God had the final say.

Do not fear, but walk in faith today. Victory belongs to the Lord! Thank you for your faithfulness. The Lord is good! #Godisfaithful #pray4bill

Day #226 August 23

Anchor Verse: Ephesians 3:20-21
Now to him who is able to do immeasurably more than all we ask or imagine,
according to his power that is at work within us, to him be glory in the church
and in Christ Jesus throughout all generations, for ever and ever! Amen. (NIV)

Our God is an Awesome God! His ways are often beyond our understanding. His faithfulness is declared from generation to generation.

This is the God I know, love, and serve. The Good Shepherd has brought me through troubled waters. God has restored my soul and saved my life from destruction.

Ephesians 3 fills me with great joy and hope. "Now to him who is able to do immeasurably MORE than all we ask or imagine, according to his power that is at work within us, to him be glory in the church and in Christ Jesus throughout all generations, for ever and ever! Amen."

What a powerful declaration of what God has already done (our testimony) and a declaration of our faith – what He will yet do.

If you have a loved one in the hospital facing a health crisis and the doctors can't figure out the solution – the Great Physician knows the answer. Maybe you have a child who has run far away from the Lord and is immersed in the muck of the world – the Good Shepherd knows where your son or daughter is right now.

Maybe your own faith has grown lukewarm. I pray that God would ignite a new fire in your soul. Lord, we pray for the miracles that will be manifested around the world today because of the healing resurrection power of Jesus Christ. We love you and praise you, in Jesus' name, hallelujah, amen!

This morning my heart is filled with praise because of God's faithfulness in our lives. Thank you for your continued prayers. God hears and answers. Hallelujah! Amen! #Godisfaithful #pray4bill

Day #227 August 24

Anchor Verse: Psalm 118:17
I will not die but live, and will proclaim (declare) what the Lord has done.
(NIV)

Sometimes you've just got to take a stand and declare the truth of the Lord over your life and over your circumstances. God calls us to be victorious in Christ, not victims of the enemy.

This verse in the book of Psalms is a powerful verse. I recall praying this and declaring this many times during the days that Bill was in ICU. Today, this is still my prayer and declaration.

I don't know what you are facing today, but I urge you to speak this verse out loud. Declare to the powers of darkness that you are not giving up, you are not checking out, God has plans for your life and they are good! You have a destiny to fulfill. There are people that can only be touched by you – your gifts, your talents, your love for the Lord.

This is your day to stand up and fight for what the Lord has promised you. Don't give in to worry, anxiety, fear, pain, or disappointment but instead declare the Word of the Lord. May His peace flow over you like a river. May His joy well up in your soul and spill over to others. Your faith in God will triumph over your fears. By His stripes you are healed – body, mind, and spirit.

In a few days, we are celebrating Bill's 75th birthday. God is rebuilding him every day. God saved Bill's life because He has work for Bill to do – a new path, the path of the redeemed that have walked through the valley of the shadow of death and come out the other side.

Join us today in declaring the works of the Lord in your life. There is victory in Jesus. Hallelujah!

Thank you for your prayers and encouraging words. Join us in this symphony of praise. #Godisfaithful #pray4bill

Day #228 August 25

Anchor Verse: Psalm 25:14
There's a private place reserved for the lovers of God, where they sit near him and receive the revelation-secrets of his promises. (TPT)

There is a place of fellowship with God that is beyond description, beyond our understanding. It is difficult to comprehend that the God who created the universe – everything from the stars in the sky to every creature on earth to the wonders in the depths of the sea, wants us to spend time with Him – not just in church, but one on one. Wow!

God doesn't come with His own agenda. Your heavenly Father just wants to spend time with you because He loves you. We can understand that concept in a human relationship but God wanting to spend time with us – we have many excuses why we aren't worthy of that invitation.

Psalm 25:14 says, "There's a private place reserved for the lovers of God, where they sit near Him and receive the revelation-secrets of His promises."

God doesn't drag us into His presence, He invites us in. After walking through Bill's health challenges this year, we both have found a new intimacy with the Lord. I have received revelation-secrets of His promises that fill me with great joy.

My heart's desire is to know Him more. His heart's desire is the same. It's a place of honor, a beautiful place that is beyond description.

As a caregiver, there are days when it's difficult to take the next step because your own strength is dwindling and the solution is not in sight. In those moments as we step out in faith, we receive strength that's not our own and wisdom beyond our understanding. God will meet your every need. He is our refuge and strength, a mighty help in our troubles.

Thank you for your faithfulness. Your prayers have moved mountains in Jesus' name. Be blessed! #Godisfaithful #pray4bill

Day #229 August 26

Anchor Verse: John 14:27
Peace I leave with you; My [perfect] peace I give to you; not as the world gives do I give to you. Do not let your heart be troubled, nor let it be afraid. [Let My perfect peace calm you in every circumstance and give you courage and strength for every challenge.] (AMP)

The words of Jesus give us peace as they impart power into our mind and spirit... and yes, our bodies too. His perfect peace. You may have experienced this perfect peace, and if you have, it's like a taste of heaven.

When we are standing in that perfect peace, no matter how great the storm that surrounds us with thunder booming in our ears, and lightning strikes at our feet, torrential rain and hail bombarding us, still we cannot be moved from that place of peace as the Lord has us wrapped in His arms of love.

The last part of today's Bible verse from John 14:27 says: "Let My perfect peace calm you in every circumstance and give you courage and strength for every challenge."

Notice it doesn't say some circumstances or some challenges... His peace is certain in anything you will face in this life.

It's when we open the door to fear that our peace disappears. Fear and peace can't coexist with each other, just like darkness and light can't be in the same place.

I pray that today you would choose His peace – in the calm and the storm. As we adjust to the ever-changing "new normal" of our lives, Bill and I are choosing to stand in God's peace and let it fill our hearts and minds as He gives us courage and strength.

May the Lord's peace be yours. Thank you for your perseverance on this long road we have traveled. You are loved. #Godisfaithful #pray4bill

Day #230 August 27

🔱 *Anchor Verse: 1 Corinthians 9:25*
*Now every athlete who [goes into training and] competes in the games is
disciplined and exercises self-control in all things. They do it to win a crown that
withers, but we [do it to receive] an imperishable [crown that cannot wither].
(AMP)*

We are all in training for the race of our lives. Some may be runners in the
athletic sense – some walk, some remember their days of walking and
running. The bottom line is that our lives should be lived with eternity in
view.

Just like a race in the natural, we must learn to run in our own lane. We
must run the race God has set before us. That takes self-discipline. Why?
Because sometimes someone else's path might look easier than yours.

Their Facebook feed might be filled with pictures of travel to exotic places
or good news of their family's accomplishments or a job promotion or a
beautiful home while your heart is burdened by the things you are walking
through – unemployment, unpaid bills, a family member's illness or your
own illness, and still trying to figure out what God's plan is for your life.

Don't be discouraged! God calls us to this walk of faith one step at a time.
He doesn't show us tomorrow's plans today; sometimes we don't even see
the plans for this afternoon. But we must choose to walk by faith. We must
discipline ourselves for the race God is calling us to walk, to walk in
integrity and honesty. To put God first and His ways and not settle for the
momentary pleasures of the world.

As 1 Corinthians 9 says, we run for the crown that we will wear for
eternity. Choose well. The seeds you sow today will bear fruit tomorrow.
Today's sacrifice is worth tomorrow's victory.

Thank you for the nights you have sacrificed sleep to pray for us. Your
prayers have illuminated our way. Great will be your reward. Have a
blessed day. #Godisfaithful #pray4bill

Day #231 August 28

🙢 *Anchor Verse: Psalm 5:11*
But let them all be glad, those who turn aside to hide themselves in you. May they keep shouting for joy forever! Overshadow them in your presence as they sing and rejoice. Then every lover of your name will burst forth with endless joy. (TPT)

Today is a day of rejoicing, a day of triumph! Today is Bill's 75th birthday (8.28.18). Woohoo!!! Not only is 75 years quite an accomplishment but considering what has happened this year, truly it is a miracle, a gift from the hands of God. Whatever celebration occurs (or not), the fact that Bill is alive and thriving is the greatest gift of all.

Let all who take refuge in you, Lord, rejoice. We can rejoice when we are covered under His wings, when we are safe in the strong tower of the Lord. Then let us sing with joy... how long? Forever!!! What a great reminder that we never stop rejoicing. In the dark hours of the night when sleep is elusive and we are wide awake with our thoughts, praise Him. In the daytime when we hit a bump in the road or the schedule is packed full and we are exhausted. Let us sing for joy – let us continue to rejoice.

We need God's protection. As God protects us, we will triumph!! That is where we are standing today, on Bill's birthday, we are triumphant. God has had the final word. As Bill's healing continues, defying the odds, God's hand of protection is over both of us. God has a plan and purpose for this suffering, the sacrifice, the pain, the loss, and ultimately, for the victory!

God is a God of love and of justice. Lord God Almighty will right the wrongs and He will restore the months, the weeks, the days, the hours that the locusts (the illness) destroyed and He will be glorified.

Trust Him today. Believe this promise to be true for you. Rejoice always. Sing with joy. Give honor and glory to His name.

Celebrate this special day with us. Thank God for the gift of life, this miracle He has given Bill. We thank God for your life too.

Our hearts are filled with gratitude this morning for your prayers these last 231 days. Thank you for your faithfulness. #Godisfaithful #pray4bill

Day #232 August 29

Anchor Verse: 1 Corinthians 10:31
So whether you eat or drink or whatever you do, do it all for the glory of God.
(NIV)

Doing it all for the glory of God... doing the dishes, taking out the garbage, reading to your child before bedtime, praying for a friend in need.

Ordinary things become extraordinary when we realize that our focus isn't just on the task but our eyes are on the Lord, our Creator, our heavenly Father, who loves us more than we can imagine.

Note what we do isn't for our glory, but for God's glory. It also keeps us humble because it keeps our life in perspective.

We aren't building our own personal empire, but we are part of God's workmanship created to honor Him and to reflect His love and light.

As we have walked through Bill's health journey, our prayer is that you have seen God in our lives. You have seen His love for His children. You have seen that obedience is what He desires.

The same power that raised Jesus from the grave is the same power that has healed Bill and sustained me both day and night these many months. Most of all, remember that it's available to you, that you might have victory in your own life and in the lives of those you love.

We are just mirrors reflecting God's glory. The radiance of light that beams from Bill's face is because God lives in him and is the source of life.

Our prayer for you today is that whatever you do, it will be done for the glory of God.

Thank you for your faithfulness. To God be the glory for great things He has done and greater things are yet to come. Hallelujah! #Godisfaithful #pray4bill

Day #233 August 30

Anchor Verse: Zephaniah 3:17
For the LORD your God is living among you. He is a mighty savior. He will take delight in you with gladness. With his love, he will calm all your fears. He will rejoice over you with joyful songs. (NLT)

You are not alone. Not only is God watching over you but He is actively involved in your life. He will save you. He will rejoice over you with gladness and singing. Weary One, He will renew you with His love.

One of the tactics the enemy loves to use is the lie that you are alone in your battle. He plays tricks in our head and our mind goes wandering off into places of pity, shame, blame, and self-condemnation, and unworthiness. You know what I'm talking about. You've wandered off the trail of grace into the dark forest of despair more than once.

The devil is a liar. God speaks the truth over us and opens our eyes to see whose we are (we belong to God) and that we can do ALL things through Christ who strengthens us.

At different points in this health journey and recovery process, Bill has hit a wall, a place where breakthrough was needed to continue on the path of healing God has for him. In that place, it's difficult to see anything but the mountain that's before you that can't be moved. You've been there too.

Please pray with me today that God would help Bill break through that wall of frustration this morning as his brain is creating a new pathway, as his body is reaching for the next step forward to walking in victory, and as his spirit man is seeking God's next step for him.

You, my friend, are an overcomer. The Lord is singing over you with joy this morning, not only for what has happened in your life but for the bright future He has planned for you.

Thank you for your faithfulness. Your prayers have moved mountains. #Godisfaithful #pray4bill

Day #234 August 31

Anchor Verse: Psalm 133:1
How good and pleasant it is when God's people live together in unity! (NIV)

United in one faith – to spread the good news about Jesus. United for one purpose – to honor and glorify God. United in prayer – to see the manifestation of God's miracles. United in this life and for all eternity.

There is so much strife and conflict in the world but in the church, it shouldn't be that way. We are called to be in the world but not like the world. We must rise above our circumstances and be united so that we can accomplish God's purposes on earth.

We are called to pray and not to faint, to pray without ceasing. Throughout the Bible, we are shown examples of the power of prayer for healing and restoration and miracles.

For the church to be salt and light to the world, we need to be united in purpose. In our own lives, we can bear witness to the power of prayer and how it has moved mountains. Not only in the physical realm with healing for Bill's body, but in the spiritual realm, we have seen the powers of darkness stopped because God's people prayed.

As this month comes to a close, I look back and see God's hand at work in our lives. I have seen physical and financial needs met as we prayed together.

Celebrating Bill's birthday was truly a miracle of God's grace. Daily I see evidence of God at work to restore Bill's brain and body to match the new creation Bill is in Christ – the old is gone and the new has come.

Living in unity, in harmony starts in your own heart. Are you willing to put God first in your life that He might live through you? "All to Jesus, I surrender, all to Him I freely, I will ever love and trust Him, In His presence daily live."

Thank you for being united with us in prayer for Bill, and for me, and for each other. Truly we have seen the hand of God move in our lives. He is worthy of our praise! #Godisfaithful #pray4bill

Our Walk of Faith

Our Walk of Faith

September 2018
His Peace, New Power

Day #235 September 1

⚓ *Anchor Verse: 1 Corinthians 12:27*
Now you [collectively] are Christ's body, and individually [you are] members of it [each with his own special purpose and function]. (AMP)

You are special and very much needed! You have gifts and talents like none other. God created you with a purpose and every day you have the honor and privilege of discovering it.

We are blessed that you are in our lives!

This passage in 1 Corinthians 12 talks about the parts of our human body and the necessity of each part. Verse 18 says, "But in fact God has placed the parts in the body, every one of them, just as he wanted them to be."

If the parts of our body understand their function and the eye isn't jealous of the ear, and the appendix doesn't wish it was the heart, shouldn't we be delighted with the way God created us? Let us choose to honor Him by loving who we are and the way God made us, every detail. Let us rejoice in God's handiwork this morning.

Likewise, we should rejoice in the way God made others. Don't fall prey to the enemy's tactics to divide us and to criticize or gossip about others.

Today we have started a new month. We have a clean slate, a fresh start. In my own life, I have declared September as self-discipline month. My challenge to myself is to stay plugged into the things that will bring me closer to the Lord and walk in health and strength.

I am so grateful that you are a part of my life. It is a blessing to see our similarities and our differences. Each one of us is a gift to the Body of Christ. Let your light shine today for His glory. Let your love touch a burdened soul today.

Thank you for your faithfulness and encouraging words. We are blessed by your perseverance and steadfastness in prayer. #Godisfaithful #pray4bill

Day #236 September 2

Anchor Verse: Psalm 139:9-10
If I fly with wings into the shining dawn, you're there! If I fly into the radiant sunset, you're there waiting! Wherever I go, your hand will guide me; your strength will empower me. (TPT)

The presence of the Lord with me brings comfort and joy. When you begin to understand that God is with you wherever you go and that in His presence there is fullness of joy, your life will never be the same.

God delights in showing you His handiwork. With the dawning of the new day as the first rays of light break through the darkness, God is there. As the day ends and the last brush strokes of pinks, and yellows, and oranges are painted on the canvas of the sky, He is sending you a love letter more beautiful than words can express.

Even as you are reading this, God is there with you. There is nowhere you can go that God's hand isn't near you. I pray that brings you comfort this morning. In your greatest joy or your deepest sorrow, He is there. Your heavenly Father will wipe away your tears but also celebrate with great joy as you accomplish something you believed was beyond your reach.

He is not an absentee father. God is invested in us. Every breath we take brings honor and glory to His holy name. God loves us with an everlasting love and He delights in who you are, just as you are.

As Psalm 139 reminds us this morning, wherever we go, His hand will guide you. His strength empowers you.

On this next leg of our journey as Bill's healing continues, we are grateful for God's guidance and strength. As Bill's brain continues to come more alive daily, it seeks the Lord. Bill's heart desires to hear God's voice to direct his steps. We can't navigate these next days and months without His wisdom and strength.

We are blessed by your prayers and encouraging words. Thanks be to God who gives us the victory. You are loved and appreciated. #Godisfaithful

Day #237 September 3

Anchor Verse: Psalm 28:7
The Lord is my strength and my [impenetrable] shield; My heart trusts [with unwavering confidence] in Him, and I am helped; Therefore my heart greatly rejoices, And with my song I shall thank Him and praise Him. (AMP)

The Lord fights for me. He is my strength and my impenetrable shield which means no challenge or trial or enemy can get past His defenses.

This fills my heart with joy this morning. This is the truth that helps me defeat the lies of the enemy.

There will be days when your own strength is small, after a restless night or a day filled with too much activity. God promised that He would never leave you or forsake you. Never – not ever!

This verse also reminds me that we live not only to win our battles but to remember to rejoice in the one who gives us the victory. Giving honor where it is due.

Praise be to God who gives us the victory!

What battle are you fighting today? Remember that you are not alone. The Lord is your strength when you think you can't take one more step. Victory is near.

On our journey through Bill's health challenges, there have been mountains and valleys, the wilderness, and the desert, but no matter the terrain God has been there.

Lord God Almighty has been our strength, and in Him, we have claimed victory.

Thank you for speaking words of life to us and over us when the battle was long and we were weary. Your prayers mean more than you know. Praise God who gives us the victory! #Godisfaithful #pray4bill

Day #238 September 4

Anchor Verse: Hebrews 11:8
Faith motivated Abraham to obey God's call and leave the familiar to discover the territory he was destined to inherit from God. So he left with only a promise and without even knowing ahead of time where he was going, Abraham stepped out in faith. (TPT)

Stepping out in faith, going to a place he doesn't know... that's how I would describe Bill's journey today. When for months your world was only as big as a hospital bed, the "whole" world can be a bit overwhelming at times.

Just like Abraham was led by God one step at a time to the destination God had for him, the mission that Abraham was called to fulfill, so God leads you and me to the place He has for us.

We are called to leave the familiar – whether that is our physical location, our workplace, and old thought pattern, and enter into a new facet of our walk with God. There we will discover the territory God has promised us – the blessing, a more intimate relationship with our heavenly Father, and greater wisdom and understanding in the days ahead.

Once you have crossed the threshold into a crisis situation – your health, a family member's health, even something good, like the birth of a new baby, a graduation, you will experience God in a whole new way. You can never "go back" to the way things once were, because that is the past.

We shouldn't live our lives looking in the rear view mirror. Why? God has amazing blessings ahead of you. Out of the pain will come a great understanding of His mercy. Out of the tears will come the familiarity of His arms of love holding you. Out of the crisis, a passion for life where victory in Jesus is our battle cry!

Thank you for your prayers. Thank you for cheering us on through our walk of faith. We are trusting the Lord to bring us to the Promised Land, to claim our inheritance. #Godisfaithful #pray4bill

Day #239 September 5

Anchor Verse: Psalm 146:5
Blessed are those whose help is the God of Jacob, whose hope is in the Lord their God. (NIV)

My hope and help come in the name of the Lord. This is the truth I believe, this is the firm foundation I am standing on. When the winds of adversity blow, when the thunder rattles the windows of my shelter and the lightning strikes of the enemy leave a burning smell in the air, I know that God has me safe in the hollow of His hands. The enemy cannot touch me there.

But I must choose to put my confidence in God. I can easily be seduced into the camp of worry or tumble down the rocky hill of fear, but God is my fortress and strength, an ever-present help in time of trouble.

Where does your hope come from? Is your hope in the Lord or in the works of your own hands? We must do what we can do and pray for the Lord to help us do the things we cannot do on our own.

On this journey, I have experienced the help of the Lord and the hope of the Lord in a whole new way. The intimacy of my relationship with God has taken on a new dimension. I "run" to be with Him in the early quiet morning hours. I know that He speaks words of peace to my soul. My mind seeks God's wisdom and knowledge in areas that are new to me.

When the God of Jacob is your help and hope, you will receive God's abundant blessings. God will shield you and deliver you from the storms of life as you sing praises to His holy name.

Thank you for your prayers today as we are off to see the neurologist. I'm praising the Lord this morning with expectation of a good report because God has done great things for us. #Godisfaithful #pray4bill

Day #240 September 6

Anchor Verse: John 15:5
I am the sprouting vine and you're my branches. As you live in union with me as your source, fruitfulness will stream from within you—but when you live separated from me you are powerless. (TPT)

In this world, we often talk about connections and being connected to the "right" people to become successful. John 15 reminds us there is only one connection that matters and that is to be connected to Jesus, the source of life. He is the vine and we are the branches.

If we live in union with Him – spending time with Him, learning from Him, and then walking out what He has taught us, fruitfulness will stream out of us. Just being busy and doing things and going places creates a hollow life. Walking with Jesus brings a rewarding life and amazing adventures, more than you can imagine.

In nature, we see a similar scenario. In the spring when a tree is beginning to get its leaves and buds appear, it is difficult to know what kind of tree it is. But when the fruit begins to form, you recognize the tree by its fruit.

So it is in our lives. Our deeds, our words, our actions reflect the source of our lives. Does your life reflect the resurrection power of Jesus? Does your faith bear much fruit? Examine the fruit of your life this morning.

Maybe Jesus needs to do a little pruning. Rest assured, God is gentle in His correction because He loves you so much. My prayer this morning is that we would all bear good fruit that comes from Him.

Thank you for your prayers. Bill's body continues to testify of the life-changing power of God. Bill is connected to the source of life. #Godisfaithful #pray4bill

Day #241 September 7

Anchor Verse: 1 Corinthians 16:13-14
Be on your guard; stand firm in the faith; be courageous; be strong. Do everything in love. (NIV)

When a teacher or leader presents a lesson, we often use bullet points. They are short instructions, points of wisdom, tools that a person can grasp and carry with them as they move ahead.

This passage in 1 Corinthians is like that this morning. These are our marching orders as believers. As you get ready to start your day, first spend time with the Lord in prayer and reading the Bible, then put on the full armor of God (Ephesians 6), and finally go through this checklist as you head out the door.

Today I will be vigilant for the enemy comes to steal, kill, and destroy. I will stand firm in my faith, because on Christ the solid Rock I stand. I fight from a place of victory. I will be courageous, because I am not fighting this battle alone – the God of angel armies is on my side. I will be strong, because the joy of the Lord is my strength and He is my strong tower.

As much as verse 13 is preparing me for the adversity, the battles that I will face this day, verse 14 says I must do everything in love – not for worldly gain or prestige, not out of jealousy or envy, not to destroy others or criticize them, but to build them up and to love them as Christ loves me.

My prayer for you is that you will walk in His way today. You will walk in love filled with hope and courage. You will speak encouraging words when you have the opportunity and you will not be overcome by the darkness and chaos around you.

Thank you for your faithfulness as you have pressed in through prayer during our trials and rejoiced in our victories. Our God is an Awesome God! #Godisfaithful #pray4bill

Day #242 September 8

Anchor Verse: 2 Corinthians 1:10-11
He rescued us from so great a threat of death, and will continue to rescue us. On Him we have set our hope. And He will again rescue us [from danger and draw us near], while you join in helping us by your prayers. Then thanks will be given by many persons on our behalf for the gracious gift [of deliverance] granted to us through the prayers of many [believers]. (AMP)

Sometimes you have to stop and remember what God has done in your life. The countless times He has rescued you from the perils of this world – even the threat of death. Don't just run through life so that everything is a blur of activity – stop and give thanks. Without His help, we would surely perish.

Yesterday Bill and I were talking about how God kept him from what looked like certain death, on more than one occasion. We were rejoicing in God's faithfulness and His love for us. Once again placing our hope in God for our future – not only for health and strength as we enter the fall and winter seasons but our path to share the story of what God has done.

If there is a book in heaven that records the prayers of God's people, there must be countless volumes filled with your prayers for Bill's healing and strength for me as we have walked this path. Together we have rejoiced in what God has done. He deserves all the glory!

This morning as Bill is still sleeping, my heart is full. My joy is overflowing as I see God's miraculous healing continue in Bill's body. As I hear him speak of his encounters with the Lord and his heart's desire to follow where Jesus leads him, my spirit rejoices. I am blessed by his laughter and the twinkle in his eye. It's not because of what I've done, but it's because of God's grace that we are celebrating today.

Thank you for your prayers, encouraging words, and arms of love surrounding us. We couldn't have made it this far without you. #Godisfaithful #pray4bill

Day #243 September 9

⚓ *Anchor Verse: Isaiah 61:1-3*

The Spirit of the Sovereign Lord is on me, because the Lord has anointed me to proclaim good news to the poor. He has sent me to bind up the brokenhearted, to proclaim freedom for the captives and release from darkness for the prisoners, to proclaim the year of the Lord's favor and the day of vengeance of our God, to comfort all who mourn, and provide for those who grieve in Zion—to bestow on them a crown of beauty instead of ashes, the oil of joy instead of mourning, and a garment of praise instead of a spirit of despair. They will be called oaks of righteousness, a planting of the Lord for the display of his splendor. (NIV)

The Year of the Lord's Favor – that's the title for this chapter in Isaiah. Jesus read this publicly as He began His ministry on earth. Jesus is the fulfillment of this passage. These are powerful words.

We have been brokenhearted or needed freedom from the darkness of our lives. We have wept and needed to be comforted in our grief. We have also been triumphant as the Lord has bestowed on us a crown of beauty instead of ashes, the oil of joy instead of mourning, and garment of praise instead of a spirit of despair.

You may be in need this morning of your Savior's touch. Your well is empty and you thirst for the living water that only God can provide. Your pillow was drenched in tears this morning and your heart is heavy with despair, but you don't have to remain there.

Jesus is holding out His hand to you this morning. He is knocking at the door of your heart. God is holding you in His arms of love and whispering peace to your soul. Don't be a defiant child that refuses to be comforted. Crawl into your heavenly Father's lap and talk to Him.

I am grateful that I have learned to lean on God in the storms of life that come in waves. I will dance in the presence of the Lord and declare His goodness as long as I have breath.

Thank you for your presence with us as we have walked through these storms and continue on this pathway to Bill's complete healing. He is all you need. Trust Him in the calm and the storm. #Godisfaithful #pray4bill

Day #244 September 10

Anchor Verse: Psalm 119:49-50

Lord, never forget the promises you've made to me, for they are my hope and confidence. In all of my affliction I find great comfort in your promises, for they have kept me alive! (TPT)

The promises of God – they are truth. They are your lighthouse in the darkness. They are brighter than the sun on a summer's day and more refreshing than a cool breeze. They offer hope to the weary and wisdom to those who have lost their way. They are your shelter in the storms of life and your anchor that will never let you go.

Confidently we can walk through this life as we hold on to God's hand. His promises keep our heads above water when the torrential rain of troubles comes our way. Stay on the narrow path, and you will never lose your way.

As I reflect on the days, weeks, and months since we started this journey, I can see God's hand at work in our lives every step of the way. I remember the days when Bill was sedated and intubated, not even aware that I was there, and I prayed over him and spoke God's promises over him. I stood on the Word of God and declared life.

God was my comfort even through my tears and His promises gave me the confidence to take a stand against the wiles and strategies of the enemy. God's promises kept Bill alive!

Where will you take your stand today? Stand on God's promises for there you will find life. You may be weary and overwhelmed by life's circumstances, but look above them and you will see Jesus reaching out to you with eyes of love. His strength can be your strength.

For those of you who are weary, I pray for God's strength. For those who have lost their way, I pray that the Good Shepherd will rescue you and bring you back to the fold.

Thank you for your continued prayers. We are grateful for each step that leads to health and life. #Godisfaithful #pray4bill

Day #245 September 11

Anchor Verse: Psalm 121:1-2
I lift up my eyes to the mountains (hills)—where does my help come from? My help comes from the Lord, the Maker of heaven and earth. (NIV)

Today is a day in our history when we look beyond our own needs, burdens and joys, and remember the needs of our nation and the moments that rocked our world.

9/11/01 – the day that great tragedy hit our nation. We can remember with shock what we saw play out before on us television screens, not only that day, but in the days that followed.

Even now I can remember the burden of that grief and how it shook our nation. But greater still the unity that rose up out of the ashes, as people not only prayed for each other but took action and became the hands and feet of Jesus. Not only in NYC, our nation's capital, and the area in Pennsylvania where the other plane went down, but in every town in America there was a camaraderie that had been missing.

What the enemy meant for evil, God used to bring out the good in people's hearts. That has been the story of our journey. You have prayed for us and encouraged us with your words and your gifts. You have stood by us day and night. You have rejoiced with us in our victories and held up our arms when we were too weary to stand alone.

As the psalmist reminds us, our help comes from the Lord, the Maker of heaven and earth. He is all we need. God is always with you. Lean on Him today and be restored and refreshed.

Today I pray each of us would take the opportunity to pray for each other and our nation. Take a few moments this day to reach out your hand to another and lift them up – with a smile, an encouraging word, or even a meal or special treat.

Thank you for this priceless gift that you have given us, over and over again. Be blessed this day. #Godisfaithful #pray4bill

Day #246 September 12

Anchor Verse: Psalm 19:14
Let the words of my mouth and the meditation of my heart Be acceptable in Your sight, O Lord, my strength and my Redeemer. (NKJV)

What we think about and what we say determine the course of our lives. Those that dwell on evil and the destructive things of this world will reap the whirlwind. Those who dwell on the goodness of God and keep their eyes on eternity will reap His blessings.

In my reading this morning I came across Proverbs 15:1, "A soft and gentle and thoughtful answer turns away wrath, But harsh and painful and careless words stir up anger."

I was reminded of the power of our words and how they not only shape our own thoughts and actions, but how much they impact others.

I was talking with a friend last night who was telling me about how often she had been wounded by other Christians. It broke my heart. As believers, we are not immune from using "harsh and painful and careless words." It is one of the enemy's methods to stir up conflict among believers.

With the help of the Lord, we don't need to fall into that pit. Our words can bring healing. Our words can bring joy and blessing. That is the cry of the psalmist's heart in Psalm 19. May it be our heart's cry today.

Lord, may the words of my mouth and the meditation of my heart be acceptable in Your sight, O Lord, my strength and my Redeemer.

As I have spoken life, healing, and God's truth over Bill, his body and spirit have responded to bring new life to his body, mind, and spirit. I have watched others walk through their valleys and witnessed words spoken in anger and frustration, words that wound and leave scars.

Thank you for the words that you have spoken to us that have refreshed our souls. May your words bring praise and honor and glory to God. #Godisfaithful #pray4bill

Day #247 September 13

⚓ *Anchor Verse: Proverbs 18:10*
The name of the LORD is a strong tower; The righteous runs to it and is safe and set on high [far above evil]. (AMP)

Over the course of our lives, we need a safe place, a place where the things of this world cannot touch us. We need the Lord.

The Bible in so many passages describes not only the character of God but invites us to commune with Him, to be at peace in His presence, to be refreshed when we are weary.

I don't know about you, but I welcome the opportunity to run to the Lord who is a strong fortress where I am safe. When I think of a fortress, a picture comes to mind of an impenetrable structure that is safe from the attack of the enemy. There are watchmen on the wall and sufficient manpower and weaponry to keep all those who are inside safe.

How much more can the Lord do for us, His children? God doesn't need to construct tall stone walls or support it with steel. His name alone is strong enough to send the enemy running.

Are you willing to run to Him today or are you determined to fight your battles alone on the battlefield of life, wounded and weary from the relentless fight?

God is waiting for you with arms open wide. He will listen to you as you pour out your heart to Him. Your heavenly Father will hold you when you are weak. The Good Shepherd will speak wisdom to you when you are lost.

Your Creator will breathe new life into your weary body. We are new creations in Christ. Behold the old is gone, the new has come.

Thank you for your faithfulness in prayer. Every day there are new mountains to conquer but we are victorious in Jesus' name. #Godisfaithful #pray4bill

Day #248 September 14

Anchor Verse: Psalm 89:15
O Lord, how blessed are the people who experience the shout of worship, for they walk in the radiance of your presence. (TPT)

Praising the Lord in all circumstances... this is the pathway of blessing for you and me. When our eyes are on the Lord, even the most difficult hill we have to climb will turn into a small speed bump we can easily walk over.

When our lips are worshiping the Lord and our heart is turned toward Him, there is no room for fear. There is no room for doubt, only for the blessing of His presence.

Are you walking through a storm right now? Maybe you have just come through a storm and you are dealing with its aftermath. Lift your hands and heart in praise to the King of kings and the Lord of lords.

Worship music is a place I have found solace on many occasions. It is through the music and the lyrics that my mind is filled with the goodness of the Lord. My eyes are taken off my present circumstances and my voice is part of the choir of angels and souls on earth that have learned what it means to praise the Lord.

I can hear some of you saying, but I can't sing, my voice sounds horrible. The Bible says, make a joyful noise unto the Lord who made heaven and earth. God's got you covered!

This morning, my heart is filled with praise. Today I choose to live in the light of His presence where I will find all I need... wisdom, knowledge, understanding, provision, and a heart filled with love and encouragement for others.

Let us lift our voices in song. May our souls be encouraged in the Lord. May our lives reflect His love. In Him, we find fullness of joy.

Thank you for standing with us and rejoicing in the God of our salvation. May His blessings flow over you today. #Godisfaithful #pray4bill

Day #249 September 15

⚓ *Anchor Verse: Proverbs 24:16*
For though the righteous fall seven times, they rise again. (NIV)

I have never been more aware of the strength of the Lord than since we began this journey. Not only in my own life, but Bill's life, and the strength that is supplied when others surround you.

As this verse in Proverbs says, the righteous may fall seven times, but they rise again... and for some of us, it's even more than seven times.

As believers, we know that our strength is in the Lord and He will help us every time we slip and fall, and that's not just in the physical world but in the spiritual realm.

You may find yourself in a time of trials this morning. The flood may be at your door. You may be in the midst of a spiritual battle or things are tough at work or at home. Know that God is with you. He will never leave you or forsake you. Your heavenly Father's hand is extended to you inviting you to take His hand. Your Savior will lift you up.

The other night during my sleep, I had a dream/vision of Jesus standing in front of me with both arms extended saying, "Come unto me all you who are weary and heavy-laden and I will give you rest. Take my yoke upon you and learn from me for I am meek and lowly of heart and you will find rest for your soul."

Run to Him this morning, my friend. He will supply your every need.

Bill has been such an amazing example to me of this verse. No matter how many times the enemy attacked him, he still kept on going. Even today, his heart and mind and spirit are set on finishing the race.

Thank you for your faithful support through prayer. Be blessed today. #Godisfaithful #pray4bill

Day #250 September 16

Anchor Verse: 2 Corinthians 9:6

Now [remember] this: he who sows sparingly will also reap sparingly, and he who sows generously [that blessings may come to others] will also reap generously [and be blessed]. (AMP)

I am often reminded that there are laws of nature that never change. The Law of Gravity remains intact or we would be floating off into space. In the same way, a fruit tree always produces the same kind of fruit – an apple tree produces apples, and a cherry tree, cherries.

This verse in 2 Corinthians 9 reminds us about how a farmer reaps what he sows. The land will only give back what has been sown into it. If a small amount of seed, a small harvest. A generous planting, likewise brings an abundant harvest.

But it doesn't stop there. It works the same way with you and me. What we sow into our own lives and the lives of others comes back to us. If we are disciplined in our lives with our finances, we will have enough to sow into God's Kingdom with our tithes, first, and pay our bills. If we spend frivolously having no thought for tomorrow, we will find ourselves in financial trouble.

When we sow love and kindness and encouraging words into others, we see them bloom and grow into the person God wants them to be. When we pray for each other, even losing sleep, God hears our prayers and not only answers them but He blesses the one who prays.

When I read this verse I thought about all of you who have been so generous in sowing into our lives. Today marks 250 days since we started this journey. It's hard to imagine that it's been that long. Our path has been strewn with blessings because of your faithfulness.

May the Lord bless you abundantly today for all you have sown so generously into our lives. Bill's continued improvement speaks to the miraculous work of God and the faithfulness of God's people. Thank you. #Godisfaithful #pray4bill

Day #251 September 17

Anchor Verse: Psalm 35:23
Contend for me, my God and Lord. (NIV)

There are times in our lives when we will face trials and challenges that are beyond our strength, beyond our comprehension. There is only one place we can run and that is to the Lord. God will fight for us. He will have the wisdom and the words. God is for us and not against us.

The God of angel armies is on our side. That truth fills me with peace. That gives me hope to take the next step. It reminds me that the storms I face in my life are not mine to face alone.

The enemy wants us to believe that we are running this race by ourselves. That no one else cares about our struggles, and in fact, that no one cares about us, and we don't matter. That's a lie from the pit of hell itself.

You are a child of the King of kings and the Lord of lords. He wrote a book about your life before you were born. You are blessed and highly favored by the Lord. Yes – you!

Contend for me, Lord. Rise to my defense. Take on my case. May justice prevail, heavenly justice. There is victory in Jesus this morning.

As I watch Bill continue to heal, I am asking the Lord to contend for him this morning. When you get to the place where so much has been restored, your desire to have your healing completed gets stronger and stronger. It can be the place where frustration sets in, where the enemy whispers crazy things that make you want to rush ahead instead of waiting for God's timing. Stay the course. Keep trusting God and His plan.

This is my prayer for all of us this morning. That God would not only fight for us but that we would be at peace as we rest under the shelter of His wings. God will protect us through the storm. Ride the waves knowing that your Savior is in the boat with you.

Thank you for your faithfulness. Your prayers have moved the hand of God. #Godisfaithful #pray4bill

Day #252 September 18

Anchor Verse: Proverbs 31:8
Speak up for those who cannot speak for themselves; ensure justice for those being crushed [for the rights of all who need an advocate.] (NLT)

There are times in our lives when we need help, when we need someone to stand up for us. The circumstances can vary from an illness to fatigue to a place where we lack knowledge, wisdom, and understanding.

If you are in a place today where you need someone to speak for you, don't beat yourself up over it. The enemy will try to use it as a weapon against you when, in fact, it can be our finest hour.

It takes grace and humility to be the recipient of this kind of help, but it also takes love and grace to be the advocate. It is a time of growth for both parties and the end result is beautiful when it is done right.

When I think about Bill's health journey and so many places along the road when Bill was not able to speak for himself, I am grateful that I could be there to be his voice and speak on his behalf. I know that not everyone is fortunate enough to have a strong advocate.

When the circumstances change and the sick person's voice begins to return, it's a tricky place to navigate. This is where Bill is right now. The desire to be independent and not have to rely on someone else is very strong, but his mind and body aren't quite ready to fly solo yet.

Please pray for us in this turn in the road. I believe this is the most dangerous part of the journey.

Thank you, Lord, for Your hand of protection over Bill. I know that Your grace is sufficient for Your power is made perfect in our weakness. We praise you this morning for the plans you have for Bill for they are good. Let not the enemy prevail as he taunts Bill to move forward more quickly than he's ready to move. Lord, I trust you with my husband. Guide him, guard him, and protect him, in Jesus' name, amen.

Thank you for your prayers. You have been our advocates in the throne room of heaven. #Godisfaithful #pray4bill

Day #253 September 19

Anchor Verse: Ecclesiastes 3:7b
A time to be silent and a time to speak. (NIV)

Communication is a powerful tool that God has given us. It also comes with great responsibility. Our words can be used to build up or destroy. Our words can also fill up all the quiet space when just the power of our presence is all that's needed.

On Bill's journey to healing, I have learned so much about what Solomon was talking about in this passage. Truly there is a time to be a silent and a time to speak. Sometimes our words can get in the way.

When you are in the presence of someone you love, whether that is a spouse, child, other family member or friend, silence can be one of the most beautiful sounds. When observing a beautiful sunset, watching with awe and wonder, silence is often most appropriate because our words would diminish nature's joy song as it proclaims the end of another day.

I have also learned that sitting in a hospital room with the one you love, praying silent prayers to God while your loved one sleeps allows the sacred presence of the Lord to fill the room.

As Bill recovers from his stroke (brain bleed), there are times I just need to be quiet as he searches for the right word. One of the most precious parts of my day is after dinner when Bill and I talk about the day or whatever is on his mind, and I have the privilege of listening to how God is moving in his heart, mind, and life. I am blessed.

In our society, we are groomed to speak, to have an opinion, and to share it on social media. We have created a modern day town square where everyone has their own soapbox.

Today spend more time listening than speaking, to intentionally choose to listen when others speak. At the end of the day, see how much you have learned, not only from others but about yourself.

Thank you for the times you have been silent with us in prayer and the times you have spoken words of encouragement. Have a blessed day! #Godisfaithful #pray4bill

Day #254 September 20

Anchor Verse: John 9:3b
This happened so that the works of God might be displayed in him. (NIV)

As human beings, we always seem to be looking for answers. Some look for others to blame for their predicament. Some will research a situation to the nth degree to figure out the cause. And there are those who look to see what God had in mind as He chose this path for them.

This verse from John 9 is the story of the man Jesus healed who was blind since birth. His disciples asked Jesus, "Rabbi, who sinned, this man or his parents, that he was born blind?"

"Neither this man nor his parents sinned," said Jesus, "but this happened so that the works of God might be displayed in him."

Even Jesus' disciples didn't always understand His ways. They were still looking at the situation from a natural perspective rather than God's perspective.

Jesus didn't scold them. He just helped redirect their perspective. "This happened so that the works of God might be displayed in him."

Wow! Have you ever thought about your challenges and deep valleys in this way? Your current circumstances are just God setting things up so that the works of God might be displayed in you or your family member or your friend.

Don't focus on "why is this happening to me?" instead praise Him in the storm. Your life is fertile soil for God's miracle!

I am grateful that God has given me a heavenly perspective. All these months of sleepless nights and challenging days happened so that God's honor and glory might be seen in our lives. We have been given the honor and privilege to let the light of the love of Jesus shine through us so that we can be a lighthouse for someone else who is lost and needs a miracle.

Thanks for your prayers of faith, believing with us for a total healing miracle. God is great and greatly to be praised. #Godisfaithful #pray4bill

Day #255 September 21

Anchor Verse: Ecclesiastes 9:4a
Anyone who is among the living has hope. (NIV)

I think we have all heard the expression, "Where there is life, there is hope." Many of you who are reading this post can testify to that truth. There have been times in your life when things looked pretty bad and the enemy tried to plant seeds of doubt and despair in your mind. You fought back because God has created us to live and there is a spirit of life, the resurrection power of Jesus that lives in us.

Hope, it's like a fire that burns inside of us. Sometimes the flame may be dim, like the brief moment of light that a match provides. Other times it is like a roaring fire that lights up the sky and spreads from ourselves to others around us and warms them.

The bottom line is that God offers hope, in our darkest hour and in our greatest victory. How can we honor Him today as we walk in hope?

I would encourage you to share your hope with another. What we share, multiplies. What we hoard, soon dwindles away. You can't out give God, it's impossible.

Many of you have been with us since the beginning, or near the beginning of this journey. Truly Bill's life is a testimony of this verse, that anyone among the living has hope. We continue to build on the hope we have in Jesus every hour of every day.

Our prayer for you is that you know Jesus, the author of our hope. And if you know Him, that you would share that hope and joy with another.

Thank you, Lord, that You are the author of hope. This morning I pray for that person who is reading this whose hope has worn thin. I pray that You, Lord, would rekindle that flame and give them the strength and the grace they need to face another day, even the next minute. The Lord is great and greatly to be praised!

Thank you for your faithfulness and rejoicing with us. Be blessed today! #Godisfaithful #pray4bill

Day #256 September 22

Anchor Verse: Ecclesiastes 12:10
The Teacher searched to find just the right words, and what he wrote was upright and true. (NIV)

Have you ever considered how powerful your words are? Words have brought people to heights of success and also ruined their careers and reputations. Words of love have brought people together for a lifetime and just as quickly words of hatred can mortally wound a soul.

Encouraging words bring people out of the depths of despair just like a ladder used to get you out of a pit. Words of doubt and anxiety have killed many a dream.

Words are so powerful yet anyone can use them regardless of their age or education. How can we harness the power of our words?

This verse in Ecclesiastes gives us a few clues about using our words for the good. We must think before we speak or write, and spend some time searching for just the right words. And then, what we write or say should be upright, honorable, and true.

Wow, if we used just this one sentence guideline how different our world would be. The good news is that the change can start with you. I encourage you to start today. Think before you speak. Take a moment to choose your words before you write them down or post them on social media. Our words can start a wildfire of good or of destruction.

On Bill's health journey, I have seen this truth in action. I carefully chose the words that I spoke to Bill and kept people's negative words away from him as much as possible. Even today as we communicate, I can see the fruit of the seeds of the good words that were sown, and definitely God's words of life that have taken root in Bill.

Thank you for the encouraging words, words of life and wisdom that you have shared with us on our journey. Let us liberally plant words of life everywhere we go today and in the days ahead. Be blessed! #Godisfaithful #pray4bill

Day #257 September 23

Anchor Verse: Psalm 68:19
Praise be to the Lord, to God our Savior, who daily bears our burdens (carries our heavy loads). (NIV)

This morning this verse brought me great joy to remember that it is the Lord who daily bears my burdens. I don't have to carry that heavy load anymore... not today, not tomorrow, not ever!

The enemy often tries to con us into believing that we are in this life alone. Then he continues to pour guilt, shame, and blame and a whole lot of other nonsense into our head. Sometimes we believe him. We open the door and the negativity and lies come pouring in.

Stop it! Stop believing the lies. Refuse to look back at yesterday with regret. Jesus took care of all that at the cross. You can have a new life of freedom with Him. This verse in Psalms reminds us that DAILY He bears our burdens. All we have to do is ask God to take our burdens, then put them in His hands, and leave them there.

There is an old Irish tale of a man carrying a heavy bag of potatoes and a kind stranger stopped to give him a ride. He got in the wagon but still held on tightly to his burden.

"The wagon owner suggested to the man that the bag of potatoes could be set down. The passenger replied, 'I don't want to trouble you too much. You're giving me a ride for which I am thankful, but I could never ask you to carry my burden too.'"

I believe this is us, this is you and me. At times in our lives, maybe even today, we don't want to bother God by asking Him to carry our burdens. We are just grateful for the gift of eternal life.

My friend, lay your burdens down at the foot of the cross today – blame, shame, unforgiveness, envy, jealousy, fear, financial burdens, unbelief, anger at God... you fill in the blank.

Thank you for standing with us through our darkest nights and glorious days of victory. May He bless you richly. #Godisfaithful #pray4bill

Day #258 September 24

Anchor Verse: Deuteronomy 31:8
The Lord himself goes before you and will be with you; he will never leave you nor forsake you. Do not be afraid; do not be discouraged. (NIV)

There are times in life when we need to be reassured that it's going to be alright. You may be battle weary this morning. Maybe you didn't sleep well last night or even if you did, there is a lot on your mind.

When life is like that, I turn to the Bible and claim God's promises as my own. His words are full of power. His promises are true. This is how we hold on to hope.

This verse in Deuteronomy reminds me of God's power and His presence. "The Lord himself goes before you" – God doesn't send a substitute into the game. Lord God Almighty, Maker of heaven and earth is on your side and personally He is fighting for you and encouraging you and calling you to walk with Him to fulfill the plans and purposes He has for your life.

"He will never leave you or forsake you" – "never" means not ever. There will be times in your life when you find yourself without others around you, but God never leaves you. His presence is always with you. God will never let you go.

This is a reminder to kick fear to the curb. "Do not be afraid" and more than that, don't even be discouraged! Don't let the enemy plant those seeds of doubt and fear in your mind because soon they take root and multiply. It spreads faster than dandelions... and we know how resilient they can be.

This morning as you start a new day, take a deep breath and take God's hand. Believe Him. Trust Him. Tune out the lies of the enemy and focus on God's truth. If you are weary, curl up in your heavenly Father's arms of love and rest. God will restore and heal you.

Thank you for your faithfulness in prayer. We are more grateful than words can express. #Godisfaithful #pray4bill

Day #259 September 25

Anchor Verse: Psalm 38:15
Lord, I wait for you; you will answer, Lord my God. (NIV)

Waiting... we spend a lot of time waiting over the course of our lifetime. As a child, waiting seems like forever! We seek instant gratification. When I want it, I want it now! Does that sound like a two-year-old having a temper tantrum? Well, maybe not just two-year-old children. I think I have heard adults speak those same words.

One thing I have learned about the Lord is that sometimes He has us wait on purpose for a purpose. It's not that He's mean and wants to withhold good things from His children – not by a long shot. We are blessed to wait because what God has for us is still in the making. The best sometimes takes a little bit longer... and if we are really honest about it, don't we want to wait for the best? Especially God's best?

Too often our flesh sneaks in and is willing to settle for a bowl of porridge rather than a seat at God's banqueting table. Instead, my friend, wait on the Lord. God will answer. It is always worth the wait. Often we wait in the silence or the pain or by the bed of someone we love... but the Lord is there with us. He supplies our strength. Jehovah Jireh will meet our every need – for shelter, food, and clothing – the essentials of life. But more importantly, peace in His presence and wisdom all wrapped up in God's love for us.

Whatever you are waiting for today, please wait. Stay the course. Trust Him. Trust Him when your eyes can't see. When that deal falls through or the job you thought was yours doesn't pan out, that's the time when God shows up in all His glory.

Live in the miraculous. Do what you can do, and pray and trust God to do the rest. He is always full of surprises.

Thank you for walking with us on this long journey. You have the best seats in the house to see the hand of God at work in our lives. #Godisfaithful #pray4bill

Day #260 September 26

Anchor Verse: 1 Corinthians 2:16b
We have the mind of Christ. (NIV)

Every moment a battle rages in our mind. God gave us free will so we can choose the path we will pursue. We can choose to do good or evil, walk in obedience or rebellion. We can choose what we think about, focus on, whether that makes us better or is harmful.

As believers, we have help, help that comes in the name of the Lord. We have the mind of Christ. It means that our minds are set toward the things of heaven that bring honor and glory to God. For example, in Philippians 4:8 it says, "Finally, brethren, whatsoever things are true, whatsoever things are honest, whatsoever things are just, whatsoever things are pure, whatsoever things are lovely, whatsoever things are of good report; if there be any virtue, and if there be any praise, think on these things."

The fruit of the Spirit will be seen in our lives: love, joy, peace, patience, kindness, goodness, faithfulness, gentleness, and self-control.

Seems like a high bar, doesn't it? We can do all things through Christ who strengthens us and we have the Holy Spirit to guide us.

As Bill continues to heal from his stroke (brain bleed), his mind is being renewed and reclaimed. There's a term they use neuroplasticity - which describes the amazing way that God created our brains so the neurons can "rewire" our brains after an injury, and even as we grow older.

Sometimes it's like the rush of white water rapids as the brain breaks through into new territory. At other times, it's like a quiet stream. All of that can be pretty confusing and hard to manage and assimilate.

As a believer, Bill has the mind of Christ that supersedes all of what is happening. God is at the helm of this reconstruction process.

Thank you for your prayers as we navigate this new adventure. He is Lord. God is in control. #Godisfaithful #pray4bill

Day #261 September 27

Anchor Verse: Galatians 6:10
Take advantage of every opportunity to be a blessing to others, especially to our brothers and sisters in the family of faith! (TPT)

Living your life watching for opportunities to be a blessing is a life filled with adventure and much joy. Being a blessing isn't always about purchasing a gift and delivering it. It is often a prayer or an encouraging word or a listening ear.

When friends and family are going through deep valleys of illness or grief, a kind word, a smile, a hug can mean so much. The apostle Paul as he wrote to the church in Galatia was urging them to take advantage of every opportunity to be a blessing to others especially those who belong to the family of God.

Here's a question for you... when you go to church on Sunday morning do you look around for those who might need to be encouraged? Do you see someone sitting or standing by themselves and go out of your way to greet them? It will not only bless them but you will be blessed.

In some of the other translations it talks about bearing each other's burdens. There have been times during Bill's health journey that many of you have done that for me, for us.

The power of your prayers has lifted us up on difficult days and multiplied our joy on days of progress. Thank you. These two words seem so small to convey our gratitude.

We will be spending the rest of our lives "paying forward" what you have planted in our lives. The seeds you have sown will continue to reap a harvest for generations to come.

Today I challenge you to follow the Lord on His divine treasure hunt to be a blessing to others. The joy and love you share will be returned to you in even greater measure.

Thank you for standing with us and lifting up our arms and dancing with joy in our victories. The best is yet to come! #Godisfaithful #pray4bill

Day #262 September 28

Anchor Verse: Isaiah 6:8
Then I heard the voice of the Lord, saying, "Whom shall I send, and who will go for Us?" Then I said, "Here am I. Send me!" (NIV)

A volunteer is someone who freely offers to do something. We do not do it for reward or recognition. We do it because we believe in the mission of an organization, or in a home setting, we may volunteer to help with chores because it lightens our parents' load of responsibilities.

As a volunteer you can learn many things, new skills, even "test drive" a job in the process of helping others.

Have you ever considered volunteering for God's work? As this verse in Isaiah shows us today, God was looking for volunteers. "Who shall I send and who will go for Us?"

Isaiah responded, "Here am I. Send me!" (They even used an exclamation point to convey his enthusiasm.)

The amazing thing about God, our Creator, our heavenly Father, He knows exactly the best place that we can serve Him. We might think we belong in the kitchen doing the dishes and God knows we are best suited to love the elderly in an assisted living facility. Your heavenly Father knows where to plant you so that you will bear much fruit.

Many times over the course of my life, I have said "yes" to God. "Yes, Lord. Here am I, send me." These last months may have been an answer to my willingness to serve Him.

The places we have gone are not places I would have chosen but He knew where His light in me could best shine through the darkness. I am honored to be a warrior for Him, to reflect His love, to speak words of life and encouragement, and yes, pray and believe for miracles.

Bill and I are willing to go wherever God needs us. Daily, He hears our cry, "Here we are, Lord. Send us!"

Thank you for standing with us and answering God's call to serve. May your day be filled with His abundant blessings. #Godisfaithful #pray4bill

Day #263 September 29

Anchor Verse: Isaiah 7:9b
If you do not stand firm in your faith, you will not stand at all. (NIV)

Standing firm takes courage. Standing firm in your faith takes a commitment that does not waver through the good times or the tough times.

Jesus showed us as He walked this earth that there would be times of blessings and times of trials. There would be times when you were misunderstood and rejected. There would be times when everyone wanted to be your friend, and other times, when you and God would be walking the road alone.

Faith in God is not just for those moments of blessings. Our faith is strengthened in the storm when the hurricane force winds are blowing and it seems that some of the things we had counted on are stripped away.

Yet in the storm comes the blessings. It was after the flood that God put the rainbow in the sky to commemorate His promise. It is our job to hold on to Him in every season.

You may be in a place where your faith is being tested today. It may be because of an illness or financial stress or a broken relationship. The bottom line is this, God is always faithful. His love floods our hearts with hope and joy. His fierce love for us will protect us in the fight. All He asks is that we stand for Him.

Over these months of Bill's illness, my one true anchor was my faith in God. When I was faced with difficult decisions and circumstances, I knew that God was always there. One day I found myself saying, "Either I trust God or I don't, there is no middle ground. Lord, I trust you with my husband's life and our future."

Where do you stand today? Are you anchored on the rock of Jesus Christ or have you fallen off the path? Think about it and ask God for help.

Thank you for standing with us, firm in your faith, and praying for the miracles we needed. #Godisfaithful #pray4bill

Day #264 September 30

Anchor Verse: Ephesians 3:16-19
I pray that out of his glorious riches he may strengthen you with power through his Spirit in your inner being, so that Christ may dwell in your hearts through faith. And I pray that you, being rooted and established in love, may have power, together with all the Lord's holy people, to grasp how wide and long and high and deep is the love of Christ, and to know this love that surpasses knowledge—that you may be filled to the measure of all the fullness of God. (NIV)

I feel an urgency to pray for you all today. God has you on my heart this morning. Just as Paul was speaking to the church in Ephesus, God's heart is stirred up for you this morning.

My prayer is for strength, strength that comes from Christ alone. That as He dwells in your heart by faith, that rooted and grounded in that love, you would have the power to face your daily challenges.

Most of all that you could understand – could grasp how wide and long and high and deep is the love of Christ. It's wider than the Grand Canyon, deeper than the deepest sea, higher than any plane can fly, and longer than any measurement known to mankind. The only way we can understand God's love is to fully surrender our heart to Him. As He fills us up with His love, we have a new revelation of who God is.

Bill and I were talking about this new life that he has been given as God continues to miraculously heal him. He described it as being a new baby in an adult body – everything is brand new. God is teaching Bill and showing him life in a new way.

Here we stand on this last day of September, about to leap into October, and my heart is filled with expectation about what lies ahead. Today, may we dwell in His presence, sit at His feet, be refreshed by the water of life, and empowered by His spirit so that we might let our light shine for Him.

Thank you for your perseverance and walking with us through this battlefield to reclaim Bill's life from the jaws of death. You are loved and appreciated. #Godisfaithful #pray4bill

October 2018
Victory through Praise

Day #265 October 1

⚓ *Anchor Verse: Isaiah 12:2*
Surely God is my salvation; I will trust and not be afraid. The LORD, the LORD himself, is my strength and my defense; he has become my salvation." (NIV)

As we start this new month, what a great reminder that God is the one who saves us. God is the one who gives us strength and keeps us safe. We don't have to do life alone. He is our defense. We call, He will answer.

We may not be able to have "do-overs" in our life, but we sure can start again from where we are. New Year's resolutions are a great example of that.

Maybe your goal was to exercise or to lose weight. You might have done well for a few weeks (or days) and then old habits flared up and you found yourself doing the very thing you didn't want to do. (The apostle Paul talked about having the same problem – you are not alone here.)

Instead of beating yourself up about it for days, forgive yourself, ask God for help and try again. His mercies are new every morning. Extend some of that grace, mercy, and forgiveness to yourself. Shake it off! Let's get started again. It's a brand new day!

Today I want to encourage you to trust the Lord with your circumstances. Circumstances are temporary, God is eternal. Choose to be strong and courageous, because God is the one who gives you strength.

It is not because you are so amazing that you can make it through this life. It's because of God's fierce love and amazing grace that you can withstand the stormy blast.

Choose to stand with God today. Find shelter under His wings. Live your life so it reflects His love as you speak words of life to each other.

Thank you for your prayers and faithfulness. We are blessed. #pray4bill #Godisfaithful

Day #266 October 2

⚓ *Anchor Verse: Matthew 20:32*
And Jesus stopped and called them, and asked, "What do you want Me to do for you?" (AMP)

Jesus hears the cries of your heart. He knows your physical pain. Your Savior knows when your heart is broken by grief and difficult relationships. Jesus knows when your heart is heavy because you are confused and don't know which way to go.

This story is about Jesus healing the two blind men who were standing by the side of the road calling out to him to have mercy on them. Although Jesus was surrounded by a large crowd as well as His disciples, with lots of noise, Jesus heard these men. Jesus stopped – He stood still.

A crowd will move you along whether you want to go or not. But Jesus stopped. I believe He had more than one lesson to teach that day. Today, Jesus still stops so you know that He is listening.

Jesus asked this question, "What do you want Me to do for you?" It was obvious. These were two blind men, surely Jesus could see that. What else would these men want than to be healed?

Mark Batterson, author of *Draw the Circle*, suggests Jesus wanted them to verbalize their specific need. Jesus wanted to make sure they knew what they wanted. The blind men replied, "Lord, we want our sight."

How often do we pray vague prayers? Maybe we want God to sort it out. Instead God is asking you to pray specific prayers. Why? So when the answer comes, you know that God is responsible for the miracle.

My journals and Facebook posts have been filled with specific prayer requests. God has not only answered them, but done even more.

As we enter this new season, God is challenging me again. What prayers do I want God to answer for Bill's life but also in my own life?

Thank you for your specific prayers. God hears and answers. #pray4bill

Day #267 October 3

Anchor Verse: Psalm 40:3
He has given me a new song to sing, a hymn of praise to our God. Many will see what He has done and be amazed. They will put their trust in the Lord. (NLT)

I have learned the power of praising the Lord in all our circumstances, whether things are going right or when it seems like they are off-track. Turn your problems into praise because we know that with God ALL things are possible.

There's a certain sense of relief when it's beyond our understanding, if God is the only one who can handle our problems.

It means that the one who hung the stars in the sky, put the stripes on the zebra and the spots on the leopard, and gave the birds a song to sing knows my name and my circumstances. God has a plan and a purpose for every situation.

The refining fire is a place where the dross is burned off, where the impurities of our lives evaporate in the heat of adversity. When we come through the fire, we are purer "gold" – God can see His reflection in us, in our lives. It's not usually a place of our choosing but down the road we can see that it was a place for our good.

We have encountered the full gamut of circumstances and emotions – from near-death to watching the hand of God restore Bill when the medicine of man couldn't explain how it happened.

Praising the Lord in ALL our circumstances did something to my heart and mind. Now I can see things from a different perspective. My heart was filled with hope and my life with God's power.

Even today as we walk through Bill's recovery at home minus the therapists for a while, we look to God to direct our day.

We are blessed to share this journey with you via social media, how else would you be able to see the hand of God at work in our lives?

Thank you for your prayers and faithfulness as God continues to move mountains in our lives. #Godisfaithful #pray4bill

Day # 268 October 4

⚓ *Anchor Verse: Ephesians 6:13*

Therefore, put on the complete armor of God, so that you will be able to [successfully] resist and stand your ground in the evil day [of danger], and having done everything [that the crisis demands], to stand firm [in your place, fully prepared, immovable, victorious.] (AMP)

The good news this morning: The battle belongs to the Lord! God prepares us to fight the battles we will face in both the physical and spiritual realm. The Bible is our instruction manual. Spending time in God's Word not only encourages us but memorizing Bible verses helps us when we need to run for shelter or to use them to fight the enemy who plants seeds of worry and doubt in our minds.

In this passage and the surrounding verses in Ephesians 6, it tells us about the full armor of God, the pieces of it, and how to use them. I hope you are familiar with God's armor. If not, dig into Ephesians 6.

Ephesians 6:13 encourages each one of us that we are not helpless. God has provided you with this armor so that you can stand your ground when crisis comes, and not only stand, but you will be unmovable and victorious! Hallelujah!

I can't imagine walking through life without the full armor of God. On this journey we have walked with Bill's health issues, many, many times, I have "prayed on" the full armor of God on both me and Bill.

Why? Because I know that it offers protection against the wiles and strategies of the enemy.

Last night when I posted the need for prayer because the evil one was up to his tricks of attacking Bill during the night, you all rose to the challenge and Bill slept for six hours straight, a peaceful sleep, before waking up.

I am here to remind you that through Christ you have the power to stand when trouble comes, and it will come. Run to the Lord! Stand on His promises through the storms and crisis of your life. You will be victorious in Jesus' name.

Thank you for your faithfulness in prayer. We declare victory in Jesus' name! #Godisfaithful #pray4bill

Day #269 October 5

Anchor Verse: Isaiah 25:1

O Lord, You are my God; I will exalt You, I will praise and give thanks to Your name; For You have done miraculous things, Plans formed long, long ago, [fulfilled] with perfect faithfulness. (AMP)

Nothing is happening to you today that is beyond His control. God often allows us to walk through those deep valleys and tight turns so that we learn to depend on Him even when our eyes can't see the path ahead.

"For you have done miraculous things, plans formed long, long ago, fulfilled with perfect faithfulness." I feel a sigh of relief escaping from my lips. Nothing is happening in our lives that is taking God by surprise.

Does that bring you comfort? It does for me. Because if God knows the way and I trust Him to lead me and guide me, I can be at perfect peace. More than trusting Him, I do it with a heart filled with praise. I watch with expectation to see what He is going to do next.

This journey with Bill has been filled with many twists and turns. Even now as he walks forward in his healing, we encounter new experiences every day. What "used to be" isn't like that anymore. For example, how Bill's body reacts to the change of seasons, his body needs more sleep as he enters a new phase of his healing. God is creating a new "normal."

The realization that 2018 is coming to an end and that the year has been spent walking through this healing adventure with so many opportunities to praise God for the miraculous things He has done.

Physical therapy continues today, a miracle that the authorization came in eight days, and not two to four weeks as they predicted. God told us this was the way to go and we trusted Him to make a way and He did.

What do you need to trust God for today? Where are you looking for the miraculous? Lift your hands in praise and thank Him for the answers.

Thank you for your continued prayers. He is worthy of our praise. #Godisfaithful #pray4bill

Day #270 October 6

Anchor Verse: Psalm 62:1
I stand silently to listen for the one I love, waiting as long as it takes for the Lord to rescue me. For God alone has become my Savior. (TPT)

Where do you find rest and peace on your journey here on earth? You won't find it in entertainment or medication or even the latest health fad. True rest and peace can only be found in God.

While we wait for our circumstances to change, walking the floor with worry won't change anything. Staying up all night seeking advice from others will not bring us peace, but through prayer and time alone in God's presence, we will find the solace that we need.

As you well know, sometimes there is waiting involved. The answers to our problems are not dispensed from a vending machine once we put in our quarters. Often it is in the waiting where we learn our greatest lessons. It is while we walk through the refining fire that we receive insight and revelation. There we let go of burdens and hurts and memories that have haunted us for years, that have weighed us down, and God says it's time to let it go.

God reminds us that the new life He has for us does not include that "stuff" from the past. When we release it, wow! – the load is lifted and we have new energy and a new focus.

Are you waiting for the Lord today? Do you need to find rest in Him? He is waiting for you. God is knocking on the door of your heart asking to come in. Only you can open the door. Do it today. Your life will never be the same. He offers rest and peace.

As Bill and I have walked this journey, we have found there is no other place to find rest and peace except in the Lord's presence. You all have offered encouraging words and faithful prayers that have helped so much.

Thank you for your faithfulness. We continue on this path to healing, one step at a time. Rejoice! God is so good! #Godisfaithful #pray4bill

Day #271 October 7

Anchor Verse: Matthew 6:20-21
But lay up for yourselves treasures in heaven, where neither moth nor rust destroys and where thieves do not break in and steal. For where your treasure is, there your heart will be also. (NKJV)

What are your treasures? As children, we read about treasure chests where men of old used to put the things they valued – gold, silver, precious jewels. Most people don't accumulate their wealth that way today. The list might look a little bit different.

Another definition of treasure is "something of great worth or value." When I think about the treasures in my life especially after walking through Bill's health challenges, what we possess does not rank high on the list of my treasures. Yes, you need some finances to survive in the world, I agree.

However, God has shown me the more valuable treasures of life. What about you? "Where your treasure is, there your heart will be also."

What I value will last for eternity, and that comes when I put God first in my life. I am investing in my legacy that will last after my life is over: the prayer seeds that are planted daily, the words of life from God's Word that are spoken into others, trusting in God and His promises, and living a life that pleases Him.

My heart belongs to God. That is where my treasure lies, in heaven with Him. Every time I look at Bill I thank the Lord for the gift of life, the gift of love, and the gift of His amazing grace.

What are the treasures in your life? May your treasure be placed in heaven's storehouses for eternity, not where rust or moth can destroy it, or a hacker can clean out your bank account. Our greatest treasures are safe in God's hands.

Thank you for your continued prayers as we press forward to finish the race that God has called us to run... Honestly... it's only just begun. Have a blessed day! #Godisfaithful #pray4bill

Day #272 October 8

Anchor Verse: Philippians 4:12
I know what it means to lack, and I know what it means to experience
overwhelming abundance. For I'm trained in the secret of overcoming all things,
whether in fullness or in hunger. And I find that the strength of Christ's
explosive power infuses me to conquer every difficulty. (TPT)

Learning to be content in every circumstance is a blessed place when you learn to live there. I looked up the definition of content. It means: "in a state of peaceful happiness." Does that describe you this morning?

The apostle Paul as he was writing to the church at Philippi was thanking them for their gifts of support. Then Paul went on to share with them these verses about learning to be content in every circumstance.

Most people have experienced circumstances when they had very little and when they had plenty. Paul describes it as the "secret" of being content at all times.

As we have walked through Bill's health journey, I have seen God provide in so many ways. Through gifts from others, by multiplying the resources we had, learning to live with less, more simply, but never lacking in the things that mattered. We have learned how to receive, when we were so used to being the ones who gave freely to others.

Bill and I have learned the richness of simplicity, the wealth we have in our love for God, and for each other. Our lives will never be the same, and I am grateful for that. You cannot see the face of God, the miracles of God and be unchanged.

I have learned that whatever circumstance I find myself to be content, peacefully happy. It doesn't mean that I will continue to dwell in that place of lack forever, but that my attitude is that the Lord will meet my need as I walk through the refining fire with His love surrounding me.

In the world's eyes, we may seem to be in need, but we know that God supplies all our needs according to His riches in glory.

Thank you for your faithfulness in prayer and walking by our side through this journey. We are blessed. #Godisfaithful #pray4bill

Day #273 October 9

Anchor Verse: Philippians 2:14
Do everything without grumbling [complaining] or arguing. (NIV)

Negativity is as contagious as the common cold. Is your attitude worth catching today? Is your cup half-full or half-empty?

As I write this, even in my mind, as I think about people complaining or arguing, it drags me down. My spirit is affected just by the thought of it, not even hearing it! Why do we complain and argue? It doesn't make sense.

We have often heard the phrase "Misery loves company" – it does. It's like a snowball running wild down a hill that will capture anyone and anything in its path.

Where is the fine line between asking for help in a difficult situation and complaining and grumbling about it? The difference lies in your heart.

Choosing to see that the Lord is with you in a difficult situation and asking others to join with you to pray through the difficulty is different than the "poor me" syndrome. The first way God is in the equation, and in the second instance, it's all about you.

Have you ever felt better after you complained about something? I think not. As my husband often says, look at the situation like a third party, be objective, and with some problem-solving skills pick it apart and you might find a solution.

We have been blessed through this journey to see God's perspective instead of complaining or asking "why us?" We are grateful that the Lord has blessed us with this opportunity to know Him in this new way.

This morning you might be weary and worn out from complaining and arguing. God has seen you hitting your head against the wall and burning up all your energy as you spin your tires and gain no traction. The Prince of Peace will give you rest. God has the answers. Trust Him.

Thank you for standing with us in prayer. Thank you for speaking encouraging words to us. We are blessed. #Godisfaithful #pray4bill

Day #274 October 10

Anchor Verse: Exodus 3:5

Take your sandals off your feet [out of respect], because the place on which you are standing is holy ground. (AMP)

Holy ground, a sacred place – it's not limited to a church building, it's wherever God is. It's the place where we meet Him – the place where He reaches out to us – at the kitchen sink doing dishes, in the hospital at the bedside of a loved one, on a tractor tilling the soil or in an office building in midtown Manhattan.

God is not restricted by geography. He knows where you are. His heart's desire is to spend time with you.

Moses had seen some challenges in his life. From the city life in Egypt, he was sent by God to the wilderness to tend sheep. Lots of lessons Moses learned tending those sheep, just like the lessons we learn when God ushers us to another place for a season.

On that day, God had a message for Moses. God's plan was about to be put in motion. But God needed Moses in the right frame of mind to receive it. If you can picture this, Moses had been tending the sheep. Likely he was dirty and smelly and sweaty, but on this day God came to visit him. Moses didn't have time to get cleaned up and put on his best clothes. God wanted something more than that. God wanted Moses to recognize he was in the presence of Lord God Almighty and it was holy ground. God asked Moses to take off his sandals, a sign of respect.

What about you and me? God can meet us anywhere, anytime. In that moment, God wants us to enter into that sacred place with Him with respect. Our Lord wants our hearts to be turned toward Him and our knees to bow, for we, too, are on sacred ground.

God had met us in many different places on this journey. When He does, His holiness, His love, His power fills the place. I'm so grateful that our heavenly Father loves to visit us where we are – all cleaned up or smelly and sweaty from life's challenges.

Thank you for joining us on holy ground. May the Lord bless you and keep you this day. #Godisfaithful #pray4bill

Day #275 October 11

Anchor Verse: Colossians 3:23-24
Whatever you do [whatever your task may be], work from the soul [that is, put in your very best effort], as [something done] for the Lord and not for men. (AMP)

Do you carry out all your work with enthusiasm? Sometimes as children when we had chores to do, it wasn't always done with enthusiasm, sometimes it was for the reward – our allowance.

As adults, now we more fully understand what the apostle Paul is talking about here, we are called by God to offer our work as an offering to Him. We need to do it with enthusiasm because we are serving God who gave us life and all the other good things we enjoy.

Maybe you are struggling in your workplace because there is conflict or you don't enjoy your job or some other reason, but for now this is where you are. God has you there for a reason. Let your light shine for Him.

Look around you. Is there someone who needs an encouraging word? Maybe someone who is struggling? This might be the place where God has placed a mentor for you to learn from to get you prepared for your next assignment.

There is so much to learn in life, and about life. When our hearts and minds are open to what God has for us, life is more enjoyable, for ourselves and others around us.

It is the Lord who will reward you for your faithfulness. Words of affirmation may not come from your employer's mouth, but listen for God's words in your heart, "Well done, good and faithful servant."

There's a song that says, "Be not seeking the praises of men but the praise of your Father in heaven."

Thank you for your faithfulness. Today we go forward knowing that God has all the details of Bill's recovery lined up. #Godisfaithful #pray4bill

Day #276 October 12

Anchor Verse: 1 Corinthians 13:4
Love is patient. (NIV)

Patience...it's not something that we desire. We get so focused on the result that we want it to happen NOW! Children and adults alike struggle with the need to be patient... to wait for what we want, what we desire, and sometimes even for what we need.

But it is in the waiting that we learn the lessons God has for us. Sometimes in the waiting we discover that our initial impulse was truly not what was best for us. Thank God our prayers weren't answered.

Bill's health journey has taken a great amount of patience because it takes time to heal properly. God can accomplish His mission in a nano-second, or it can take years. Sometimes the answer is delayed because of us and our unwillingness to submit to His best for us, we want to do it our way.

In this last week, we went from elation that Bill's physical therapist had returned to help Bill continue to rebuild his strength to the shock a few days ago that the full authorization wasn't completed, so physical therapy was stopped. It was like slamming on your brakes at 70 mph!

My first thought was, how will it affect Bill? Bill said he wasn't disappointed but would be much stronger when we resumed therapy again. Patience – being willing to wait for God's appointed time.

Bill and I have seen God's hand writing a new chapter in our love story. I am grateful for this "world" that God had created for us, this place where we often get to spend time together. It's a beautiful place.

From the beginning God showed me that He would rebuild Bill's body one "brick" at a time, just like building a new house, each piece would be perfect and strong. There would be no weakness, no flaws, if we allowed God to take His time and do it His way.

I am so grateful for God's patience with me and loving me enough to allow my old caterpillar self to be transformed into a beautiful butterfly that will soar for His glory. Thank you for your patience as you have prayed for us all these months. #Godisfaithful #pray4bill

Day #277 October 13

Anchor Verse: Isaiah 41:13
*For I am the Lord your God who takes hold of your right hand and says to you,
Do not fear; I will help you. (NIV)*

God holds our hand through every season of our lives. This morning as I was reflecting on this verse, I was thinking about the times in our lives that holding a person's hand is so important and meaningful.

When a child begins to walk, an adult holds their hand to help them stay balanced and to catch them if they fall. When children get a little older, how often have we said or heard, "Hold my hand while we cross the street"?

And then when we get older and start dating or fall in love, holding hands is done to signify the beginning of a dance that may last a lifetime. When a loved one is sick, we hold their hand to comfort them. Many friends have shared lately how in the final moments of a loved one's life, they have held that person's hand as they traveled from this world to the next.

This verse in Isaiah says that God will not only hold your hand but He whispers these reassuring words, "Do not fear; I will help you."

If the God who created the universe is willing to help us, we truly have no reason to fear. When we place our trust in the One who created us, who knows us inside and out, we can rest securely in His presence.

When a journey is long, we can grow weary at times and we need to take time to rest and be restored. God is our guide and He knows that too.

This morning you may be in a place where not only do you need God to hold your hand, but you need Him to carry you. Just like a good father, God will pick you up in His arms of love and hold you, listen to you, and speak words of life and love over you.

Thank you for your faithfulness in prayer. Thank you for being His hands and feet. You are loved. #Godisfaithful #pray4bill

Day #278 October 14

Anchor Verse: 1 Thessalonians 1:3
We remember before our God and Father your work produced by faith, your labor prompted by love, and your endurance inspired by hope in our Lord Jesus Christ. (NIV)

How are you remembered by others? I don't mean your legacy, after you're gone, but how are you remembered today? What does your life reflect? Is it like what Paul outlines above?

We remember "your work produced by faith, your labor prompted by love, and your endurance inspired by hope in our Lord Jesus Christ."

Fruit like this in your life comes from a relationship with God. There is no other way that your life can bear this kind of fruit.

You may be going through a valley right now. Life might be really difficult and you don't see an end to your suffering. The good news – God does! He is with you through those sleepless nights and tough days. God whispers words of hope and reminds you that He is with you. Your heavenly Father will NEVER leave you or forsake you.

Hold on to hope. It's amazing how far you can go when you take each step with God. When I look at the fact it's been 278 days we have been on this journey... but for God's help, I don't know how we would have successfully made it this far.

We have made it this far, and we will cross the finish line of Bill's healing. Seeing Bill's bright eyes in the morning and long discussions with him throughout the day bring a smile to my face. When Bill talks about the goals he has of walking and doing "normal" things, it warms my heart.

God is doing a work in you, too. Every minute, every hour, every day, week and month, He is creating something beautiful out of your life.

Stay the course. Finish the race. Let it be said that God found you faithful.

Thank you for holding up our arms on difficult days and raising your arms to rejoice with us on our victorious days. #Godisfaithful #pray4bill

Day #279 October 15

Anchor Verse: Isaiah 46:4
Even as you grow old and your hair turns gray, I'll keep carrying you! I am your Maker and your Caregiver. I will carry you and be your Savior. (TPT)

Isn't it great news that God has the strength to carry you for your entire lifetime? Whether you are in your youth or middle years or older years, God has all that you need.

Fatigue isn't reserved just for the old. In Isaiah 40:29-31 it says, "He gives strength to the weary and increases the power of the weak. Even youths grow tired and weary, and young men stumble and fall; but those who hope in the Lord will renew their strength. They will soar on wings like eagles; they will run and not grow weary, they will walk and not be faint."

I can appreciate the specific words of this verse as I grow older and my hair has been gray, even white, for quite some time. It is a crown of glory from the Lord, but also a daily opportunity to proclaim my dependence on Him. Thank you, Lord, that you are my Maker, Caregiver, and Savior. You will carry me through every season of my life.

Even as God is there to carry us and rescue us, we need to do our part. Time spent in God's presence will refresh our spirit and our mind. We need to honor our bodies and rest when they say rest.

Yesterday Bill and I took a day of rest. We needed to pull back and hide under the shadow of God's wings. Sleeping and eating good food and talking and laughing, and as Bill would say, just being "us." It was a great day. And we slept so well last night! Hallelujah!

My encouragement is to praise the Lord for carrying you through the deep waters of your life as you do your part. There is a time to step away from social media. Turn off your phone. Be present with those you love. Take a walk. Engage in conversation. Learn to listen with your ears and your heart.

Thank you for your faithful prayers. They have moved mountains in our lives. Be blessed! #Godisfaithful #pray4bill

Day #280 October 16

Anchor Verse: Isaiah 48:17
This is what the Lord says— your Redeemer, the Holy One of Israel: "I am the Lord your God, who teaches you what is best for you, who directs you in the way you should go." (NIV)

I am so glad that the Lord directs our path, and most of all, that He teaches us what is best for us. Did you catch that?

This verse in Isaiah says the Lord teaches us what's best. That means that as we learn what's best, we can continue to make good choices and not repeat the same mistakes.

That's a Hallelujah moment for sure!

The other thing that is powerful to remember is that God wants what is best for you. Sometimes we get in our own way and fall short of His best for us. That doesn't mean that all of us will be rich and famous. It means that God has a best plan, a place most suited to us and how He created us; we just need to find it.

In the process of getting to that "best" place, sometimes we go through the desert or the wilderness or the refining fire, because we have some "stuff" we need to get rid of – pride, unforgiveness, an entitlement mentality, low self-esteem, anger, and the list goes on.

God can use us best when we are closest to Him. Spend time in His presence daily. Dive into God's Word – the Bible – His instruction manual and you will learn more about a life that pleases God. The whole book of Proverbs has nuggets of wisdom!

Be committed to follow Him, no matter the cost. There will be a price to pay for His best for you, but it is worth it.

Thank you for your faithfulness in prayer. Thank you for the hours of sleep you have sacrificed on our behalf. The Lord will reward you. #pray4bill

Day #281 October 17

Anchor Verse: Isaiah 52:12b
For the Lord will go before you, And the God of Israel will be your rear guard.
(NIV)

You do not have to face this life alone. The Lord will go before us and the God of Israel is our rear guard to protect us from behind.

Those with military experience will value this trait about the Lord. There is a scout to see what dangers might lie ahead and the rear guard will protect from any attacks by the enemy from ground that has already been won.

Our heads don't swivel around 360 degrees (for that I am grateful), but God can see it all. His heart's desire for His children is that we proceed through this life in safety, to run the race that He has for us. More than desiring it, our heavenly Father sets the stage for us to accomplish it.

Even with these provisions from the Lord, it does not mean that we will not encounter difficulties – it's guaranteed as long as we live on this earth, we will. Jesus reminded us in John 16:33, "These things I have spoken to you, that in Me you may have peace. In the world you will have tribulation; but be of good cheer, I have overcome the world." We are overcomers! There may be blood, sweat, and tears in the process, but in the end, we will overcome the world.

Sometimes just taking the next breath is difficult. Take that next step. Take a deep breath. Know that God is on your side, and more than that, He often brings others alongside of you to support you. Even if you are going through a rough patch "alone" – God promised that He would never leave you or forsake you – NEVER!

On this journey, my faith in God has been my life line. Even now our heavenly Father is ahead of us in the future preparing the place He has for us and the way we can best serve Him.

Thank you for walking with us as part of the great cloud of witnesses that surround us. #Godisfaithful #pray4bill

Day #282 October 18

⚓ *Anchor Verse: 2 Thessalonians 1:3*
We ought always to thank God for you, brothers and sisters, and rightly so, because your faith is growing more and more, and the love all of you have for one another is increasing. (NIV)

Nothing is wasted in God's economy. Our joys, our sorrows, our challenges have a purpose even for those who are walking with us.

This has been the story of our journey since Bill's entrance to the hospital on January 10, 2018. From the minute I called 911, God started placing people around us that would impact our lives – and save Bill's life with God directing every action.

Prayers starting that first day have continued to be raised to heaven. I can only imagine how many prayers include Bill's name in them (and my name too). When we get to heaven, Bill and I might take a look at that book, or should I say volumes, that contain your prayers on our behalf.

This verse from 2 Thessalonians seemed so appropriate to thank you for your prayers and your love and to see how your faith has grown on this journey. You have watched God's miracles unfold in Bill's life. You have seen what the doctors and the world said was impossible happen, because God says ALL things are possible with Me.

We are so grateful for how you have surrounded us, in the spirit and the flesh. Most of all I am grateful to see how your faith has grown. God is not finished with us yet. God is not finished in your life either. Months ago, God gave me a prayer to pray for you, and I renew my prayer to God on your behalf this morning.

Lord, may a tsunami of blessings come into the lives of all those who have prayed for us. May healing and restoration and deliverance and miracles be seen in their lives and may they give testimony that it was by Your hand these things came to fruition. In Jesus' name I pray, amen.

Thank you for your prayers for they have moved mountains in our lives. #Godisfaithful #pray4bill

Day #283 October 19

Anchor Verse: Isaiah 56:7b
    ...For My house will be called a house of prayer for all nations. (NIV)

Prayer is powerful. I am not telling you something you don't already know. If you are reading this post, you know that Bill's miracle health journey has been the result of much prayer, prayers offered by those who know that prayer moves the hand of God.

Today I want to take you to a wider circle, the world. Our prayers have no boundaries. I may not be able to travel to Ghana or India or Japan or Antarctica like the speed of light, but my prayers can.

I can't imagine my life without prayer. When others I love are facing challenges of illness or death or discouragement, the first thing I can do is take their troubles to God in prayer. He loves them more than I do and knows how to comfort, encourage, and provide for them.

This verse specifically points out that "My house" will be called a house of prayer for all nations. That's a call to the church to pray and touch the world.

We are a little more than halfway through the month of October. Our church has set aside the month of October as a month of prayer and fasting, particularly for our nation but also for our individual lives and our church. We want to see God move in our lives. We want a greater intimacy with Him so that our faith will shine like a lighthouse to the nations. That begins on our knees in prayer.

I am reading *The Circle Maker* by Mark Batterson - an excellent book on the power of prayer. "Sometimes the power of prayer is the power to carry on. It doesn't always change your circumstances but it gives you the strength to walk through them. When you pray through, the burden is taken off of your shoulders and put on the shoulders of the Him who carried the cross to Calvary." This is the power of prayer, my friends. May you walk in His power and His peace today.

Thank you for your faithfulness. #Godisfaithful #pray4bill

Day #284 October 20

⚓ *Anchor Verse: 2 Thessalonians 3: 16*
Now may the Lord of peace himself give you peace at all times and in every way.
The Lord be with all of you. (NIV)

Peace – it's what nations long for. It's what people strive for. And it seems to be the most elusive thing in the world to find. But as Christians, we know that we can find peace in God, and God alone. That is the only destination where we will always find peace.

It is interesting to note that as the apostle Paul was writing this letter to the church at Thessalonica, that the people there were struggling with finding peace just as we do today. As King Solomon says in the book of Ecclesiastes, there is nothing new under the sun.

Are you pursuing peace today? Have you been awake all night filled with worry and fear? Do you pace the floor or scroll through Facebook or buy things online when you can't find the answers to your problems?

There is only one place you will find the peace that you desire, you need and that is in the arms of Jesus. This verse reminds us that God will grant you His peace not just once in a while, it says, "May the Lord himself give you peace at all times and in every way." That means day and night, 24 hours a day, seven days a week, and God does not take holidays off.

Instead of running away or running to drugs or alcohol, run to God and surrender your will to Him. Stop trying to figure it out on your own.

One thing I have learned on Bill's health journey is the power of God's peace in the midst of the storm. I have experienced that peace and still do when I rest in God's presence. It is there I find the answers to my questions. I am filled with His peace and His power and walk through this life knowing that all things are possible with God.

My prayer for you today is that you would lay down your burdens and exchange them for His peace. You are loved. Thank you for your faithfulness. #Godisfaithful #pray4bill

Day #285 October 21

Anchor Verse: Isaiah 64:8
Yet still, Yahweh, you are our Father. We are like clay and you are our Potter. Each one of us is the creative, artistic work of your hands. (TPT)

As a young child, we often sang a hymn at church (Have Thine Own Way Lord) about this verse, "Have thine one way, Lord, have thine own way, Thou art the potter, I am the clay. Mold me make me after thy will, while I am waiting, yielded and still."

How often are we willing to let God have His own way in our lives, to completely surrender to Him and His best for us?

Sometimes we may struggle with our flesh in those moments of surrender. Like a two-year-old child, we think we know what is best and throw a temper tantrum when we don't get our own way. God still loves you there.

When we get a visual picture of a potter working with clay, we see a craftsman at work. As the potter works, he can see the finished product in his mind before it is formed by his hands. God does that with us.

Before you were born, God knew exactly the gifts and talents He had placed in you so that you would shine for His glory here on earth. Many of us are still discovering those talents.

Another translation of the verse reminds us that we were "shaped and formed into something of worth." This is one of the areas that the enemy rushes in to destroy our effectiveness for God's Kingdom.

The devil tries to get us to believe we are worthless and unworthy of God's love and we will never accomplish anything worthwhile. They are lies!

We are blessed to see God, the potter, continue to reshape and rebuild Bill's body of clay and activate the gifts that God has placed in Bill.

Thank you for circling us in prayer. #Godisfaithful #pray4bill

Day #286 October 22

Anchor Verse: Isaiah 65:24
Before they call I will answer; while they are still speaking I will hear. (NIV)

God is an Awesome God and a loving heavenly Father. There is not one second of our lives that He leaves us alone. Even those who walk away from His love, God's heart is broken by their absence from Him.

One of the amazing gifts of being a child of God is the blessing of prayer and communicating with our heavenly Father. It's not just a one-way street where we ask for something and He delivers it. God is not a vending machine or a phone app where we plug in our request and He delivers.

God knows the desires of our heart. He knows our needs. Our heavenly Father knows our requests often before they are even formed on our lips.

How many of you have had situations in your life like what is described in Isaiah 65:24? The verse says, "Before they call I will answer, while they are still speaking I will hear."

As I walk in fellowship with the Lord, as I hear His voice and let Him guide my life, this happens even more often. Just like in a relationship you have with someone you love, for example, a husband and wife or a mother and her child, when you can anticipate their need or finish their sentence, that's how well God knows us.

On this journey to Bill's healing, we have encountered many places like this. Many times you were the answers to our unspoken prayers.

It is with great joy that God fulfills our requests, or better yet, God provides His best, which is far greater than we could ever imagine.

My heart is full of anticipation this morning as we step into this new week. There are many appointments on the calendar. Bill described it last night as "next steps" that will be taken. God is up to something special: the authorizations that are still outstanding. The healing Bill still needs. Holy surprises. Timely answers to bold prayers.

Thank you for your prayers. They have moved mountains in our lives. You are loved! #Godisfaithful #pray4bill

Day #287 October 23

Anchor Verse: Joshua 3:8, 13
...When you reach the banks of the Jordan River, take a few steps into the river...The priests will carry the Ark of the Lord, the Lord of all the earth. As soon as their feet touch the water, the flow of water will be cut off upstream, and the river will stand up like a wall. (NLT)

How many of you like to get your feet wet before God does the miracle? We want to walk through on dry ground after God has already parted the waters and our troubles have been washed away.

In Joshua 3, the Israelites are getting ready to enter the Promised Land after 40 years in the wilderness. God would do the miraculous but wanted them to have some "skin in the game."

This is a déjà vu moment, just like when God asked them to walk by faith into the Red Sea with the Egyptian army in pursuit. God did a miracle then and they needed a miracle now.

Just as God promised, as the priests got their feet wet, the water parted, and the priests stood there in the middle of the Jordan River while all the people passed through on dry ground. Then the Lord restored the river to its normal course once again.

This story is not just about the end result – the completion of God's promise and their arrival in the Promised Land. It's about walking by faith, walking in obedience where and when God says to go.

Where is God calling you to step out in faith? What mountain would He have you climb? What raging river do you need to pass through?

We have been blessed to see God part the waters for us many times. Each time we had to get our feet wet. During the time when Bill was still sedated, God called me to walk by faith for both of us into those raging waters knowing without a doubt He would deliver us.

Thank you for getting your feet wet as you walked forward by faith with us. Hallelujah! #Godisfaithful #pray4bill

Day #288 October 24

Anchor Verse: Psalm 4:8
In peace I will lie down and sleep, for you alone, O Lord, will keep me safe. (NIV)

Laying down to sleep is one of the greatest acts of trust that you do every day. We are vigilant during the day but when we lay down to sleep at night, we are the most vulnerable.

Some of our scariest moments have happened during the night. Like the night in March when I got a phone call telling me that Bill's blood oxygen levels had dropped. They took him by ambulance to the nearest hospital 45 minutes away from me. I woke up a dear friend for help.

During the darkness of the night with snowflakes falling, we zoomed down the highway not knowing what we faced on the other end.

Bill was in ICU and they were trying to get him stabilized. They had "bronched" him to clear his bronchial passages, his lungs now had blood in them. That night with blankets wrapped around me, I watched the monitors, not knowing if I dared close my eyes.

Last night we did an oxygen assessment to determine his night oxygen needs. Bill was supposed to sleep WITHOUT any oxygen support! Scary!

After being on oxygen for many months, now we were being asked to trust God and Bill's lungs and heart to keep him alive. We made it through the night without having to put his oxygen on. Bill's numbers were in the 80s at times but he was never short of breath.

I don't know what is on your heart and mind today. Be willing to put your troubles, your family, your job, your finances in God's hands as you lay down to sleep tonight, trusting Him to keep you safe and at peace.

Thank you for your faithfulness in prayer. #Godisfaithful #pray4bill

Day #289 October 25

Anchor Verse: Jeremiah 6:16
This is what the Lord says: "Stand at the crossroads and look; ask for the ancient paths, ask where the good way is, and walk in it, and you will find rest for your souls. But you said, 'We will not walk in it.' (NIV)

It matters where you choose to live your life. It matters the road that you take and the decisions you make. One path leads to life and the other to destruction.

When we stand at the crossroads of our lives, we must decide if we will walk with God or walk our own way. There is a difference. Time after time God has shown us the best way to live, the way that is in accordance with His Word, the path that leads to life.

Countless times since the creation of the world, human beings have chosen to run off the other direction and do what was right in their own eyes. History is littered with the disasters that have occurred when people chose folly instead of righteousness.

As I read this verse, I was reminded that God gives us the same instructions today. As we approach places in our lives where we need to make decisions, we need to look where the good way is and walk in it. And yes, we will find rest for our souls. That's His promise.

Today many will respond the same way as those addressed in this Jeremiah passage. "We will not walk in it." Blatant disobedience. Choosing evil over good.

My heart is filled with a yearning for those who are standing at the crossroads this morning. My prayer is that today they would say, "Yes, Lord, we will follow You. We will choose the way that leads to life."

Seek God's wisdom and walk in it. There you will find His love, His grace, and His power to overcome the trials of this world.

Thank you for your faithfulness in prayer. We are blessed. #Godisfaithful #pray4bill

Day #290 October 26

Anchor Verse: 1 Timothy 6:12
Fight the good fight of faith. Take hold of the eternal life—you were called to it, and you made the good confession for it in the presence of many witnesses. (NIV)

Fight the good fight. Hold on. Persevere. The Lord will give you the victory. It will not be an easy life – the life of a believer, a follower of Jesus Christ. But God promised that it would be worth it.

When you go through deep waters, God will hold your hand. He will rescue you. He will keep your head above water - above the trials that you face. Your heavenly Father will keep your warm when the world is cold and others have turned away to their own troubles. God will never leave you or forsake you.

Hold on to the prize that God has promised, eternal life, not just in heaven once we pass from this life, eternal life begins today. Why? Because we are a new creation in Christ when we say "yes" to God. We are daily renewed. Our minds are transformed. Hallelujah for that!

The apostle Paul in this letter to Timothy reminds him that it is a "good" fight. You are on the Lord's side. There will be a reward.

Share what God has done for you. Let others know the faith that you hold on to. May God be glorified in your life. Bill and I have seen God's hand move in mighty ways during this year of Bill's illness. We know that without God and His miracles our story would have a different ending.

We are committed to holding onto God's hand, letting Him have the glory, and declaring victory as we continue on Bill's healing journey.

Thank you for being our traveling companions and prayer warriors. Be blessed today. #Godisfaithful #pray4bill

Day #291 October 27

Anchor Verse: 2 Timothy 1:12
For I know whom I have believed and am persuaded (convinced, certain) that He is able to keep (guard, protect, take care of) what I have committed (entrusted) to Him until that Day (the day He returns). (NKJV)

It all starts with trusting God and it ends with trusting God. This is the only safe place to stand. It is the solid rock. It is the impenetrable fortress.

This morning my prayer is that you believe in God and His saving grace. And that you know that He is able to guard those you have entrusted to Him. I think of the many days and nights on this healing journey when I have placed Bill in God's hands.

Trusting God with the person I love the most and knowing that God would fight for Bill, fight for Bill's life and the future God has planned for him. In our humanity, our resources are limited. In God, in the spiritual realm, we have the resources of eternity and they are beyond our understanding!

The devil will try to sow seeds of doubt. He will attempt to distract you and get you focused on the past – the "old man." Your past is gone as a believer in Christ. You have been set free. It no longer has a hold on you. Trust God. Walk in the resurrection power available to you.

It has been a very full week, lots of places of testing and trusting. I know my Redeemer lives and that victory is ours. Just like the apostle Paul I will say, "I know whom I have believed and am persuaded that He is able to keep that which I've entrusted unto him until the day that He returns."

Thank you for holding up our arms on the days we were too tired to lift them. You have been a blessing. We thank God for you every day. #Godisfaithful #pray4bill

Day #292 October 28

Anchor Verse: Psalm 116:8-9
God has rescued my soul from death's fear and dried my eyes of many tears. He's kept my feet firmly on his path and strengthened me so that I may please him and live my life before him in his life-giving light. (TPT)

God has a purpose for your life. He saved you from destruction for a reason. As these verses in Psalm 116 remind us, God has delivered your soul from death even from the fear of death, your eyes from weeping, and your feet from stumbling. God has planted your feet firmly on His path and strengthened you.

Why? So that you may walk before the Lord in the land of the living and that your life would please Him!

Wow! God has plans for you and they are good. There are tasks that only you can do, gifts that only you have been given. It's time to step up and use them for God's glory. Today would be a good day to start.

During our journey toward Bill's healing, we have walked through all of these places – deliverance from death, from weeping, and Bill's feet from stumbling. As we continue to walk on this journey, we know that our God is the one who saves. Our God reigns!

As we continue to walk before the Lord, our hearts and minds are turned toward Him asking the question, "Where can we be of service to you, Lord?" God has a place for you even as you heal.

Every day on earth is a gift. Use every opportunity to speak words of life to each other, to just be there to listen or to hold your loved one's hand or pray. There is no act too small or too big when we are about the Master's business.

Thank you for your faithfulness in prayer. As God continues to stir up new life in Bill, we are grateful and filled with great joy, for greater things are yet to come. Have a blessed and restful Sunday. #Godisfaithful #pray4bill

Day #293 October 29

🛟 *Anchor Verse: Jeremiah 20:11*
But the LORD stands beside me like a great warrior. Before him my persecutors will stumble. They cannot defeat me. They will fail and be thoroughly humiliated. Their dishonor will never be forgotten. (NLT)

The Lord is with you like a great, strong warrior. He is fighting for you, not against you. If God is with us, who can be against us? No one, no one that will succeed.

We are involved in a daily battle – the battle of good against evil. Some days we can hear the battle cry of our enemy, and other days, the peace of God that passes all understanding muffles the noise.

On those tough days, we need to remember this truth – we are victorious in the Lord. Those who are pursuing us will not defeat us.

There may be days when you feel overwhelmed by the battle, weary of the fight, where you would rather stay in bed than face the day. God will lead you through the twists and turns of those rocky roads and along steep cliffs, but He will also lead you to green pastures where you can lay down and rest, and be restored.

As we come near the end of this month, I praise the Lord for His faithfulness. Before we started the month of October, God showed both of us that it would be a game changer month. God has not disappointed us. And there are still three days to go!

Whether you are in the winner's circle of victory, lying in the ditch alongside the road, barely holding on, or only steps away from meeting your goal, know that God is for you, not against you. Trust Him in this fight. Hold on to hope and never let go. Victory is yours in Jesus.

Thank you for your prayers, day and night. They have moved mountains in our lives. We are grateful. #Godisfaithful #pray4bill

Day #294 October 30

Anchor Verse: Jeremiah 29:12
Then you will call on Me and you will come and pray to Me, and I will hear [your voice] and I will listen to you. (AMP)

When you are in the midst of troubles, how often do you remember that you have God's ear?

The God who created the universe, who knows each star by name, who knows the number of hairs on your head, who has plans for you, hears your voice, and will listen to you when you pray.

You won't find that kind of promise of faithfulness here on earth. We all have great intentions but we often fall short of the mark.

How often do you take God up on His promise? Do you have a quiet place where you come to Him and spend time with Him? God has wisdom He would love to impart to your heart. Sometimes we are so busy trying to fix our own problems that we leave Him out of the equation... big mistake on our part.

No matter your past practices, you can change that today. Come to Him. Come on your knees, whether that is physically or mentally. Acknowledge that He is not only your Savior but your Lord. Ask Him for wisdom. Praise God for what He has done and the miracles that are yet to come.

Take time now before you rush into your day to run to Him. Your prayer doesn't have to be long or eloquent. Speak from your heart. He longs to hear your voice. God has called you by name and you belong to Him. May His strength be yours today in the battles you face.

Thank you for your faithfulness in prayer as you held both Bill and me up to the throne room of grace. We are praying that we finish this month strong! He is able. #Godisfaithful #pray4bill

Day #295 October 31

Anchor Verse: Colossians 4:2
Be persistent and devoted to prayer, being alert and focused in your prayer life with an attitude of thanksgiving. (AMP)

Prayer... I'm not sure how anyone can live without it. I really can't imagine trying to make it through life without having a conversation with God on a daily basis. Life is filled with so much more than we can handle. To survive, we must run to God and lay our cares at His feet and ask for His wisdom and provision for ourselves and others.

We have seen how faithful, consistent prayer has changed things in our life again and again. The apostle Paul reminds the church to be persistent and devoted to prayer. That means it's a habit. It's not something you pull out of your back pocket when you face desperate times that call for desperate measures. Prayer is woven into the tapestry of your life. God can see you coming and welcomes time with you. He knows that you are serious when you stand in the gap for others. God answers your prayers.

Do you have a prayer list? Do you have prayer requests that others have shared with you that you regularly bring to the Lord? If the devil wants you to be ineffective, he will keep you busy and distracted as you stop to pray. Stay focused on the Lord's tasks for you.

We thank the Lord for you and your commitment to pray for us through this year. It has been a blessing greater than you can imagine unless you have walked through a deep valley like this yourself.

We rejoice in the plans God has for us. We are grateful for the revelation He continues to give as we walk in obedience to Him. Today I celebrate the gift of prayer and praising God for the great things He has done.

Give thanks with a grateful heart. You are loved and appreciated.
#Godisfaithful #pray4bill

Our Walk of Faith

November 2018
Give Thanks

Day #296 November 1

Anchor Verse: Psalm 56:8
You have seen me tossing and turning through the night. You have collected all my tears and preserved them in your bottle! You have recorded every one in your book. (TLB)

God is with you 24 hours a day, seven days a week. He cares about you on those sleepless nights when all you do is toss and turn. God speaks peace to you when the world shouts with loud voices of chaos and confusion.

As we enter November, my heart is filled with thanksgiving as I recount the path where God led us this year. It has not always been easy, but God has been so faithful.

My heavenly Father knows every tear that I shed – tears of sorrow and tears of joy. God knows every ache that Bill has experienced, and with His gentle healing touch, God has restored him.

As we enter another new bend in the road with the therapists returning to propel Bill forward on the path God has for him, I am mindful that God will make things smooth once again. Where God leads, we will follow. When an obstacle arises in our path, we will overcome it with God's help. Likewise, there will be days of rejoicing when there is a breakthrough.

This is true in your life too. God sees you and loves you. He was with you last night as you laid awake sorting out your troubles. He heard your cries for mercy. Your heavenly Father bathed you with His peace and His grace.

The Lord will walk with you through this day, this month of thanksgiving that lies ahead of you. He will restore what the locusts have destroyed. There will be rejoicing forevermore.

Thank you for your faithful prayers day and night. Lift your hearts and hands in thanksgiving this morning. He is worthy of our praise. #Godisfaithful #pray4bill

Day #297 November 2

Anchor Verse: Luke 6:38
Give generously and generous gifts will be given back to you, shaken down to make room for more. Abundant gifts will pour out upon you with such an overflowing measure that it will run over the top! Your measurement of generosity becomes the measurement of your return. (TPT)

The gift of giving is not so you can receive but to know the joy that comes from giving from your heart. That's one thing about God's economy – it's not the same as our worldly marketplace.

A penny saved is a penny earned. The money lessons that we learned as children about putting money in our savings account so we could buy something special down the road are important.

This lesson Jesus taught was greater than that, it has a greater meaning. It is an attitude about life. When God created you, He gave you specific gifts and talents to use in this world to support yourself and your family but also for the greater good.

I know in my life that some of the most joyful moments have been when I gave freely to another, not because it would benefit me personally, but to meet their need. The greatest reward we have are words from the Lord, "Well-done, thou good and faithful servant. Enter into the joy I have prepared for you."

Your reward from the Lord cannot be contained in your hands or your heart. It will continue to flow not only in this generation but generations to come. We have no idea how the seeds of goodness sown today will bear fruit tomorrow, but God does.

Thank you for all the prayer seeds and other acts of kindness you have sown into our lives this year. Truly our arms and heart and home cannot contain them. Your love continues to flow through us to benefit others.

Be a blessing today. Soak in the joy that comes from being Jesus' hands and feet. There is joy in serving Jesus. #Godisfaithful #pray4bill

Day #298 November 3

Anchor Verse: Jeremiah 31:25
I will refresh the weary and satisfy the faint. (NIV)

I love the promises of God! There are nuggets of truth and promises of hope and joy buried throughout the Bible. All you need to do is start reading your Bible and you will find sustenance for your soul.

"Refresh the weary and satisfy the faint" – this is the perfect verse to end this week. It's been a long week in many ways as we bridged the gap between October and November. What I do know is that God is faithful.

I have learned to hold on to the Lord and never let go. Whether we were navigating sharp corners or steep mountains, He has been our guard rail. After sleepless nights, God has come to speak peace to our weary souls. Your heavenly Father will do the same for you.

As we enter the month of November with thanksgiving in our hearts, time and time again I can share with you stories of God's faithfulness and His miraculous hand at work. You have seen it in your own lives. Just when you thought you couldn't handle any more, something changed and God gave you hope or help or a new direction.

Last night we both had a great night's sleep after several nights of restlessness. God was hovering over us during those nights as well.

Are you weary or weak this morning? Run to the Lord. Cry out to Him. He will restore you. Your heavenly Father has you wrapped in His arms of love. Lean in. Listen to His still small voice. He will turn your mourning into dancing. God is for you, not against you. He is your peace.

Thank you for lifting up our arms when we were weary. May you be blessed as you have been a blessing to us. #Godisfaithful #pray4bill

Day #299 November 4

Anchor Verse: Jeremiah 32:17
Ah, Lord God! Behold, You have made the heavens and the earth by Your great power and outstretched arm. There is nothing too hard for You. (NKJV)

Sometimes we just need to declare the power of God in our lives and say it out loud! Say it where you are right now, "There is nothing too hard for You, God!"

If there is nothing too hard for God, then there is nothing too hard for you! Because as believers, we are walking with God alongside of us. We lean on Him, God who made the heavens and the earth. Every detail, every leaf, every brushstroke of the color painted on the birds, every sunrise and sunset were designed for His honor and glory and to give us pleasure.

God loves us so much because He is a good, good Father. God wants you to grow into His likeness. Your heavenly Father wants you to walk in the calling He has for you. God doesn't want you to walk in fear but in faith. Trust Him when you cannot see. Trust Him when all you can take is a small step forward only because He is holding your hand.

This is the Lord's day – we celebrate Jesus' resurrection every Sunday, the same resurrection power that lives in us. Own it today. Do not be overcome by evil but overcome evil with good.

I challenge you to dare to dream big dreams, to invite God to carry out His best plans for your life. Hold on as you walk through deep waters, they will not overcome you. Once again, He will bring you back to dry ground.

We are excited about what God has planned for us – for it is good. We rejoice today in the God of our salvation. We believe that nothing is too hard for God, including Bill's complete healing! #Godisfaithful #pray4bill

Day #300 November 5

⚓ *Anchor Verse: 1 Peter 1:6-8*
In this you rejoice greatly, even though now for a little while, if necessary, you have been distressed by various trials, so that the genuineness of your faith, which is much more precious than gold which is perishable, even though tested and purified by fire, may be found to result in [your] praise and glory and honor at the revelation of Jesus Christ. Though you have not seen Him, you love Him; and though you do not even see Him now, you believe and trust in Him and you greatly rejoice and delight with inexpressible and glorious joy. (AMP)

The troubles that have come to purify your faith… you have them and I have them. The good news – there's a reason and a reward.

We are willing to jump through many hoops when we know we're going to get something out of it in the end. Your sufferings are like that.

Today is day #300 since Bill first entered the hospital on January 10, 2018. We never planned that recovery from pneumonia would take this long. Of course, we didn't know all the other illnesses and complications that were in store for us. But God did.

Did you know that your troubles come in order to prove that your faith is real? If your faith isn't tested, how do you know if it's genuine? Rejoice that the Lord sees such potential in you.

Did you know that your faith is worth more than gold? Many of you would rather have gold in your hand than the fiery trials you are going through.

Bill and I know that daily He fights for us. His love fills our hearts and our home. And the peace that passes all understanding guards our hearts and minds every hour of the day and night.

Thank you for standing with us and loving us and praying for us. Great will be your reward in heaven. #Hallelujah #Godisfaithful #pray4bill

Day #301 November 6

⚓ *Anchor Verse: Deuteronomy 29:29*
There are secrets the Lord your God has not revealed to us, but these words that he has revealed are for us and our children to obey forever. (TLB)

Life is like a book. In a book you start reading the first page and as you continue to read page by page, the story is revealed.

Our lives are like that too. We can't see into the future, we live in the present and we walk each step in faith. With God guiding our footsteps, we can walk securely even when our eyes can't see the path ahead of us.

God's Word, the Bible, gives us instructions for living. It is filled with examples of people, just like you and me, who walked through difficult times in their lives. Think about Abraham. God told him to take his family, leave his home, and go to a land that God promised. Abraham stepped out in faith not knowing where he was going but trusting God to lead him.

The Ten Commandments are a good place for us to start living a life that is pleasing to the Lord. Walking in holiness. Loving God first and our neighbor as ourselves. There are many things that are unknown, but we know that God is unmovable, unshakable, and unstoppable, and He desires the best for us.

This verse in Deuteronomy reminds us that there are secrets the Lord has not revealed to us, but there are many truths that God has revealed. We must walk in obedience to God and He will open up the path to the bright future He has for us.

What is the next page in your story? Trust Him to write it. Believe that God is for you and not against you. We are more than conquerors through Him who loved us so.

Thank you for walking this path with us. God is faithful every day. We trust in Him even when our eyes can't see. We love you, Lord. #Godisfaithful #pray4bill

Day #302 November 7

Anchor Verse: Acts 16:25
About midnight Paul and Silas were praying and singing hymns of praise to God, and the other prisoners were listening to them. (NIV)

When you are faced with difficult circumstances, would we find you praying and singing hymns of praise to God at midnight? I have friends who are amazing intercessors that regularly pray during the night hours.

Often insomnia comes when people are worried about something happening in their lives – finances, employment, family, health issues, our nation, the list goes on. They tell stories of lying awake for hours as thoughts go flying through their heads.

In Acts 16, Paul and Silas give us another look at how to deal with adversity – praying and singing hymns of praise to God. Praise and worship unlock a vault of joy inside of us. Our spirit is set free from the bondage of earth and rises to the heavens where we join the angels in singing praise to the King of kings and the Lord of lords.

What if instead of our weeping or ranting to God those in our household heard songs of praise and thanksgiving? It says the other prisoners were listening to Paul and Silas. They weren't sleeping either.

A strong earthquake shook the prison and the doors were opened and the chains came loose. That's powerful praying and praising! It's also a picture of what God can do when we enter His presence with praise and thanksgiving and prayer, trusting God with the outcome.

Instead of complaining and being filled with worry about our difficulties, we should lift our voices in praise and thanksgiving, and surrender our lives completely to Him.

Do you trust Him with your present and your future? Do you believe that God can do the impossible in your life? Trust Him. Believe Him.

Thank you for your faithfulness in prayer, day and night. Thank you for rejoicing with us in our victories. #Godisfaithful #pray4bill

Day #303 November 8

Anchor Verse: Ecclesiastes 11:4
He who watches the wind [waiting for all conditions to be perfect] will not sow [seed], and he who looks at the clouds will not reap [a harvest]. (AMP)

Are you a perfectionist? Does everything have to be perfect before you move forward? The truth is, in this world, conditions will never be perfect before you move into the plans God has for you. You need to take a leap of faith!

This verse in Ecclesiastes reminded me this morning of the many places in my life where conditions haven't been perfect but God showed me that His plans for me are perfect. Are you spinning your wheels trying to connect the dots? God can take a path that is crooked and make it beautiful. He will bring order out of the chaos.

Is there beauty in the perfection? No. The beauty comes from the spirit of our Creator, God in us the hope of glory. We are called to let His light shine through us even when the circumstances are messy, when we don't know the path, when we can't even find the map!

When God calls you to a task, never doubt that He will equip you for it and God will bring the resources. Our purpose is to bring glory and honor to God, not for ourselves. God has called us to work in His Kingdom. Our call is to obedience and faithfulness.

I challenge you today to haul out that list of projects you want to do "someday" and get started. Maybe you want to write a book. Start with writing a story. Maybe you want to learn to cook. Get a recipe book or ask someone you know to help you. Maybe you want to travel. Get some travel guides and start planning.

If you wait for perfect weather, you'll never plant the seeds. If you are afraid that every cloud will bring rain or snow, you will never harvest your crops or achieve your goals. I'm checking my own list today. Lord, I'm willing! Now is the time. This is the place. Let's do it!

Thank you for jumping in to help during our journey. Your prayers and actions and words have lightened our load. #Godisfaithful #pray4bill

Day #304 November 9

Anchor Verse: Hebrews 6:10
God is not unjust; he will not forget your work and the love you have shown him as you have helped his people and continue to help them. (NIV)

This morning God's message is that He remembers you. He remembers the good you do for others. What we do for others rises like a pleasant aroma to the throne room of grace. God is a proud Father when He sees you, not only loving others by your words, but putting your words and thoughts into action.

Most, if not all of us, have been recipients of God's love through human hands. When I think about my childhood, my parents lived out that example of helping others through their actions, not only through the church but in everyday life. It was part of the legacy they were passing along to us, their children. I am grateful for that blessing.

God doesn't forget. You might think your labor for the Lord is going unnoticed. Your reward may not be in this life but we know that great will be your reward in heaven.

When God's love fills us, we don't do acts of kindness to be rewarded or recognized, we serve from the overflow of God's love in our hearts.

I know the joy of serving others, and in this season, Bill and I have been the recipients of that love from so many people as you have prayed and spoke encouraging words, cooked for us, helped with transportation, and so much more. You have been Jesus' hands and feet in our lives. Thank you so much.

"He will remember that you showed your love to him by helping his people." God sees your acts of kindness this morning. Do not grow weary in well-doing. Great will be your reward.

Thank you for your faithfulness. You are loved and appreciated. #Godisfaithful #pray4bill

Day #305 November 10

Anchor Verse: Psalm 33:20-21
We wait in hope for the Lord; he is our help and our shield. In him our hearts rejoice, for we trust in his holy name. (NIV)

The Lord is our hope and our help. I have experienced this truth in a whole new way in these last 10 months. I have learned to trust God when my eyes couldn't see the way ahead of us.

In those dark hours, it was the light of the love of Jesus that lit our way. It still does today, both for us and for you. The truth is we will always face challenges in this life. If it's not in our family, it's your family or friends or colleagues or church family who are walking through deep waters where God's hand is their only stability.

Listen to these words in Psalm 33:21, "In Him our hearts rejoice, for we trust in His holy name."

Is your heart rejoicing today? Mine is. And it's not just because of the evidence I see of God's work in Bill's life as he gets stronger, and walks, and talks, and laughs, and shares his conversations with God. It's because of the hope burning in my heart and because God has proven Himself faithful.

When I trust and obey the Lord, His joy is multiplied and magnified in me. Have you experienced that kind of intimacy with God? He wants to know you more. He wants to spend time with you. God wants you to rest in Him. He will fill you up with joy in His presence.

Today we celebrate 10 months since Bill entered the hospital early the morning of January 10, 2018, into an unknown situation, which we thought would be as "simple" as pneumonia. And you know the rest of the story... there hasn't been anything simple about our journey. God's faithfulness has never faltered.

Thank you for your faithfulness. Please take a moment to rejoice with us today. Since God has done it for us, He can do it for you. #Godisfaithful #pray4bill #Hallelujah

Day #306 November 11

Anchor Verse: Psalm 105:4
Look to the Lord and his strength; seek his face always. (NIV)

We often jest about the image of the "98 lb. weakling" but there are times and circumstances in our lives where our own strength is comparable to that.

The good news: God's strength is ALWAYS sufficient. His power is made perfect in our weakness.

It's like going on a road trip. If you look at the map, or these days, follow your GPS instructions, you will arrive at your destination on time and in good shape. Life is like that too. If we look to the Lord and seek His face, God promised to give us the strength to face any circumstance that we might encounter.

Whether it is an illness, a diagnosis, a broken relationship, financial hardship, even death of a loved one, God is able to carry you through.

There will be times when He will take you up in His arms and literally carry you through the difficult times.

I can't imagine how else we would have made it through Bill's health issues this year without God's help. With God helping us and fighting for us as we transferred our load of care to His shoulders, we walk in victory every day as we walk toward Bill's complete healing.

Whatever you are going through today, God will surround you with songs of deliverance. He will take your hand and lead you through the deep waters.

You will feel His love and experience His grace, His peace, and His power in a whole new way. Seek God's face always, in the good times and the challenging times.

Thank you for your continued prayers. We know that the prayers of a believing heart move the hand of God. #Godisfaithful #pray4bill

Day #307 November 12

🪝 *Anchor Verse: Luke 11:9-10*
"So I say to you, ask and keep on asking, and it will be given to you; seek and keep on seeking, and you will find; knock and keep on knocking, and the door will be opened to you. For everyone who keeps on asking [persistently], receives; and he who keeps on seeking [persistently], finds; and to him who keeps on knocking [persistently], the door will be opened." (AMP)

A couple of weeks ago, God gave me a living illustration of this verse. He broke it down for me because sometimes we need His lessons simplified.

Day #1: "Ask and keep on asking and it will be given to you." It was a day I was making phone calls that had been put off because I didn't have time. We had been asking and praying for authorization for Bill's therapy. After one phone call, God connected me with the right person. Within a half hour, the last piece was in place, and by afternoon, the physical therapist called to schedule Bill's first session. Wow! I was surprised. When it's His perfect timing, it happens. We just need to be persistent.

Day #2: "Seek and keep on seeking, and you will find." I had lost something. It wasn't actually lost but misplaced. I was relentless. Looking under things and in drawers and in my office (that's still a mess) and I found it! Just like the story of the woman in the Bible who was looking for the lost coin. Again, persistence won the day. I was beginning to get the message that God was showing me.

Day #3: "Knock and keep on knocking and the door will be opened to you." A lot of doors have been closed, some by me and some by God. There were things I used to do or activities that I participated in that were stripped away. We have been praying about new doors of opportunity. New opportunities were explored that day as I asked more questions. There was a stirring in my spirit, an open door in my heart.

Walking this path, I have learned that surrendering to God's perfect will is the only place I want to be. Don't believe the lie that surrendering to God's will means that horrible things are going to happen. God won't force His best on you. You must take action, persistent action.

Thank you for your persistence in prayer. It has moved mountains in our lives. #Godisfaithful #pray4bill

Day #308 November 13

⚓ *Anchor Verse: Colossians 3:12*
So, as God's own chosen people, who are holy [set apart, sanctified for His purpose] and well-beloved [by God Himself], put on a heart of compassion, kindness, humility, gentleness, and patience [which has the power to endure whatever injustice or unpleasantness comes, with good temper]. (AMP)

In this month of thanksgiving, God is calling us to be more like Him. That includes "a heart of compassion, kindness, humility, gentleness, and patience."

This list sounds like qualities I would like to have in a friend. These are all qualities that our friend Jesus has. As we walk with Jesus and learn from Him, we will become more like Him.

Every day I am more aware that so many people are hurting so much right now – physically, emotionally, mentally, spiritually, and financially. Our very souls are being sifted as God brings us through the refining fire. His goal is not to destroy us but to make us more like Him. Are you willing to walk that path with Him?

In some translations it says that we should be "clothed" with a heart of compassion, kindness, humility, gentleness, and patience. Just like putting your clothes on in the morning, I am going to challenge you for the next week as you are getting dressed to pray that God would fill your heart with compassion, kindness, humility, gentleness, and patience.

This means God will put you in situations where each of these qualities will be tested. Step up to the challenge. If we want to be beacons of light for the Lord, it won't be easy but definitely it will be worth it!

Lord, may each person who reads this be transformed into a lighthouse that reflects compassion, kindness, humility, gentleness, and patience. If we are willing, so are You. And through our obedience, we will change the world. Thank you, Lord.

Thank you for your compassion and kindness as we walk this road to Bill's healing. #Godisfaithful #pray4bill

Day #309 November 14

⚓ *Anchor Verse: Lamentations 3:21-23*
But this I call to mind, Therefore I have hope. It is because of the Lord's lovingkindnesses that we are not consumed, Because His [tender] compassions never fail. They are new every morning; Great and beyond measure is Your faithfulness. (AMP)

It is in the presence of the Lord that we find hope. It is because of His lovingkindness that we can walk through the storms of life and not be destroyed. His tender compassion NEVER fails. This morning they are brand new and tomorrow morning they will be as well. Yes, great and beyond measure is God's faithfulness.

Over this last year, I have tested and proved these verses over and over again. What we fix our mind on is crucial to getting us through the hard times. If we focus on the negative, we are drawn just like a magnet over the cliff into the pit of despair. If we look to the Lord and the hope that He offers, God reaches down to pull us up, to help us to stand, to help us to our knees in surrender and worship.

Many of you are walking through some of the most difficult challenges you have ever experienced in your life right now. In some moments, it's difficult to even breathe because your pain is so intense. God is in charge of each breath, each heartbeat, and each step we take. Always remember that He loves you, no matter what the world says or what your circumstances may be screaming at you.

God hurts when you hurt. He holds you when you cry. He will give you wisdom when you can't even pull your thoughts together.

One step at a time. That's all you need to do. God will provide. He will equip you. Your heavenly Father will sing songs of deliverance over you.

Your job is to hold on to hope. "But this I call to mind. Therefore I have hope." Fix your mind on these things. Know that God loves you. He is faithful. Praise Him in the storm and know that you are surrounded by our prayers.

Thank you for holding on to hope with us as Bill continues to recover. Your faithfulness encourages us. #Hallelujah #Godisfaithful #pray4bill

Day #310 November 15

🔱 *Anchor Verse: Psalm 89:15*
O Lord, how blessed are the people who experience the shout of worship, for they walk in the radiance of your presence (TPT)

Learning how to praise Him no matter your circumstances comes from a heart that is filled with His power and His presence. It is not our natural human instinct to rejoice during times of testing. As believers, we walk in the joy of His presence, the light of His love.

There's a song we sing in church that talks about how God can work through those who praise Him. God inhabits our praise. And when we praise Him, the chains, the enemy's hold on you, the lies that have bound you, will drop powerless at your feet when you praise Him.

Praising the Lord is one of the best tools we have to neutralize the enemy!

One of the lessons that has been driven home to me this year is that praising the Lord, lifting our voices in song sends the devil running. Your heart and mind cannot be praising the Lord and be filled with fear and doubt at the same time.

When you're tired, praise the Lord! When you're afraid, praise the Lord! When you're seeking wisdom, praise the Lord! When you feel alone, praise the Lord!

It is in our darkest nights and deepest valleys that our praises echo through the night and rise to heaven. I believe they are the sweetest music our heavenly Father hears when we choose to unite our voices with the angels that surround His throne.

Whatever your circumstances, turn on some praise music! Run to Him. Sing! Make a joyful sound even if you can't sing. God longs to hear your voice because He can then exchange your troubles for His peace.

This morning know that you are loved. Your heavenly Father is faithful. With His help, you can make it through anything!

Thank you for your faithfulness in prayer, day and night. We are blessed. #Godisfaithful #pray4bill

Day #311 November 16

Anchor Verse: Hebrews 11:30
It was faith that brought the walls of Jericho tumbling down after the people of Israel had walked around them seven days as God had commanded them. (TLB)

When you read about the "giants" of the faith, does the thought "I could never do that" run through your mind? They were ordinary people just like you and me who followed an extraordinary God.

It wasn't the strength of the army. It wasn't that the walls were poorly constructed. It was "faith" that brought Jericho's walls tumbling down after the army followed God's instructions for seven days.

What are the walls in your life that God wants to bring tumbling down?

What is the obstacle that your faith, your obedience will remove?

On Bill's healing journey, the greatest victories were won in prayer as I surrendered to God's best for Bill. I stood in faith and declared victory over his illness, and even what appeared to be impending death. It is only because of God that Bill is alive. He deserves all the honor and glory.

Joshua and his army walked by faith for those seven days around the great walled city of Jericho. It was not their normal fighting tactic, but they walked in obedience.

Because of their faith in God, the entire army believed the city of Jericho would be delivered into their hands.

Today God is calling you to walk by faith and in obedience to His commands so that you might receive the reward He has for you.

Walk with Bill and me on this faith journey. Believe in the God of miracles and that the outcome will be for your best and give God the glory.

Thank you for your faith and your faithfulness. God has seen them and is proud of you. #Godisfaithful #pray4bill

Day #312 November 17

Anchor Verse: Hebrews 12:12-13
So be made strong even in your weakness by lifting up your tired hands in prayer and worship. And strengthen your weak knees, for as you keep walking forward on God's paths all your stumbling ways will be divinely healed! (TPT)

Are you weak, tired, and weary this morning? Lift your tired hands in prayer and worship. God can work through those who praise Him!

This passage in Hebrews 12 reminds us that it's not just about prayer and worship. We must keep walking forward on God's path, and in the process, you will be divinely healed!

I have learned so much about walking with the Lord during these days of Bill's healing journey, not only in the physical realm but the spiritual realm too. Even as Bill was confined to a hospital bed for months and not able to walk, God was at work on the spirit man, and also in me, to refresh, restore, rejuvenate our love for God and our love for each other.

As Bill continues on this path of healing, God walks with him every step he takes. Now I see the joy and fire in Bill's eyes when he walks with his four-wheeled walker and says, "I want to walk!" I can imagine the lame man Jesus healed had the same joy in his eyes.

As we walk on God's path for us, it is not only about our physical healing. God wants to transform us and heal us mentally, emotionally, and spiritually. His plans for us are good. Walking in His healing power we will experience the greatest joy of our lives even as we walk through deep waters.

Today God is holding your weak and tired hand as you walk those stumbling steps. His heart's desire is not only that you would run to Him but that you would walk in relationship with Him and know God's healing power for your soul.

Thank you for your faithfulness and believing with us. Thank you for cheering us on during every season of this journey. The best is yet to come. #Hallelujah #Godisfaithful #pray4bill

Day #313 November 18

Anchor Verse: Ecclesiastes 5:4
When you make a vow to God, do not delay to fulfill it. (NIV)

"Do not delay." These are the words I woke up hearing yesterday morning. There was something I needed to do that was time-sensitive. The week had been busy, but God reminded me that time was running out. Do it now! There was no more time for procrastination or excuses.

Are there things in your life that you have been putting off? The really important things often sit in the corner or on our computer waiting for us to pay attention to them, to tend to them, to complete them.

We don't need to raise our hands to identify that we are part of the human race that has an unfinished "to do" list. There is a book that needs to be written. A note of thanks for a gift or a kind gesture. A note of encouragement to someone who has lost their way. A phone conversation with a friend. Maybe even a visit that needs to be paid to a loved one. You have a list similar to mine.

In three short words God can get your attention: do not delay. It's like a parent who uses your full first name and middle name(s)... they definitely have your attention. It's time to take action!

My encouragement and challenge to you today as we enter this week of Thanksgiving is to give the gift of your time, your words, and your listening ear. God may be the one you owe that time. He is waiting for you even now. If it's a loved one or a friend who needs to hear from you, do it today. Please don't put it off until tomorrow, because tomorrow isn't promised to any of us.

When I have heeded God's warning, "do not delay" I have been blessed by a conversation, a visit, a note sent, love received, because I put aside "my plans" in exchange for "God's plans." Even during the night when God wakes me up, my first thought is, "Who do I need to be praying for right now?" Your nighttime prayers have often hit the target in our lives.

Thank you for continuing to surround us with your prayers and words of encouragement. #Godisfaithful #pray4bill

Day #314 November 19

Anchor Verse: Ezekiel 11:19
And I will give them singleness of heart and put a new spirit within them. I will take away their stony, stubborn heart and give them a tender, responsive heart. (NLT)

God wants to make you brand new! His desire is to have you walk in harmony and communion with Him.

Singleness of heart – an undivided heart – what a gift! In this world in which we live, it seems that we are torn first one way and then another. The world tells us we should do one thing or believe this or that, and God's Word stands unshakable and unchanging and clearly shows us the way we should live.

Do you have a stony, stubborn heart this morning? Is there something that God is asking you to do that you have not done? Not only have you not done it but you throw a temper tantrum every time He asks you to act on His behalf?

This morning all that can change. God wants to exchange your heart of stone and replace it with a heart of flesh – a tender, responsive heart that hears His voice and walks in His way.

Living in fellowship with your heavenly Father is a blessing. You have new eyes to see the beauty of God's creation and the beauty of those who are around you. You have new ears to hear God's voice as He leads you beside still waters and restores your soul. Your feet have been renewed so you can walk on the path He has for you. Your new heart is tender and compassionate as you see the needs of others in a new way.

As I continue to see God renew, transform, and remake Bill, I see the new man emerging. This journey has not been wasted. In both of us, God has made our hearts more tender and compassionate with a greater love for God, each other, and others.

May the Lord continue to use your compassionate heart in a world that needs His love today. #Godisfaithful #pray4bill

Day #315 November 20

Anchor Verse: Proverbs 27:17
As iron sharpens iron, so a friend sharpens a friend. (NLT)

Are you blessed with a friend who desires to see you grow in your gifts and talents, in your Christian walk? If you have such a friend, you have a treasure that is greater than gold.

God's desire for us is that we would continue to grow and not remain babies, when it comes to wisdom and understanding. We need to grow up and mature, so you and I can fulfill the mission He has for us.

How do we do that? We can't do it alone. Not only do we have God's Word, the Bible, to teach us and a community of believers to fellowship with as we learn more about Him, but God also places people in our lives to encourage and challenge us.

Over my lifetime, I have been blessed by friends, mentors, and coaches who have helped me not only in my personal life, but in my spiritual growth and in my business. It has been a blessing to see Proverbs 27:17 lived out in my life.

Just as iron sharpening iron creates sparks, the sharpening of our skills and smoothing the rough edges of our lives isn't always pretty. We like to hold on to things the way they are, even if it's not the best for us.

God loves you so much He will send other people into your life to encourage you to take that leap of faith, that next step in becoming the man or woman of God He wants you to be. Are you brave enough to submit to the growth process?

Yesterday (11.19.18), my friend Julie Sheldon who sharpened me, God called home to her eternal reward. Her time here was way too short. I will cherish the things Julie set in motion in my life. Do you have a person who sharpens you? Ask God to show you how you can be that kind of friend.

Thank you for your faithfulness in prayer. #Godisfaithful #pray4bill

Day #316 November 21

Anchor Verse: James 3:17
But the wisdom from above is first pure [morally and spiritually undefiled], then peace-loving [courteous, considerate], gentle, reasonable [and willing to listen], full of compassion and good fruits. It is unwavering, without [self-righteous] hypocrisy [and self-serving guile]. (AMP)

Wisdom – it is something we all long for, but are we willing to pay the price to gain it?

In the book of James, the author outlines what wisdom consists of: first of all, it comes from heaven, not earth. Wisdom comes from God alone. We must seek His face and know His heart to truly be rooted in wisdom.

It is pure. Not tainted by the world or "what's in it for me." Wisdom flows from the heart of God. It gives peace. When you are trying to make a decision and you are tossed like a boat in a storm, and suddenly God reveals the answer, you are filled with His peace.

It is gentle and willing to obey. A wise person is not like a bull in a china shop. When we are wise, we move into a situation like a gentle summer breeze that refreshes the soul. And willing to obey, the first step begins in our heart. When we submit to the Lord and are willing to obey, we exchange our tainted sense of what is wise for God's higher perspective. We are willing to surrender our will on the altar of praise.

It is full of loving-kindness and of doing good. We do not seek to destroy, but to build up and leave mended fences rather than what looks like the aftermath of a hurricane.

It has no doubts and does not pretend to be something it is not. We are not swayed by the wind or the opinions of others but we remain true to who God has called us to be. On Christ the solid rock we stand. We will not stray from the truth found in God's Word.

Thank you for standing with us this year. We are grateful for your friendship and your prayers. #Godisfaithful #pray4bill

Day #317 November 22

Anchor Verse: Psalm 69:30
Then my song will be a burst of praise to you. My glory-shouts will make your fame even more glorious to all who hear my praises! (TPT)

My heart is filled with thanksgiving this morning and not just because it's Thanksgiving Day. I am grateful that Bill is alive! Just like the psalmist in this passage, my song will be a burst of praise to God. I will bring Him glory by giving Him thanks.

Through this journey, God has worked through the hands of men and women in the medical field but He has also worked through your prayers and petitions on our behalf. Most glorious of all are the miracles God has performed in Bill's body just because God loves him and has plans for Bill's future.

The good news is that God wants to do that for you. He has plenty of love to share with each one of you. One thing I have learned on this journey is that what our heart and mind feed on is reflected in our lives.

If you focus on the positive and believe God's promises are true, that is what you will see in your life. Even if there is a lot of darkness, you will find a ray of light. On the other hand, those who focus on the negative and are critical will be consumed by the darkness. Remember the laws of nature, you reap what you sow. The same principles apply in your thought life as much as the seeds you plant in your garden.

This morning I invite you to dine at the table not only with a healthy appetite to fill your stomach, but a grateful heart that will satisfy your soul. Give honor and glory to God because it is only by His grace that we can enjoy the good things in our lives and weather the storm as we hold on to His hand.

Each one of you has contributed to our lives in some way on this journey – with your talents, your prayers, financial blessings, your encouraging words. Thank God for the miracle of Mr. Bill.

Have a blessed day with your family and friends! #Godisfaithful #pray4bill

Day #318 November 23

Anchor Verse: Psalm 32:7
You are my hiding place; You, Lord, protect me from trouble; You surround me with songs and shouts of deliverance. Selah. (AMP)

So grateful this morning that God is my hiding place. When you watch the news or even review your Facebook feed, you can see the troubles that surround us – they are many. God invites you to come under His wings of protection, a safe place, a place free from trouble.

As a child, you may have had a hiding place. It was a place where you could go for some much needed quiet time away from the hubbub of your family life. We all need a quiet place, even children, to process the demands of our lives.

It is there in that quiet place where God meets us, as adults or children. It is there that we hear His whispers of wisdom and instruction. It is there our peace is restored and we can face life with a new perspective, new courage, and holy boldness.

This morning I would challenge you to listen for the songs and shouts of deliverance that permeate, that transcend the circumstances of your life. Are your ears tuned to His message of peace or focused only on the worst of life?

As we have walked on this healing journey, daily I have found the Lord to be my shelter in the storm. I won't know until I get to heaven the number of times He has kept me out of danger, even spared my life. I can praise God today for what I know He has done. He has brought me joy in the midst of trouble. God has brought peace in the storm. My heavenly Father has encouraged me when others only saw impending doom. The Great Physician has given us victory when in our flesh it looked like defeat!

My God can do the same for you. The choice is yours. My prayer for you this morning is on this Black Friday you would run to God and let Him be your hiding place knowing that He will protect you.

Thank you for your love and your prayers. #Godisfaithful #pray4bill

Day #319 November 24

Anchor Verse: Psalm 62:6
Yes, he alone is my Rock, my rescuer, defense, and fortress—why then should I be tense with fear when troubles come? (TLB)

I will not be shaken or discouraged. Life will always be filled with opportunities to run to God. When you conquer one mountain, another mountain looms in the distance.

The good news is that God is always faithful. He is my Rock, my rescuer, defense, and fortress. That sounds like everything I need to face life.

The psalmist makes a powerful statement without any exceptions, "I will not be shaken or discouraged!" Do you have that kind of boldness? Do you trust in God so much that you will boldly declare: I will not be shaken or discouraged?

Not even a moment of discouragement? Wow, I call that being totally sold out to God. This is what I have discovered during these months of Bill's health journey. If I keep my eyes on the Lord and listen to His voice, and keep my mind fed with good food from the Bible, then I can stay above the fray of life.

It's when I begin to look at circumstances and listen to the doubts and fears of others that the water starts to come into my boat. Enough!

I have said this before and I will say it again, "Lord, either I trust you or I don't. I choose to trust You... all the time."

Bold declarations of faith encourage us. We need to speak it out loud so we can hear it and it makes the enemy flee. If God is for me, who can be against me? No one will succeed. No weapon formed against you will prosper.

Thank you for standing with us in prayer and fighting this battle for Bill's complete healing. We are more than conquerors through Jesus Christ. #Godisfaithful #pray4bill

Day #320 November 25

Anchor Verse: 1 Peter 2:21
For God called you to do good, even if it means suffering, just as Christ suffered for you. He is your example, and you must follow in his steps. (NLT)

Doing the right thing is not always easy. Even doing the good that God has called you to do is not always the path of least resistance, it will cost you something.

But it is the path of eternal joy. When we reach the end of our life here on earth, we will hear the Lord greet us with, "Well-done, good and faithful servant, enter into the joy I have prepared for you."

There was a book written in 1896 called *In His Steps* by Charles Sheldon. The novel features a pastor that challenged his congregation for one whole year not to do anything before they asked the question, "What would Jesus do?" It changes their lives.

This verse is not only a challenge for us today to follow in His steps, the steps of Jesus, but really it is God's command to believers to do what is good without counting the cost.

We will walk through seasons in our lives when we are called to do difficult things. We walk through the valley of the shadow of death. We will walk the narrow road, the lonely road but Christ will always be our companion. And at times, we will see only one set of footprints as Jesus carries us.

Christmas is one month from today. My challenge to you, and to myself, is that in these days before Christmas that we would follow in His steps and do the good Jesus calls us to do. It might be as simple as listening to a friend talk or holding someone's hand. It may involve fixing something that's broken or making a meal for a friend who is ill. Know that in all that we do, it is to honor God, not for our own glory.

Thank you for the sacrifices you have made as you have walked this path with us. You have been Jesus' hands and feet. We are grateful. #Godisfaithful #pray4bill

Day #321 November 26

Anchor Verse: 1 Peter 3:15
But in your hearts revere Christ as Lord. Always be prepared to give an answer to everyone who asks you to give the reason for the hope that you have. But do this with gentleness and respect. (NIV)

Jesus offers us hope that will never fail. It is that hope that burns in our hearts and helps us make it through the difficult days. The days when your eyes are red from crying, your mind is filled with all the "what ifs" of life, and you're exhausted because you can't sleep because of the anxiety that is flowing through your veins.

As believers, we can run to God at anytime, anywhere, and His fountain of life will never run dry. When our hearts are full of love and respect for the Lord, we cannot be moved from the faith we hold dear.

When that hope is secure, others will see the difference. They will wonder how you can walk through the fires of life and not be overcome by them. Our hope is in Christ alone.

Through Bill's health journey, hope has been our anchor through the most challenging days and sleepless nights. It is the confidence we have in the Lord that has helped us navigate this bumpy road. We have been upfront about where our hope comes from and the fact that Bill is alive is because of God and the miracles we have seen Him perform.

Bill's life is a living testimony about what God can do. We have been blessed to be surrounded by great medical professionals on this journey. But our hope does not rest in the hands of men but in the hands of God. We know that God will carry us through.

What about you? Do you have that hope today? Do you know that Jesus will walk with you through the greatest challenges you will face in this life? He will. You just have to ask and He will hold your hand and speak peace to your soul.

Thank you for your prayers. Thank you for your kindness. We are blessed by the hope we share with you. #Godisfaithful #pray4bill

Day #322 November 27

Anchor Verse: Colossians 3:15

Let the peace of Christ [the inner calm of one who walks daily with Him] be the controlling factor in your hearts [deciding and settling questions that arise]. To this peace indeed you were called as members in one body [of believers]. And be thankful [to God always]. (AMP)

Peace and thankfulness are great companions on our life journey. Now that we've passed Thanksgiving, we've turned the corner and we're looking at Christmas, it's easy to get caught up in the flurry of shopping and baking and Christmas cards, etc.

Through it all, we are called to be at peace. Often our peace comes when we say "no" to the activities that get us all wound up. The first part of Colossians 3:15 says, "Let the peace of Christ [the inner calm of one who walks daily with Him]..." Isn't that beautiful?

That inner calm will come only as we walk daily with Christ. It's when we run ahead of Him or lag behind that we are robbed of our peace. Nothing in this world is worth exchanging God's peace for it because it will only pass away.

We still have a few days to go in the month of November, the month of thanksgiving. I encourage you to find that place of peace in these final days and hours. Find a quiet place and go and sit with your heavenly Father. God wants to hear your voice and longs for you to hear His voice.

Lift your voice in praise and your hands in thanksgiving. I was reading in a devotional this morning this phrase, "A life of praise and thankfulness becomes a life filled with miracles." That's the place I want to walk. That's the place where truly I have seen the miracles of God happen.

Thank you for your faithfulness. Thank you for rejoicing with us in God's miracles, it makes the victory even sweeter. #Godisfaithful #pray4bill

Day #323 November 28

Anchor Verse: 1 Peter 5:9

But resist him [the devil], be firm in your faith [against his attack—rooted, established, immovable], knowing that the same experiences of suffering are being experienced by your brothers and sisters throughout the world. [You do not suffer alone.] (AMP)

One of the enemy's most powerful weapons is to make us believe that we face the battles of life alone. When you are alone, it's easier to get picked off and knocked off track. It's easier to believe the lies that you don't have anything to offer and your life doesn't matter. They are all lies!!

The truth is that the Lord will fight for you. The Bible is filled with the truth that we do not face life alone and that your brothers and sisters around the world are experiencing the same kind of suffering that you are.

There are others that do not speak the same language as you do nor do they look like you, yet they have the same heartaches. They have family members that are in the hospital and are fighting cancer or heart disease. There are mothers and fathers who live on the ocean shore, in the desert, or on the mountaintop that have prodigal children and are experiencing hunger and financial distress.

We are all one. We experience the same challenges but we also have the same victory in the Lord. Today celebrate the joy that comes with being a member of the body of believers. Know with certainty that our God reigns. In the twinkling of an eye, your circumstances can change.

Hold on to God's hand and never let go. Stand firm in your faith against the attack of the enemy... be rooted, established, and unmovable! Face the challenges of each day with the full armor of God in place (Ephesians 6:10-18) and you will be victorious in Jesus' name.

On this health journey, I have learned the power of prayer and standing firm on the promises of God. His truth remains the same. Hold fast to the anchor we have in Christ and you can weather the storms of life.

Thank you for your continued prayers. Daily, we continue to see the miracles of God in Bill's life. #Godisfaithful #pray4bill

Day #324 November 29

Anchor Verse: 2 Peter 1:2
May grace and peace be yours in abundance through the knowledge of God and of Jesus our Lord. (NIV)

This is my prayer for you this morning... that grace and peace would be yours in ABUNDANCE through the knowledge of God and of Jesus our Lord.

Not just a little bit of grace and peace, not just a thimble full of it, but oceans filled with grace and peace that would quench any lack in your life.

It is when we run to the Lord and seek His face and spend time in His presence that God opens the floodgates of heaven in our soul. It is only there that we will know this measure of grace and peace because in our humanity we cannot earn it; we don't even really know how to seek it.

Because we are spiritual beings, created in the image of God, our heart's desire is to know Him more, to know the One who created us, who sustains us, who provides for us. We yearn to see the miracles that He has planned for us. Deep within us, we want to walk where God has plans for us because it is only there that we will find true happiness and peace.

On the days when we are fussy like a little child, I would venture to say that we have gone off track and are walking in the light of our own understanding. It is there that the enemy comes to sink our boat and destroy our confidence.

This morning grace and peace can be yours in abundance. It will light your way. It will fill your heart with peace instead of worry. And you will extend God's grace to others you meet along the way.

My prayer today is that others would find me faithful in my Christian walk long after I have departed this earth for heaven's gates.

Thank you for your faithfulness as you have walked with us. We are blessed to have you in our lives. #Godisfaithful #pray4bill

Day #325 November 30

Anchor Verse: 1 Samuel 30:6
But David found strength in the Lord his God. [but the Lord his God gave him
courage]. (NIV)

As this month comes to a close, this month of thanksgiving, I am reminded
that our strength is found in the Lord. It is the Lord that gives us courage
to face whatever giants are before us. It is that hope, courage, and strength
that allows us to survey the battlefield that lies behind us and see the
enemies that have been slain – doubt, fear, blame, shame, pity, inadequacy,
and in some cases, even death itself.

My friends, on this last day of November, we are victorious in Jesus' name.
No matter what your earthly circumstances look like today, know that God
is with you. Don't panic! He has a plan. And His plans often unfold one
footstep at a time. There are moments when things go into hyper-speed
but often it is our daily walk that determines our destination.

Many of you have faced difficult things this month, a difficult diagnosis of
cancer, the death of a loved one, unemployment, still waiting for the
healing that is long in coming, or financial struggles that you can't seem to
conquer.

Hold on to hope. Hold on to His hand. Your heavenly Father will never let
you go. And in that moment when you think the battle is over, the tide
turns and there is victory in Jesus' name.

This month has been like a roller coaster – the therapists are coming! Then
the therapists are leaving in two weeks. Greater clarity in Bill's mind. Signs
that his physical body is getting stronger... one step at a time. Yes, there are
still mountains to conquer but daily in the "little things" we have victory.

As we face this last month of 2018, we do so with hope. God has given us
courage to face the days ahead – days of healing, days of dodging cold
weather, and days to evade any winter illness.

Thank you for standing with us. Thank you for your continued prayers.
The battle belongs to the Lord. #Godisfaithful #pray4bill

December 2018
The Greatest Gift of All

Day #326 December 1

Anchor Verse: 2 Peter 3:8
But don't forget this, dear friends, that a day or a thousand years from now is like tomorrow to the Lord. (TLB)

The first day of a new month, the last month of 2018 – another year that has flown by so quickly. We try and harness our time with clocks, phones, alarms, and calendars. Yet we never truly can capture time. One slight change, one bump, one unforeseen illness, and all our plans are altered.

On God's timetable – God sees the whole picture – the picture of eternity. We see this brief moment of our lives. We want to achieve goals rapidly and check them off our "list", while God wants us to enjoy the journey.

Some of the greatest treasures of our lives cannot be squeezed into slots on our calendar or minutes on the clock. Think about time spent with a loved one or a beautiful sunrise/sunset or enjoying a good meal with a friend or family member. These are moments we want to experience fully and we don't want them to end. Too quickly the time passes.

How do we reconcile this time issue? The reference made here about God's view of time, comes from Psalm 90:4: "A thousand years in your sight are like a day that has just gone by, or like a watch in the night."

Time spent in the Lord's presence is one of those great treasures. God stretches time there. In His presence, we experience the fullness of His joy. When I am writing, through the inspiration of God and the direction of the Holy Spirit, it is a sacred place where time does not exist. It's a sweet treat that feeds my soul.

In this month of December, I invite you to spend time with God. Spend time in God's Word, the Bible. Spend time in silence so that you may taste and see that the Lord is good.

God loves you with an everlasting love and His desire is to know you more. Step into God's timetable, even if only for a few moments this Christmas season. May you experience His peace and grace and joy.

Thank you for your prayers every month this year. They have changed the course of our lives. Be blessed. #Godisfaithful #pray4bill

Day #327 December 2

Anchor Verse: 1 John 1:5
This is the message which we have heard from Him and declare to you, that God is light and in Him is no darkness at all. (NIV)

We were born into a world of darkness and light. When God brought order into the world, He created day and night, a time of light and a time of darkness.

Before electricity was discovered, people would get up when the sun came up and go to bed when the sun went down. Today many people have strayed far from that simple lifestyle.

This verse goes beyond the contrast of day and night, it speaks to life itself. God is pure and holy, full of light, hope, joy, and peace in contrast to the world which is imperfect and filled with the consequences of sin. Every day we get to choose whether we walk in the light or in the darkness.

In the presence of God, our doubts, fears, and shame all disappear. We are filled with the light of His love. We reflect the heart of God and desire to follow Him.

In this world, we will never 100% of the time reflect light as God reflects light, that is a pleasure saved for eternity.

Every time you make a good choice and reach out a helping hand to another, a little more light enters your life and your soul.

Jesus called us to be the light of the world, to be a lighthouse to those who have lost their way. Step into the light today. Spend time with Him as you get to know Him more. Then your light will shine brighter against the darkness of the world.

Be the hands and feet of Jesus this Christmas season and see how many lives you can impact with the light of His love. It's not just about the gifts you purchase, but the gifts of love given from your heart.

Thank you for the gift you have been to us this year. We are grateful. #Godisfaithful #pray4bill

Day #328 December 3

Anchor Verse: 1 John 2:5-6
But if anyone obeys his word, love for God is truly made complete in them. This is how we know we are in him: Whoever claims to live in him must live as Jesus did. (NIV)

We have heard the expression in our lifetime, to walk the walk and talk the talk, but do you walk the talk? Do we just talk about doing the right thing or do we actually do it, and live it?

It's easy to speak the words but are you willing to put your commitment to the test and do what Jesus would do and walk where Jesus would walk?

We know that Jesus' life wasn't smooth and easy, He ran into many bumps in the road. There were many times when Jesus spoke the truth and others were offended. Even when He healed others, Jesus was questioned about the miracle He performed. Jesus loved all people – from the outcasts of society to the religious leaders who hated Him... Jesus' love was without boundaries. Jesus loved the saint and the sinner.

How then shall we live? Jesus has given us an example that we should walk in His steps. It is only when we walk in obedience that "love for God is truly made complete" in us.

During this Advent season leading up to Christmas, when Jesus gave us the greatest gift of all, I challenge you to love as Jesus loved. I challenge you to love those you may disagree with and to love those who may have hurt you. It's a season to mend fences and it's a season to break the wall down that you have built to keep out God's love.

Every day I am blessed to know that God loves me and I see how much God loves Bill, as He has given us a second chance at life. Whatever your circumstances, God's love transcends them. He is a miracle-working God. As you are waiting for your miracle, He will love you, hold you, and comfort you.

Thank you for your prayers – day and night. We are blessed by your willingness to pray. You are loved! #Godisfaithful #pray4bill

Day #329 December 4

⚓ *Anchor Verse: Psalm 115:1*

God, glorify your name! Yes, your name alone be glorified, not ours. For you are the one who loves us passionately, and you are faithful and true. (TPT)

The world was created to reflect the glory of God and for our lives to bring honor and glory to His name. On the night that Jesus was born, the heavenly host filled the skies praising God and proclaiming, "Glory to God in the highest and on earth peace and goodwill to all men."

That should be our heart's cry today that in our own lives God would be honored and glorified. It's not for own glory and honor, but for His glory we should strive to live each day.

How do we do that? We do our best in everything God sends us to do. That includes loving each other, taking care of our families, doing the work of God's Kingdom, and spreading the good news of Jesus. God is glorified when His light and love are reflected in our lives.

It is not our finest hour when we encourage the world to "see what I have done". The "life is all about me" mentality is not very attractive.

God is faithful and true. We are alive to sing praises to His name because He is good and He loves us passionately. God wants you to excel and receive His best for you. He is your heavenly Father and God loves you so very much!

This Christmas season, how can you reflect His love? How can you praise God and with the heavenly host walk in His love and honor and glorify His holy name?

There are numerous opportunities available to you today to be God's hands and feet.

Thank you for the ways you have helped us walk through Bill's healing journey so God could be honored and glorified in our lives. It is by His love and grace that we celebrate Bill's life and progress today. God alone is worthy of our praise! #Godisfaithful #pray4bill

Day #330 December 5

Anchor Verse: Genesis 28:16
Surely the Lord is in this place... (NIV)

What a powerful declaration to see that God is everywhere! When we find ourselves in unfamiliar surroundings, places that could fill us with fear – like a hospital or a cancer center or an ICU unit or the bedside of a loved one who is in pain, choose to see God in that place too.

He is never absent. God is ALWAYS with us. His Spirit hovers over us to bring us comfort. Sometimes all we need is to see our circumstances from a different perspective – a heavenly view.

It may not change the reality of what we face but we do not face it alone. God is with us. He is infinitely creative in the way He brings deliverance and healing. What seems like a dead end to us is the beginning of the new life God has planned for us.

You or your loved one may be facing a mountain of illness today. In the flesh, it may not look good, but in the spirit, God has plans for you!

This year I have learned to praise Him in the storm. To take my eyes off the circumstances and look to my heavenly Father. As I laid my requests and my fears before Him, they were bathed in my tears. I have found Him faithful. I can trust God even when my eyes can't see the outcome.

May we declare everywhere we go today – work, grocery store, sports event, hospitals, chemo centers, our homes, our churches, even government buildings, "Surely the Lord is in this place!" It's an invitation for God to enter in and show us His glory.

Let's transform the world today! Let's transform our perspective and experience His miracles!

Thank you for standing with us on those difficult days and praying. And celebrating with us on the days we stand on the mountaintop of accomplishment! He is worthy of our praise. #Godisfaithful #pray4bill

Day #331 December 6

⚓ *Anchor Verse: Daniel 3:17, 27*

If we are thrown into the blazing furnace, the God we serve is able to deliver us from it...and there was no smell of fire on them. (NIV)

The refining fires of our lives are not meant to destroy us but to get rid of the impurities in our lives, our heart and soul, to make us more like Jesus. The good news: Jesus walks through the fire with you. You are never alone as you walk on this path of adversity.

Even in those moments when the heat is the hottest and it's hard to take a deep breath, know that the Lord is your breath of life. There is a purpose. There is a plan. There is a reward.

This passage in Daniel was speaking of an actual fire that Shadrach, Meshach, and Abednego endured and God preserved them. So too, He will save you as you navigate the trials of your life.

Are you being tested today? Are you being called upon to stand up for your belief in God? Is this a place where you will walk in integrity and not stumble on the slippery slope of the praises of men?

Is God calling you to a new place even as the last days of 2018 are upon us? Be strong in the power of His might. Walk forward in confidence that your best days are still ahead of you.

Bill and I have been blessed to see the hand of God at work throughout the course of Bill's healing journey. We have walked through the fire again and again and every time God has delivered us. Hallelujah!

Thank you for your faithfulness and your trust in God as you have stood with us and prayed. Your heavenly Father will reward your faithfulness. #Godisfaithful #pray4bill

Day #332 December 7

Anchor Verse: Daniel 6:16
The king said to Daniel, 'May your God, whom you continually [faithfully] serve, deliver you!' (NIV)

When we go through the most difficult times of lives, our encouragers and advocates will come from the most unlikely places.

This scripture passage is spoken by King Darius who had been "tricked" into issuing a decree that everyone in the land must bow down and worship the king. The king thought it was a good idea and played right into the hands of those who opposed Daniel. Daniel was not deterred from serving God even though he knew the consequences of his actions would result in a trip to the lion's den – certain death.

Daniel, in obedience to God, got down on his knees and prayed to God three times a day in front of an open window. The king tried to figure out a way to rescue him from the punishment. There was no way... except that God would deliver Daniel.

Daniel was thrown into the lion's den. The king stayed up all night awaiting the outcome. I wonder if King Darius prayed that night for God's protection over Daniel... we don't know.

At the first light of dawn, King Darius hurried to the lion's den, "Daniel, servant of the living God, has your God, whom you serve continually, been able to rescue you from the lions?" Daniel responded that the angel of the Lord had shut the mouths of the lions and he was unharmed.

Why did I share this story? 1. Your daily obedience to God is crucial. If you walk in obedience, God will honor you. 2. Your behavior is on display for believers and unbelievers. Daniel was living in a foreign land, serving in a government position where the Lord has placed him to be God's ambassador. God gave him abilities that made him stand out and he was promoted to the third highest position in the land. Why? Because God had plans for Daniel.

Thank you for your faithfulness in prayer. It has been the greatest gift you could give us. #Godisfaithful #pray4bill

Day #333 December 8

Anchor Verse: 2 John 6
And this is love: that we walk in obedience to his commands. As you have heard from the beginning, his command is that you walk in love. (NIV)

Love - we hear a lot about it. Millions and billions of dollars are spent each year in the name of love or creating products that are signs of our love. Yet, when God talks about love in the Bible, there is no dollar figure attached to it. It's not purchased for $1.98 nor does it have a $1 million price tag. Love is about obedience and that is shown through our actions – how we love God and one another.

During this Christmas season, there are many opportunities to walk in love. Giving the gift of your time is one of the greatest gifts you can offer another. Spontaneously showing your love is a surprise gift that a friend or family member will never forget.

In this verse in 2 John, our love starts with obedience to God's commands. It is only out of obedience that we can live a life of love. If the root of your actions is sin and selfishness then the result of your actions will be self-serving. God's love at work in us is never self-serving. It's about reflecting God's love.

Are you willing – willing to walk in God's love? Then I have a challenge for you.

My challenge to you today (and for me) is that we walk in that love today. Take the time to show our love to just one person today. Taking time for coffee or cooking a meal, maybe a phone call or reaching out to visit someone. You know the person that's been on your heart. It's time to reach out to them today.

What a blessing it has been to both of us this year as you have walked in obedience to God and loved us so well. We will be forever grateful. Thank you for your continued prayers. #Godisfaithful #pray4bill

Day #334 December 9

Anchor Verse: John 12:26
If anyone serves Me, he must [continue to faithfully] follow Me [without hesitation, holding steadfastly to Me, conforming to My example in living and, if need be, suffering or perhaps dying because of faith in Me]; and wherever I am [in heaven's glory], there will My servant be also. If anyone serves Me, the Father will honor him. If anyone serves Me, he must [continue to faithfully] follow Me [without hesitation, holding steadfastly to Me, conforming to My example in living and, if need be, suffering or perhaps dying because of faith in Me]; and wherever I am [in heaven's glory], there will My servant be also. If anyone serves Me, the Father will honor him. (AMP)

"Be willing to go out on a limb with Me." That was the first line of my devotional reading today. God will never lead you to a place that He cannot save and protect you. There will be times when following God might lead you to some unusual places, places where we would not choose to go on our own.

However, God in His wisdom, mercy, and grace knows the places we need to walk so that He can help us become the men and women of God that we were created to be. It may be out on a limb or in a deep valley or on a mountain top, but God's ways are not our ways, God's thoughts are higher than our thoughts.

We are called into His service. We are called to stand up and be a lighthouse for the lost. We are called to reflect His love. We are called to extend a helping hand. We are called to be ready at a moment's notice to respond to His voice and answer His call.

God honors our obedience. He will reward those who serve Him. The fullness of His joy is greater than any gift you can imagine. Today, please rest in His arms of love. Today, ready yourself for the journey He has planned for you – for it is good. Be the spark that lights the way for others.

Thank you for your faithfulness. Your prayers continue to move mountains. We continue to stand and believe for Bill's complete healing in Jesus' name! #Godisfaithful #pray4bill

Day #335 December 10

Anchor Verse: 1 Corinthians 13:5
Love does not demand its own way. (TLB)

The gift of love is a beautiful gift. It originates from God's heart and He gives us an example of how we should love. In 1 Corinthians 13, the "Love" chapter, there are specific attributes that are highlighted.

The one that jumped out at me this morning was that love is not selfish. The Message version states it this way, "isn't always 'me first'."

This world is filled with people who live in one camp or the other. When I think of those who do live like the world revolves around them, where "me" and not "we" is the sole pronoun in their vocabulary, it makes me sad for them. Truly it is a barren life when the world is all about you.

When I think about the opposite of that, where we focus on loving others and our world is enriched as we love, I find a life filled with joy.

On this journey to Bill's healing, we have been blessed to have our lives touched by so many that are not selfish – from prayer warriors to those in the medical field. Our lives are richer because we have been touched by their loving hands and prayers.

Today is a special day for us. Twenty-five years ago, Bill declared his love for me when I was coordinating a luncheon and he presented me with a dozen red roses and an orchid corsage. It took my breath away. We hadn't even been out on a date yet! Bill's love was shown through his actions.

Our daily challenge is to put God's love in action. We should love as Jesus loves and not be so caught up in the cares of our own lives that we fail to reach out a hand to another or lift up a friend in prayer.

Thank you for the many ways you have reached out to us this year. #Godisfaithful #pray4bill

Day #336 December 11

Anchor Verse: Revelation 2:3
I also know how you have bravely endured trials and persecutions because of my name, yet you have not become discouraged. (TPT)

The Lord is always near. God walks with you through your deepest valleys. He knows what you have endured in your life because you have chosen to follow Him. God rewards those who diligently seek Him.

This verse in Revelation reminds us that when we go through trials and persecutions we should do it without becoming discouraged. It is not enough to just endure, but we must be encouraged! Do you understand what I mean?

It is not only our actions but our attitude. You may be going through the motions and doing the work, but if your disposition is sour and your heart is filled with bitterness, what have you gained? What joy have you left behind in your wake? It's not going to make you the poster child for what it looks like to have a positive attitude. Likely people won't be choosing you to be their role model. As the chapter continues, it speaks of them (the church) losing their first love, their love for Him.

My prayer for you this morning is that as you endure trials and tribulations because you are following God, you would not lose your love for Him. You would not grow bitter, resentful, frustrated, even angry, at the path you are called to walk. May your testimony be that you finished the race triumphantly, with love in your heart and words of praise on your lips.

Ladies and gentlemen, we are MORE THAN conquerors through Him who loves us so. Walk in that hope today. Be empowered by Jesus' victory over death and the grave.

May the power of our testimony be that Jesus saves and He delivered us from the storms of our lives. Thank you for your faithfulness. The Lord will reward you. #Godisfaithful #pray4bill

Day #337 December 12

Anchor Verse: 2 Corinthians 5:7
For we walk [live] by faith, not by sight. (NKJV)

Faith – it's what makes life worth living. It's our guiding light. It gives us hope when our eyes can only see the challenges and difficulties in our path.

Our eyesight is very limited, even if you have 20/20 vision. If you only see the world as "flat", not three-dimensional, plus the spiritual dimension God created, how much you are missing.

Walking with the Lord and seeing the beauty of creation through His eyes is like a National Geographic movie super-sized!

As a believer, we not only have the mind of Christ, but we have "new" eyes to see. As we live and walk by faith, God shows us things that others cannot see. We can see the look of pain on your face and ask what's wrong and if we can help carry your burden. The joy in another's heart is seen on their face and it encourages our soul. Life is so much richer when we live by faith, not just by what we see.

Most of all, I believe we can walk through those deep valleys when we walk by faith, because we know we don't walk alone. We have no doubt that Jesus is holding our hand and sometimes He carries us through our most desperate circumstances.

It is our walk of faith that allows us to see hope on the horizon and know that we will walk out of these difficult circumstances into the bright future God has planned for us.

As we approach Christmas and the end of the year, our eyes are set on the things to come as we rejoice in God's gift of love. We are so grateful for the many miracles we have seen in 2018. There are more to come.

Thank you so much for your prayers that have carried us through the difficult nights and encouraged us on our days of victory. May the Lord bless you and keep you safe this day. #Godisfaithful #pray4bill

Day #338 December 13

Anchor Verse: 2 Timothy 1:9
It is he [God] who saved us and chose us for his holy work, not because we deserved it but because that was his plan long before the world began—to show his love and kindness to us through Christ. (TLB)

We are called to be holy. The word "holy" doesn't mean goody-goody, it means set apart for sacred use.

Once we understand God's plan and purpose for us, we will choose to walk with Him in the light of His presence rather than fumbling around in the darkness of sin.

Walking in the light of His love and letting God's love be an extension of our lives. When others see you walking down the street, the radiance of His love is seen on your face. People wonder what's different about you – different in a good way and they are drawn to the light of His love. Have you had that experience? I have.

When people do a double-take as you pass by, it's not because you are so handsome or beautiful, but they caught a glimpse of Jesus in you.

Holiness is clean living because we are God's ambassadors here on earth. It's following in Christ's steps and loving those who can offer us nothing in return. To pray for one another and encourage each other even when you may be carrying your own burdens.

As I was reading this passage in Revelation 4:8 describing the scene around God's throne in heaven and the words, "Holy, Holy, Holy, is the Lord God Almighty, who was and is and is to come."... God whispered to me of my own call to holiness.

"Be holy as I am holy" – these are the words of Christ to us. It reminds me of an old hymn we used to sing in church, "Take Time to Be Holy."

May the Lord bless you and keep you. You are safe in the hollow of His hands. Receive God's blessings in Jesus' name. #Godisfaithful #pray4bill

Day #339 December 14

Anchor Verse: Psalm 91:2
I will say of the Lord, "He is my refuge and my fortress, my God, in whom I trust." (NIV)

It's a Psalm 91 kind of day. Daily we live in a world where the forces of good and evil battle against each other. Sometimes the disasters happen in the world around us but we are at peace.

Other days, it is in our own lives that the battle is raging – physically, mentally, emotionally, or spiritually. It is on those days that the promises of God are the rungs of the ladder we hold on to as we ascend into the presence of our heavenly Father.

This declaration from Psalm 91:2 is our declaration: "He is my refuge (my place of safety) and my fortress (my stronghold), my God, in whom I trust."

The enemy wants to fill you with doubt and fear. All it takes is one little crack in our armor and the rushing waters of doubt and fear flood the solid ground of our lives.

Stuff those cracks of doubt with the promises of God. Ask others to cover you in prayer. Get down on your knees, whether physically or in your heart, and ask God to help you. The joy of the Lord will be your strength. Hold on to hope and don't let anything pry it from your hands.

Maybe you are on the battlefield this morning and the storm is raging around you, praise the Lord. Know that the battle belongs to the Lord and He will fight for you. God will never leave you or forsake you, never!

As we enter this new season of our lives, looking forward to the plans that God has for us, please continue to cover us with your prayers. The enemy is not happy about Bill's progress and our plans for the future, but we are victorious in Jesus' name. We will not be moved. We will not retreat. We are more than conquerors in Jesus' name. #Godisfaithful #pray4bill

Day #340 December 15

Anchor Verse: Luke 1:37
Not one promise from God is empty of power, for nothing is impossible with God. (TPT)

God's promises are tucked in like little gems throughout the Bible. There are seeds of hope scattered through some of the most difficult circumstances. God knows that when you are going through deep valleys or hear unexpected news you will need the rope of hope to hold on to when you feel like letting go. God is your anchor in the storm.

With Christmas only 10 days away, the Lord turned my head and heart away from my daily battles to the chapter of Luke and the circumstances surrounding Christ's birth.

In this passage in Luke 1, the angel of the Lord has just appeared to Mary and told her that she would give birth to the son of God. The angel tells her of another miracle that is in the process of happening, "Even Elizabeth your relative is going to have a child in her old age, and she who was said to be unable to conceive is in her sixth month." (A miracle indeed!)

And then this gem is slipped in, "No word from God will ever fail." or in the translation above, "Not one promise from God is empty of power, for nothing is impossible with God." WOW!

This promise is something to hold on to when the storms of life are about to sink your boat. This truth keeps you company on the sleepless nights when you are laying there in pain or worried what the tests will show and what the future holds for you and your family.

Jesus is the hope of the world. He is your hope on the darkest nights and during the days when wave after wave of adversity hit you.

The promises of God have been the truth I held on to when the enemy was whispering words of doubt and fear. I boldly proclaimed the words of truth, the promises of God out loud so that I could hear them.

Thank you for your faithfulness in prayer. He is the God of miracles. #Godisfaithful #pray4bill

Day #341 December 16

🜨 *Anchor Verse: Luke 1:38*
Mary said, "I am the Lord's servant, and I am willing to do whatever he wants. May everything you said come true." And then the angel disappeared. (TLB)

Mary was born an ordinary girl, just like you and me. But God had an extraordinary task for her; she would give birth to Jesus, the son of God.

An angel came to Mary to give her the news of what was to take place and how it would happen. Even as I read this passage, it's hard to comprehend what must have been going through her mind. Yet, she said "yes" to God, wholeheartedly, "I am willing to do whatever He wants, May your word to me be fulfilled."

It's not like Mary had time to think about "the offer" for a week or two or talk to someone to counsel her. In those moments as the angel was speaking to her revealing God's plan for her life, Mary surrendered her heart, her will, and her body completely to the Lord.

Are you willing to do the same for Him today? Each of us has a call on our lives. Each of us has been given gifts and talents. We were uniquely designed by our heavenly Father before we were born. There are qualities that are still untapped in our hearts and minds, dreams that God still wants to make come true.

Just like Mary, we need to say "yes" to God. We need to be willing to lay down our agenda and willingly walk with God on the path He has for us. There may be joy and sorrow, suffering and victory, but through it all He will be honored and glorified. It will be for our best and His glory.

We can never be completely ready for that moment when God says, "It's time. I'm ready to use you." but daily we prepare for that day as we spend time with Him, reading the Bible, praying, and listening. Are you ready to do whatever He wants? I pray that your answer is "yes."

We walk in victory because God holds today and tomorrow in His hands. Be blessed. #Godisfaithful #pray4bill

Day #342 December 17

Anchor Verse: Proverbs 8:34
If you wait at wisdom's doorway, longing to hear a word for every day, joy will break forth within you as you listen for what I'll say. (TPT)

Oh the blessing and wisdom that comes from listening to God and seeking His face every day – in everything. The blessings come not only when we seek God about the big decisions, the big roadblocks in our lives but the so-called "little things."

God desires the best for you in ALL things. He loves you more than you can imagine. Just as you want the best for those you love, God's desire to provide for you and protect you is even greater.

The part of the verse that caught my attention in the VOICE translation it says, "and delays action until my way is apparent." We often get caught up in the momentum of the moment, the pressure of the world and we think we have to "hurry up" and do something. It is often in our hurry that we get in trouble.

Be willing to wait on the Lord. Be willing to delay action until the path is clear. Think about the men who walked around Jericho for six days as God directed, and then on the 7th day was the day of victory according to God's command. For soldiers, this was not the way they were trained to fight and win. But it was God's way.

As the last two weeks of the year are before us, lay your requests before the Lord. Review the prayers you have prayed and are still waiting for answers. Seek His face. Wait until His pathway is made apparent and when it is, Go for it!

We are grateful for God's leading in our lives in 2018 and for the plans He has for us in the days ahead. We continue to wait on God for Bill's complete healing and trust God to do what He promised. Thank you for praying. It has changed the course of our lives and encouraged us in so many ways. #Godisfaithful #pray4bill

Day #343 December 18

Anchor Verse: Isaiah 30:20
Though the Lord gives you the bread of adversity and the water of oppression, yet your Teacher will no longer hide Himself, but your eyes will [constantly] see your Teacher. (AMP)

There are times in our lives when we walk through deep valleys; the Lord allows it to be so. It is not a punishment. It is an opportunity to go to a deeper level with our heavenly Father.

God desires an intimate relationship with us. His heart's desire is that we would know His heart and walk and talk with Him. Just like a good earthly father, God wants you to run to Him in your joy and in your sorrow.

Isaiah talks about the "bread of adversity and the water of oppression." For many of you, this is your diet right now. All you can do is cling to God because He is the source of your strength.

From my own experience this year on Bill's health journey, I learned that through those darkest hours, God's love and faithfulness shine even brighter. It is God's face that we see. It is His voice that we hear in the silence of our sleepless nights. It is His strength that helps us to stand as the wind and rain come against us.

Once you have emerged from the valley, just like the gold that comes out of the refining fire, your life will reflect God's love, your face will shine with His radiance. And you will never be the same... hallelujah!

Today I stand with you as you face that tempest in your life. I lift your name to heaven's throne room and ask that God would touch you, heal you, and reveal Himself to you in a more powerful way. Your labor is not in vain. Hold on to hope. Holding on to God's hand is not reckless or foolish. It is your best choice. God will lead you and never forsake you.

Thank you for standing with us through our days and nights of adversity. The battle is not over, but the war is already won in Jesus' name. #Godisfaithful #pray4bill

Day #344 December 19

Anchor Verse: Matthew 6:33
But first ana most importantly seek (aim at, strive after) His kingdom and His righteousness [His way of doing and being right—the attitude and character of God], and all these things will be given to you also. (AMP)

Are you consumed by your list of things to get done before Christmas arrives? Are you so caught up in the whirlwind of the season that you have forgotten what Christmas is really all about?

It is so easy to be consumed by the "little things" in our lives that we put God on the shelf. Isn't our greatest joy in life to bring honor and glory to Him why we are alive?

If we want to be in alignment with God and His ways, Jesus reminds us that we must "seek first God's Kingdom and what God wants us to do." Seek first... what's first on your list when you wake up in the morning? Is it spending time with the Creator of the universe, your heavenly Father who gave you the gift of another day of life?

On this journey through Bill's health challenges, God has reinforced again and again, our need to run to Him first. Our hope is in Him. Our help comes from Him. Most of all, God is worthy of our praise. He is the author of miracles; we have seen that again and again.

Matthew 6:33 reminds us that when we put God first, He will meet our needs... not necessarily our wants, although in His kindness sometimes those are fulfilled too.

It reminds me of the words of the apostle Paul, "I have learned to be content whatever my circumstances." We have learned obedience brings life and God has supplied our needs for a simple life that honors Him.

Is God on the throne of your heart? Are you giving Him the honor and glory due His name? May our lives reflect His love and His glory as we bow our hearts before Him and give thanks for all He has done.

Thank you for your faithfulness and your prayers. The Lord is good and His love endures forever. #Godisfaithful #pray4bill

Day #345 December 20

Anchor Verse: Proverbs 18:21
Death and life are in the power of the tongue, And those who love it ana indulge it will eat its fruit ana bear the consequences of their words.]. (AMP)

The power of our words – wow! We all have been both the "speaker" and the "receiver" when words were spoken that brought life and when words were spoken that brought harm.

The little verse we used to "sing" when we were children, "Sticks and stones may break my bones but words will never hurt me" really isn't true. Even as you read this, there may be circumstances that pop up in your mind where words wounded you. My prayer is that they have been replaced by the places where words brought life and empowered you.

Every day, every moment of every day, we get to choose the words we speak and the ones we respond to, the ones we take in. Choose wisely, it will impact your thought life and often the course of your day.

On Bill's healing journey, I have observed firsthand the power of words at work. When Bill wasn't able to communicate with us and was heavily sedated, I made sure that the words that were spoken to him and over him were words of life. I prayed over him. I quoted the Bible, God's promises. I sang hymns of praise. I called him by name and spoke truth to him when words of "death" were spoken within hearing distance.

Words are the seeds that are planted in our heart and soul, and in due time, there will be a harvest. Choose carefully what you "hear" and take in. Choose carefully the words that you speak to yourself. The power of life and death are in your tongue, and everyone else's mouth on the face of the planet.

During this Christmas season, let's bring life with our words – words of peace and goodwill to all men.

Thank you for your encouraging words and your words spoken in prayer for us. #Godisfaithful #pray4bill

Day #346 December 21

Anchor Verse: John 11:40
"But didn't I tell you that you will see a wonderful miracle from God if you believe?" Jesus asked her. (TLB)

This verse has so much more meaning to me than it did a year ago. This year on Bill's health journey truly we have seen the glory of the Lord fill Bill's hospital rooms and fill our home. Actually, wherever Bill goes the glory of the Lord radiates from him because Bill is a miracle. The touch of God's hand on his life is visible.

In my devotional book this morning, it was talking about God's plan for your life unfolding before you and sometimes the road is blocked, and then suddenly the roadblocks are resolved and you move forward. It's the way that God works in our lives.

"Do not fear your weakness for it is the stage on which My Power and Glory perform most brilliantly.... expect to see miracles - and you will."

I know that in our flesh our goal is not to go through suffering, in fact, we try to avoid it if at all possible. But when it is the path God has called you to walk, the nuggets of blessings abound. You will not only survive the struggle, but you will thrive through it. And yes, you will see miracles.

I don't have the words to describe how incredible this journey has been for us this year. Sure, there have been some hairpin curves. As you know there have been many life and death moments, but that is not where our focus remains. Instead what I remember are the moments when God showed us His glory. Where He turned around what seemed impossible, and not only made it possible, but He was honored and glorified.

Our faith has grown by leaps and bounds, because often, our faith was the only thing we had to hold on to – faith and each other's hand.

Christmas is only a few days away. May your eyes be opened so you stand in awe and wonder as the night sky is lit up with the stars and the moon reflecting the glory of the Lord.

You have been given a front row seat to see the miracles of God in Bill's life. #Godisfaithful #pray4bill

Day #347 December 22

Anchor Verse: Micah 6:8
He has told you, O man, what is good; And what does the LORD require of you
Except to be just, and to love [and to diligently practice] kindness (compassion),
And to walk humbly with your God [setting aside any overblown sense of
importance or self-righteousness]? (AMP)

The Lord has shown you what is good, now are you willing to do it? So often we know the right thing, but are we obedient and walk it out?

You know the dilemma, do I attack that pile of work or laundry or dishes or cleaning the house or do I see what's happening on Facebook or follow some other form of entertainment? Often, it's not what we do; it's what we don't do that gets us in trouble.

You must act with justice, do what is right and fair. We think of a court of law where the judge looks at the law and then judges your actions. Did you do the right thing? God asks us to do the right thing every day in every area of our lives. He wants our obedience, not just lip service.

You must love to show mercy. Do you act like a tyrant or do you act with compassion? None of us is perfect. We all make mistakes. Be quick to forgive and act with grace just as God is gracious and merciful to you.

You must be humble as you live in the sight of your God. One translation says, "…don't take yourself too seriously, take God seriously." The world doesn't revolve around you, and it doesn't revolve around me.

We need to live in a right relationship with God and listen to what He has to say and then walk in obedience. Less of me – more of God.

Please join with me today as we act with justice, love to show mercy, and walk humbly with God. The world will notice. The world will be changed where we walk. God will be pleased.

Thank you for all your prayers. They give us the strength to stand and fight the good fight another day. #Godisfaithful #pray4bill

Day #348 December 23

Anchor Verse: Luke 12:24
Consider the ravens: They do not sow or reap, they have no storeroom or barn; yet God feeds them. And how much more valuable you are than birds! (NIV)

God's provision: libraries would be filled with countless volumes if every person that has ever lived wrote down the times that God provided what they needed, when they needed it.

It is good to have a journal and write down those miraculous provisions so that we can be encouraged on the days when the enemy sows seeds of doubt and fear into our minds and hearts.

The other thing I have learned on this journey, especially this year, is that we need to do all that we can do, and then God will make up the difference.

I was listening to a video training the other day, and the speaker was talking about money and times when an unexpected financial situation caught them off guard. God taught her how to pray for "God ideas" – ways that she could raise the money to pay the bill. When she followed God's path, she had sufficient funds. I was really struck by the power of this method.

We all have been in situations where we had more month than money. Instead of crying out to God that I need "x" amount of dollars, asking God to show you how to pay that bill or meet that need, invite God into the conversation and He will empower you to meet that need.

With just a couple of days left until Christmas, you might be running around still shopping for gifts or feeling guilty that you don't have the finances to give gifts this year. Give the gift of yourself – your time, your talents, your listening ear, your prayers.

Bill and I have the greatest gift we can imagine – his life. The three of us – God, Bill, and me will be spending Christmas together celebrating the gift of life, and Jesus, the greatest gift of all.

Thank you for your faithful prayers. Our prayer for you is that you would recognize how valuable you are in God's eyes. #Godisfaithful #pray4bill

Day #349 December 24

Anchor Verse: Luke 2:14
Glory to God in the highest, and on earth peace, good will toward men. (NKJV)

Praise and worship lit up the sky the night that Jesus was born. God sent an angel to the shepherds to announce His son's birth. The angel gave them directions to find the long-awaited Messiah. Then in the most spectacular birth announcement the world has ever seen, the sky was filled with the heavenly host saying/singing, "Glory to God in the highest and on earth peace, good will toward men."

These were just ordinary men living a solitary life tending their sheep and keeping them from harm and danger. The shepherds were entrusted with these animals who would suffer harm on their own or lose their way, and be hurt or killed by their enemies.

We are just like those sheep. Without God's hand of protection over us and His loving care, we can easily be snatched up by the enemy of our souls.

So easily words of doubt and fear lead us off the path of life into the ditch or the brambles and briers, where we get hurt and lose our way. And there we cry out to God. He lovingly comes to tend to our wounds and speak words of comfort to us, and restores us to the path of life.

This Christmas Eve, I encourage you, I challenge you to look away from the cares of this world, to turn away from your lack, your doubt, your fears, even your pain, and join the heavenly host and sing, "Glory to God in the highest and on earth peace, good will to all men."

It is in the light of His glory that our souls are refreshed. It is in the radiance of His majesty that our hearts are filled with His light and His love. As we enter into that place of awe and wonder, the things of earth grow strangely dim and we see Jesus, the hope of the world, our hope in time of trouble.

May you and your families be blessed on this Christmas Eve! You are loved. #Godisfaithful #pray4bill

Day #350 December 25

Anchor Verse: Isaiah 9:6

For unto us a Child is born, unto us a Son is given: and the government shall be upon His shoulder: and His name shall be called Wonderful, Counsellor, Mighty God, Everlasting Father, Prince of Peace. (NKJV)

Hallelujah! It's Christmas Day! It is the day the hope of the world was born in the form of a tiny baby, Jesus. He was born that we might have a second chance at life, eternal life with Him.

Jesus is the best gift that any of us could receive this Christmas. Everything in life is brighter and filled with hope, love, joy, and peace because He lives.

The magnitude of this gift of love is even more powerful after the health challenges we have walked through with Bill this year. We have felt His grace. We have been bathed in His peace even in the scariest moments on our journey. We have been wrapped in His arms of love as He whispered words of hope in our darkest hours. We have stood in victory over death and illness when He proclaimed that Bill would live and not die.

These are not gifts that we will see today under the Christmas tree but they are gifts that we are given each day – every day is Christmas for us.

When I think about the names of Jesus from this passage in Isaiah 9:6: "Wonderful, Counsellor, Mighty God, Everlasting Father, Prince of Peace" my spirit rises within me with praise and thanksgiving. Truly it is beyond our human comprehension that God would give us such a gift, but with open arms and hands raised to heaven this morning, Lord, we thank you.

As you join with family and friends, or if you are far away from home and among strangers, know that God is with you. Jesus has come that you might have life, abundant life, not just on Christmas Day but every day.

Thank you for your precious gifts throughout this year. May the Christ of Christmas fill your heart with love and peace and joy and hope this day and the days to come. Merry Christmas! Glory to the newborn king! #Godisfaithful #pray4bill

Day #351 December 26

Anchor Verse: Jeremiah 31:3
I have loved you with an everlasting love; I have drawn you with unfailing kindness. (NIV)

As I spent time with the Lord this morning, I thought what is God's message to us the day after Christmas? There are so many "big" events in our lives like weddings, birthdays, etc. and the day after that "big" event, there is a letdown. Some fall into a pit of despair or depression.

Christmas isn't like that! God whispered these words into my spirit this morning, "I have loved you with an everlasting love." Everlasting means that it never ends! God's love for you today is the same as it was yesterday and even as far back as that first Christmas Day. He will love you unconditionally tomorrow and the days and years after that as well.

God loves YOU! He wants the best for you. Your heavenly Father has planted dreams and desires in your heart, and He wants them to come true. If we could absorb just a smidgen of how much God loves us, our lives would be forever changed.

It's not about the fancy packages or big celebrations. It's that God's love is just as present on your sleepless nights, the days your children are sick, as when it's just you and God together during those early morning hours.

My hope and prayer for you today is that you remember that the Christ of Christmas will always love you. He draws you with unfailing kindness. Jesus is the greatest gift of all and His love continues yesterday, today, and forever.

We have been so blessed by God's unconditional love. He is the hope we have held onto during this tumultuous journey. And we love Him more and more every day.

Thank you for your faithfulness. Thank you for the many prayers you have prayed. God has heard them and answered. #Godisfaithful #pray4bill

Day #352 December 27

🫀 *Anchor Verse: Psalm 36:9*
For with You is the fountain of life [the fountain of life-giving water]; In Your light we see light. (AMP)

God is preparing us for our next steps, the road ahead, what's around the bend in 2019. Now that we have celebrated Christmas and the birth of Jesus, it's time to shift our focus to God's plans for us in the new year.

I am focused on cleaning up the remnants of 2018 that are strewn around my office and clear the path for the revelation about what's ahead.

These are days of preparation in every area of our lives. Are you getting ready? This verse in Psalm 36 reminded me that God is able to fully equip us for what is to come. He is the fountain of life that quenches our thirst. He is the living water, the well that never runs dry. As we run to Him, God replenishes and rejuvenates our body, mind, and spirit.

Have your eyes grown dim this year? Have the cares of the world clouded God's vision for your life? There's good news! "Your light has opened our eyes and awakened our souls." Lord, we know the truth that "In Your light, we see light."

God wants you to "get it." He doesn't want you to miss your calling, your purpose, and His best for your life.

As Bill and I have been talking about what lies ahead of us in 2019, we are excited. A lot of healing has happened and there are areas that need a lot of work, but God is faithful and what He started He will complete.

Drink deeply from the fountain of life-giving water that the Lord is offering today. There is abundant life waiting for you, life forevermore.

Thank you for your faithfulness to us in 2018. Thank you for walking with us on these next steps of our journey as God completes Bill's healing and prepares him for this new chapter of our lives. #Godisfaithful #pray4bill

Day #353 December 28

Anchor Verse: Isaiah 59:19b
For He will come in like a narrow, rushing stream which the breath of
the LORD drives [overwhelming the enemy]. (AMP)

Good news! No matter how difficult the battle you face today, the Lord
will fight for you. The imagery from Isaiah 59:19 is an accurate picture of
what happens in our lives. Often the enemy comes in like a flood, totally
unexpected, out of nowhere. If there were signs to prepare us, we missed
them. But just like a thief in the night, we find ourselves in the midst of a
calamity, a challenge, a testing.

However, God does not leave us alone. He is greater than the enemy of
our soul. "The Spirit of the Lord will lift up a standard against him and put
him to flight!" The enemy loses the battle. Remember that truth. It may not
be instantaneously, but God wins, the enemy loses. Those are the facts and
that will never change.

It's a great reminder as this year comes to a close that there is hope, there is
help that comes in the name of the Lord. There are still a few days left in
this year. Your victory may yet come in these final hours. Don't give up
hope. Press in. Hold on. God always has the final word, no matter how
dark the night may seem right now.

This year we have had a front row seat on this battlefield. We have seen the
enemy come rushing in like a flood that landed Bill in the hospital, actually
many hospitals. But then, God showed up again and again and again, and
declared that Bill was His child and that God would fight for him and we
would be victorious in Jesus' name.

Even as we wait on the Lord and move forward toward Bill's complete
healing, we wait with expectation and assurance that God is for us and not
against us. We rejoice in the God of our salvation and we sing praises to
His holy name. Hallelujah!

Thank you for your encouragement and fighting alongside us through
prayer. Truly it has moved mountains. We are forever grateful.
#Godisfaithful #pray4bill

Day #354 December 29

Anchor Verse: Psalm 62:8

Join me, everyone! Trust only in God every moment! Tell him all your troubles and pour out your heart-longings to him. Believe me when I tell you—he will help you! Pause in his presence (TPT)

Trust in God at all times – in the calm moments and the crisis situations. When you are full of joy or grieving, He is your help and your glory.

In the MESSAGE translation, the description of God is really powerful: "granite-strength and safe-harbor-God."

Why is granite so strong? Granite is so strong because the quartz and feldspar that compose it are harder than steel and as the magma (its source) cooled, it did so very slowly. It took time to make granite strong.

Stronger than steel – granite-strength – that is the God who loves you and protects you – every moment of every day. He is a hedge of protection around you. God is your strong tower, run to Him.

God is also a "safe harbor" – a place that is safe from the weather or attack, something that protects and allows something to flourish, and a refuge or break from suffering.

The psalmist challenges us to trust God absolutely! No room for doubt. There must be total surrender of all our doubts and fears, so all that remains is faith in the God who loves you so much.

Why is it so important to trust God at all times? Because we can easily fall prey to the wiles and strategies of the enemy, when life is difficult or when life is comfortable and you don't think you need God's help.

My granite-strength God has saved Bill's life from destruction. I have felt the arms of the "safe-harbor-God" wrapped around us as we needed to feel His tenderness and power in the middle of the storm.

Thank you for your faithfulness. Thank you for standing with us when we didn't have the strength to stand. Thank you for your prayers that have moved the hand of God. #Godisfaithful #pray4bill

Day #355 December 30

Anchor Verse: Isaiah 26:3-4
You will keep in perfect peace those whose minds are steadfast, because they trust in you. Trust in the Lord forever, for the Lord, the Lord himself, is the Rock eternal. (NIV)

Perfect peace – it's something we long for in this world. All around us we see signs of chaos and confusion. The news is filled with horrific things happening, yet through it all, God is our shelter in the storm. He offers peace – peace that passes all understanding.

What is our part? Our mind must be steadfast. Or another way to put it, our minds must be committed and focused on Him. It's not going be easy all the time, because the enemy distracts us, he comes to steal, kill, and destroy. With God's help, we have victory in Jesus' name.

The second part of what we must do is trust God. Trusting is a choice. Trusting when your eyes can't see. Trusting that God is faithful and that nothing is too difficult for Him. Peace and trust – they go hand in hand as we walk through our life journey.

As Bill and I have walked through his health journey this year, I have found peace in the most unlikely places because I chose to trust God and not be overcome by fear. In the middle of the ICU ward, where people were very sick and dying around us, God gave us hope and His perfect peace. God would whisper words of peace and power in my ear as I knelt before His throne of grace asking for His help.

There is great power in God's promises. Speak them. Write them. Memorize them. As the passage in Ephesians 6 regarding the armor of God tells us, the last piece of your armor is the sword of the Spirit, which is the Word of God. God's Word defeats the enemy every time. Jesus used Scripture to defend Himself from Satan's attack in the wilderness.

Thank you for your sacrifice of sleep and time as you prayed for us this year. Thank you for your continued prayers as we seek Bill's complete healing in Jesus' name. Hallelujah! #Godisfaithful #pray4bill

Day #356 December 31

Anchor Verse: Revelation 22:13
I am the Alpha and the Omega, the First and the Last, the Beginning and the End. (NIV)

The last day of the year... 365 days of 2018 are coming to an end. It has been quite a journey for all of us. But the consistent theme has been the faithfulness of God.

As I was reading the last chapter of Revelation this morning, I was struck by Jesus' words that seem to so accurately sum up where we stand today, "I am the Alpha and the Omega, the First and the Last, the Beginning and the End." God and Jesus were with us as we stepped into January 1, 2018 and have walked with us every moment of every day until the end of this day, December 31. He is the Alpha and the Omega, the beginning and the end of all things.

God knows that path that we take. He created a plan for our lives before we were born. Your heavenly Father wrote a book about your life filled with amazing plans for you. This should fill you with hope and joy!

My hope is that on this last day of 2018 you would take a moment to review the year and thank God for His abundant blessings in your life. Apologize to God for the times you went your own way. Thank Him for when He rescued you and lovingly brought you back home to safety in His arms of love. Thank God for drying your tears when your heart was broken, and when you were in physical pain and God healed you.

I am grateful for the many miracles that I have witnessed and the magnitude of His amazing grace. I stand in awe and wonder of the works of God's mighty hand. Most of all, I am overwhelmed by His love for me and Bill, and for all of you. God is great and greatly to be praised!

As I look ahead 24 hours into 2019, I do so with assurance that God is there too. In Malachi 3:6 it says, "I the Lord do not change." This is my comfort and joy. His faithfulness precedes us as we walk forward. He has Jeremiah 29:11 plans for us – and they are good!

We cannot begin to express our gratitude for your prayers and faithfulness in 2018. #Godisfaithful #pray4bill

About the Author

Barbara Hollace is a Christian woman who loves the Lord. God has called her to be a prayer warrior and a writer. Her greatest joy is to pray for others and see God's miracles happen. Through her own husband's health challenges, Barbara has learned that prayer can move mountains.

Her love of writing blossomed from an early age when she started creating her own greeting cards for family and friends. In 1985, Barbara self-published her first poetry book, "From Dust to Dust." Since that time Barbara has been published in 19 books as well as numerous newspaper articles. She has written 14 novels and is pursuing publication options.

Professionally, she is an author, editor, writing coach, and speaker. Owner of Hollace Writing Services, Barbara's goal is to "identify the good and magnify it!" This includes helping a person get the story in their heart on the page, editing the story, and pursuing publication options. She recently opened her own publishing company, Hollace House Publishing, and will be expanding its reach in the upcoming years.

Barbara has a Bachelor's degree in Business Administration from Western Washington University and a Juris Doctor degree from Gonzaga University School of Law. She is also the Communications Director for Spokane Dream Center church in Spokane Valley, Washington.

Barbara and her husband live in Eastern Washington and love to vacation at the ocean. For more information about Barbara and her business, go to www.barbarahollace.com

A Personal Note

From Bill

I thank God for saving me and those of you who prayed to keep me alive. You gave of yourself to me as you reached out to God, and for that, I thank you. I know that God is always here with us. We may lose sight of Him but He never loses sight of us.

At one point, I was ready to give up because of the pain, but God wouldn't let me. God said He had things for me to do and Barbara to do. God has taught me patience on this adventure even though I am not a patient person. If God can teach me patience, He can do the same for you.

I don't know what the future holds but God is a lot smarter than me, so I will follow where He leads me. I am grateful to God for saving me and I will be paying homage to Him for the rest of my life.

Be safe and may God bless you,

Bill

From Barb

I never imagined that our journey would touch so many lives. But in God's economy, nothing is ever wasted. Our hope and prayer is that the miracles God has done in our lives will inspire and encourage you. Support from around the world has been amazing. When we needed prayer support, I knew someone in the world was awake to pray, day or night. I reached out and people prayed. God heard, and answered, and the rest is history.

Bill's healing journey continues, so will this series. At the end of 2020, the second book featuring our 2019 journey will be released. We are excited to share the "greater things" God has planned for us.

If your life has been touched by our journey, please contact us and share your story. Email: Barbara@barbarahollace.com Facebook: Hollace Writing Services. Watch my website for announcements of coming events: www.barbarahollace.com.

Be blessed as you have blessed us!

Barb

www.ingramcontent.com/pod-product-compliance
Lightning Source LLC
Chambersburg PA
CBHW021351090426
42742CB00009B/811